International Studies in Entrepreneurship

Volume 44

More information about this series at http://www.springer.com/series/6149

Mark Sanders · Axel Marx · Mikael Stenkula
Editors

The Entrepreneurial Society

A Reform Strategy for Italy, Germany and the UK

Springer Open

Editors
Mark Sanders
Utrecht School of Economics
Utrecht University
Utrecht, The Netherlands

Mikael Stenkula
Research Institute of Industrial Economics
Stockholm, Sweden

Axel Marx
Leuven Centre for Global
Governance Studies
University of Leuven
Leuven, Belgium

ISSN 1572-1922 ISSN 2197-5884 (electronic)
International Studies in Entrepreneurship
ISBN 978-3-662-61006-0 ISBN 978-3-662-61007-7 (eBook)
https://doi.org/10.1007/978-3-662-61007-7

This Springer imprint is published by the registered company Springer-Verlag GmbH, DE part of Springer Nature.
The registered company address is: Heidelberger Platz 3, 14197 Berlin, Germany

To Cedric, Merel, Luka and Milo. Look out for opportunities and have the guts to act on them.

Foreword

Building Entrepreneurial Societies with a Multidisciplinary Perspective

The Entrepreneurial Society is always in the making. At the micro level, entrepreneurial people and organizations develop valuable new combinations, enabled and constrained by structures at the macro level. This book provides an excellent overview of how to improve the Entrepreneurial Society in the context of the European Union, and more particular its member states Italy, Germany and the UK. Improving the Entrepreneurial Society is a process of trial-and-error. One can go through this process in the dark or be illuminated by multiple scientific disciplines. This book, and the FIRES project at large, is a multidisciplinary endeavor that sheds light from multiple scientific disciplines on the question and challenge of how to build a more Entrepreneurial Society. It might look like the parable of the blind men and the elephant, in which each blind man feels part of the animal and creates his own version of reality from that limited experience and perspective. The FIRES consortium has been able to connect the blind men, with teams of scholars from law, economics, history, economic geography and innovation studies. This has delivered insights into the process of improving the Entrepreneurial Society and a diagnostic toolkit to uncover the key institutions of entrepreneurial societies. The proposed improvement process provides seven steps to achieve the ultimate aim of inclusive, innovative and sustainable growth. With this book, we will have the best starting point available to start and guide this journey!

Prof. Dr. Erik Stam
Dean, Utrecht University School of Economics
Utrecht, The Netherlands

Preface

This book marks the end of a three-year intense collaboration among some 40 excellent scientists and colleagues from nine institutes in as many countries. As not all their names appear in the author lists of the chapters in this book, we want to thank them here for all their patience, insights and discussions. We also extend our gratitude to many guests and partners that got involved at some stage in our project and Prashanth and Ruth at Springer Publishers in creating this book. Also, it would not have been possible to make this project a success without the support of Mischa, Martina and Mike at the LEG research support office, our project officer at the European Commission, Danilla Conte and the Commission's reviewers during the project. It was a great ride for all of us.

Utrecht, The Netherlands
Stockholm, Sweden
Leuven, Belgium
December 2019

Mark Sanders
Mikael Stenkula
Axel Marx

Acknowledgements

The editors thank Elisa Terragno Bogliaccini for research assistance and Erik Stam and participants of the workshop of September 5–6, 2019, in Utrecht for useful comments on the draft chapters. Mark Sanders thanks Montpellier Business School for their kind hospitality while drafting the manuscript during his sabbatical in the first half of 2019, and Mikael Stenkula gratefully acknowledges financial support from Jan Wallanders och Tom Hedelius stiftelse and from the Marianne and Marcus Wallenberg Foundation. Finally, financial support for open access publication of this book was provided by the European Commission under the Horizon 2020 project Financial and Institutional Reforms for the Entrepreneurial Society (FIRES), Grant Agreement Number 649378.

Contents

Contributors

Selin Dilli Department of History and Art History, Utrecht University, Utrecht, The Netherlands

James Dunstan Utrecht School of Economics, Utrecht University, Utrecht, The Netherlands

Saul Estrin Department of Management, London School of Economics, London, England, UK

Michael Fritsch Friedrich Schiller University of Jena, Jena, Germany

Luca Grilli Department of Management Economics and Industrial Engineering, Politecnico di Milano, Milan, Italy

Andrea M. Herrmann Innovation Studies, Copernicus Institute of Sustainable Development, Utrecht University, Utrecht, The Netherlands

Gresa Latifi TUM School of Management, Technical University of Munich, Munich, Germany

Axel Marx Leuven Centre for Global Governance Studies, University of Leuven, Leuven, Belgium

Balázs Páger Department of Management Science, University of Pécs, Pécs, Hungary

Mark Sanders Utrecht School of Economics, Utrecht University, Utrecht, The Netherlands

Tamás Sebestyén Regional Innovation and Entrepreneurship Research Center, MTA-PTE Innovation and Economic Growth Research Group, University of Pécs, Pécs, Hungary

Mikael Stenkula Research Institute of Industrial Economics, Stockholm, Sweden

Norbert Szabó Regional Innovation and Entrepreneurship Research Center, MTA-PTE Innovation and Economic Growth Research Group, University of Pécs, Pécs, Hungary

László Szerb Regional Innovation and Entrepreneurship Research Center, MTA-PTE Innovation and Economic Growth Research Group, University of Pécs, Pécs, Hungary;
Department of Management Science, University of Pécs, Pécs, Hungary

Elisa Terragno Bogliaccini Utrecht School of Economics, Utrecht University, Utrecht, The Netherlands

Attila Varga Regional Innovation and Entrepreneurship Research Center, MTA-PTE Innovation and Economic Growth Research Group, University of Pécs, Pécs, Hungary

Michael Wyrwich Faculty of Economics and Business, University of Groningen, Groningen, The Netherlands

Chapter 1
Seven Steps Toward Inclusive, Innovative, and Sustainable Growth

Mark Sanders, Axel Marx and Mikael Stenkula

Abstract In this chapter, the editors introduce and motivate the approach in this volume. Although this volume brings together contributions from different authors, the chapters all flow directly from the work that was done in the European H2020 research project Financial and Institutional Reforms for the Entrepreneurial Society that was conducted between 2015 and 2018. The first four chapters present and illustrate the multidisciplinary tools that fill the diagnostic toolkit developed in the project. Then three chapters illustrate how these tools can be usefully applied in different institutional contexts in the European Union, namely in Italy, Germany, and the UK.

Keywords Entrepreneurship · Entrepreneurship policy

1.1 Introduction

A good 50 years after its birth, the European Union is, arguably, in a serious midlife crisis. The global financial crash of 2007–2008 plunged several member states in a prolonged recession and the Syrian crisis strained already troubled relationships in the European family. With the Brexit referendum, the rise of *Alternative für Deutschland*, populist movements in Spain, Italy, and Greece and the revolt of the *Gilets Jaunes* in France, it is fair to conclude that Europe is losing its appeal among a vocal and perhaps growing share of European citizens. We believe that this decade of discontent is rooted in feelings of injustice and of being confronted with decisions and their consequences, rather than being involved in them. The solution in a globalizing

M. Sanders (✉)
Utrecht School of Economics, Utrecht University, Utrecht, The Netherlands
e-mail: m.w.j.l.sanders@uu.nl

A. Marx
Leuven Centre for Global Governance Studies, University of Leuven, Leuven, Belgium
e-mail: axel.marx@kuleuven.be

M. Stenkula
Research Institute of Industrial Economics, Stockholm, Sweden
e-mail: mikael.stenkula@ifn.se

M. Sanders et al. (eds.), *The Entrepreneurial Society*, International Studies in Entrepreneurship 44, https://doi.org/10.1007/978-3-662-61007-7_1

world, however, is not a retreat to the nation-state. Europe needs to deliver on its initial promise of providing security, well-being, and opportunity for all European citizens. We believe that doing so is also our best chance of restoring Europe on the path to innovative, inclusive, and sustainable growth.

Between 2015 and 2018, some 40 researchers in 9 institutions and countries across Europe have worked on the Horizon2020 project *Financial and Institutional Reforms for the Entrepreneurial Society* (FIRES; www.projectfires.eu). The chief aim of FIRES was to translate the insights of some three decades of entrepreneurship research into actionable institutional reform proposals. In the project, a strategy was formulated to bring inclusive, sustainable, and innovative growth back to the European Union by reforming Europe's institutions to promote a more open, contestable Entrepreneurial Society. This book, together with its companion volume published as *The Entrepreneurial Society: A Reform Agenda for the European Union*, presents the core results of this project in a comprehensive way.

In the companion volume, FIRES-researchers Niklas Elert, Magnus Henrekson and Mark Sanders introduced and motivated 50 proposals for reform in six key areas of policy making (Elert et al. 2019). These six areas go well beyond the areas that policymakers traditionally associate with entrepreneurship policy. They give us a list of possibly useful interventions that would have to be implemented at different levels in the European Union. In recognition of the complexity of multilayered policy competencies in the European Union, the authors carefully analyzed the relevant policy-making institutions and their legal and political competencies on the six areas of policy making identified in that volume.

Inevitably, however, these proposals are general and motivated from a broad base of evidence and scientific debate. The resulting menu of options, therefore, should still not be interpreted as a blueprint for a reform strategy that will work in all EU Member States and regions. It would be naive and possibly even damaging to implement all reforms in all regions across the very diverse entrepreneurial ecosystems of the European Union. Each region and state has its specific history and institutional trajectory, and we have therefore always stressed the need for tailoring reforms to local needs and conditions.

In this volume, we collect, present, and illustrate the application of the tools we have developed to do so. Before one can decide what reforms are most suitable in any given context, one needs to distinguish the deep rooted from the more reformable institutions in a region and identify the strengths, weaknesses, and bottlenecks in Europe's entrepreneurial ecosystems. Doing so requires a multidisciplinary approach and the tools illustrated in this volume therefore build on such diverse disciplines as history, geography, economics, and law.

1.2 The FIRES Seven-Step Procedure

In our project, we presented a seven-step approach to formulating an effective reform strategy:

- Step 1: Assess the most salient features of the institutions of a country or region and trace their historical roots.
- Step 2: Assess the strengths and weaknesses of the institutions and flag the bottlenecks in the entrepreneurial ecosystem using structured data analysis.
- Step 3: Identify, using careful primary data collection among entrepreneurial individuals, the most salient features characterizing the start-up process and the barriers that entrepreneurs face.
- Step 4: Map the results of Steps 2 and 3 onto a menu of evidence-based policy interventions to identify suitable interventions for the region or country under investigation.
- Step 5: In light of the historical analysis under Step 1, fit the proposed reforms to the existing local, regional, and national institutional setup.
- Step 6: Identify the relevant policymakers and procedures, i.e., who should change what and in what order for the reform strategy to achieve the greatest chance of success.
- Step 7: Experiment, evaluate, and learn—and return to Step 1 for the next iteration.

With a menu of options and corresponding attribution to the adequate policy making levels in place, we can use this seven-step approach, to formulate an effective reform strategy tailored to the needs of a specific country or region. The book before you shows how to prioritize and adjust the broad, evidence-based menu of reforms presented in Elert et al. (2019) to the specific Member States across Europe.

1.3 Book Outline

In Part One of this volume, consisting of four chapters, we discuss how we addressed Steps 1–3 in the FIRES project. This part of the book sets the stage and illustrates how the FIRES-toolbox can be used to diagnose weaknesses in an entrepreneurial ecosystem and select reforms to strengthen them. In the three chapters that make up Part Two of this book, we apply these tools and go through the cycle from Steps 1 to 6 for three countries—Italy, Germany and the UK—representing three rather distinct institutional clusters in the European Union. As we cannot actually implement the proposed policies to execute Step 7, this step is outside the scope of this book, but how this is to be done responsibly is briefly discussed in our conclusion.

In Chap. 2, *Selin Dilli* illustrates the importance of historical research in Step 1 for institutions shaping the allocation of labor, knowledge, and finance in Europe. Historical research shows that the differences in these institutions are often the result of long-term historical processes. A reform strategy can only be successful if it builds on these historical foundations. Using the Varieties of Capitalism (VoC) framework, the chapter provides insight into the different patterns of institutional change and its implications for different forms of entrepreneurial activity across European countries. The historical approach presented in Chap. 2 constitutes the first step in designing a tailored reform strategy.

In Chap. 3, *Attila Varga, László Szerb, Tamás Sebestyén* and *Norbert Szabó* present the Regional Entrepreneurship and Development Index (REDI) methodology for assessing the quality of the entrepreneurial ecosystem at the regional level in step 2. In this chapter, the authors also show how improvements in the ecosystem generate macroeconomic impacts in a Geographic Macro Regional (GMR) model simulation. The focus of the analysis here is more on the cross-sectional and geographical dimension. The simulations communicate an important message to policy makers by demonstrating that the impact of reforms will vary across regions and countries in Europe, creating a tension between the level at which policies can be implemented and where they generate positive or negative impacts.

In Chap. 4, *Andrea M. Herrmann* illustrates how "varieties of entrepreneurial ecosystems" form distinct institutional constellations that facilitate different types of entrepreneurship. More specifically, she stressed that slow-growing incrementally innovative ventures constitute a distinct type of entrepreneurship next to radically innovative, high-growth entrepreneurship. This reveals a second potential tension in formulating reform proposals that build on existing strengths or rather strengthen existing weaknesses. These findings invite policy makers to target entrepreneurial support measures more specifically to their economy's institutional environment and carefully consider institutional complementarities that exist in different varieties of entrepreneurial ecosystems.

To conclude Part One of this volume, *Axel Marx* presents a legal analysis of European entrepreneurship policy in Chap. 5. In this chapter, he elaborates on how European policy making should be affected when implementing reforms. Changing the institutional environment responsible for the quality of the entrepreneurial ecosystem will require changes on multiple levels. The chapter shows that fostering entrepreneurship will require a multi-level approach with a strong focus on the level of EU Member States.

In Chap. 6, representing the first chapter of Part Two, *Mark Sanders*, *Mikael Stenkula,* and co-authors outline a reform strategy to promote a more entrepreneurial society in Italy, classified as a Mixed or Mediterranean Market Economy (MME). Italy historically boasts a vibrant entrepreneurial economy of locally embedded, often family-owned small- and medium-sized firms. But the Italian entrepreneurial ecosystem has a bureaucratic business environment that feeds back into low levels of productivity and ambition in entrepreneurship. To address the problem, Italy could reform its educational system to promote a more experimental attitude and reduce the bureaucratic business environment and recruitment culture that stifles ambitious entrepreneurs. For Italy, important tensions arise between the tendency for entrepreneurial venturing to concentrate in already well-off regions and creating opportunities for all Italians.

Mark Sanders, Mikael Stenkula, and co-authors follow up in Chap. 7 with a reform strategy to promote a more entrepreneurial society in Germany. Germany can be classified as a coordinated market economy (CME) and is historically characterized by a strong and regionally embedded *Mittelstand* and an economy where high productivity growth is driven by on-the-job learning and firm-specific skill accumulation. Germany's entrepreneurial talent could be encouraged to take on more risk. The education system could promote creativity, and a more equal playing field between new and incumbent ventures in attracting finance, labor, and knowledge could be created. For Germany, an important tension exists between supporting its traditional incrementally innovative *Mittelstand* and channeling resources into somewhat riskier and radically innovative ventures to also push out the global technology frontier.

In Chap. 8, *Mark Sanders, Mikael Stenkula,* and co-authors finally present a reform strategy to promote an entrepreneurial society in the UK. The UK is typically classified as a liberal market economy (LME) and has a deregulated environment, flexible labor markets, well-funded elite universities, and strong protection of intellectual property rights. The UK should aim at strengthening the workforce's knowledge base and talent pool as well as the capital base. It furthermore is advisable to open opportunities for not only starting but also for growing, perhaps less radically innovative, firms in all regions in the UK. For the UK, both the geographical and the variety of entrepreneurship tension will require careful consideration in designing and evaluating our proposed reforms.

The country case studies in Chaps. 6–8 are substantially shortened and reworked versions of the country reports that were submitted as reports to the European Commission and published earlier on www.projectfires.eu, where the reader can also find the policy briefs and a report on the policy round tables that were organized around them in the spring of 2018 in Rome, Berlin, and London, respectively. For the purpose of this book, this material has been merged and significantly revised and updated.

We conclude this volume with Chap. 9, where the editors of the book sum up the main points concerning theory, method, and policy proposals. The editors also elaborate on tensions that exist between the chapters.

Reference

Elert N, Henrekson M, Sanders M (2019) The entrepreneurial society: a reform strategy for the European Union. Springer, Berlin

Part I
Historical Roots, Ecosystem Assessment, Firm Formation Processes and Legal Competences

Chapter 2
A Historical Perspective on the Evolution of Finance, Knowledge, and Labor Market Institutions in Europe

Selin Dilli

Abstract Both policymakers and academics offer various strategies concerning institutions on how to stimulate entrepreneurial activity in Europe. However, historical evidence shows that the cross-national differences in these institutions are the result of long-term historical processes. A successful entrepreneurial strategy would therefore benefit from looking at the past to build and improve current institutions in the future. To provide such a historical insight, this chapter aims to answer the question: How and to what extent have the institutional factors relevant to entrepreneurial activity evolved over time? It discusses the changes in the financial, knowledge, and labor institutions over the twentieth century across European countries to be able to distinguish between institutions that are dynamic and those that are slowly changing. Using the Varieties of Capitalism (VoC) framework, it provides insight into the different patterns of institutional change and the implications of this change for the different forms of entrepreneurial activity across European countries. The historical approach presented in this chapter thus contributes to the development of more diversified and better-informed policy tools to stimulate entrepreneurship.

Keywords Entrepreneurship · Varieties of Capitalism · National institutions · Institutional complementarities

2.1 Introduction

A widely acknowledged explanation for the difference in terms of entrepreneurship outcomes between the USA and Europe, as well as across countries around the world, is institutions (Bruton et al. 2010). Institutions are defined as the formal

The author gratefully acknowledges funding from the European Union's Horizon 2020 research and innovation program under grant agreement No 649378. Thanks to Axel Marx, Mark Sanders, and Mikael Stenkula for comments on earlier drafts of this chapter.

S. Dilli (✉)
Department of History and Art History, Utrecht University, Utrecht, The Netherlands
e-mail: s.dilli@uu.nl

M. Sanders et al. (eds.), *The Entrepreneurial Society*, International Studies in Entrepreneurship 44, https://doi.org/10.1007/978-3-662-61007-7_2

and informal sets of rules which shape individuals' preferences and behavior (North 1990), which promote or hamper entrepreneurial activity via the reduction or increase of uncertainty and costs (Baumol 1990). The starting point in the FIRES project is that the institutions in finance, knowledge, and labor markets are key institutions in shaping entrepreneurial activity. This chapter aims to provide a historical perspective on the evolution of these institutions to be able to identify those that are more rapidly changing versus ones that persist over time. This is important information for policymakers aiming to build up institutions for a more entrepreneurial society.

In our earlier works, using the Varieties of Capitalism (henceforth VoC) framework (Dilli et al. 2018; Dilli and Westerhuis 2018a; Dilli and Westerhuis 2018b; Dilli 2019), we showed that the variations in the finance, labor, and knowledge institutions and their complementarities explain the differences both in terms of the level and type of entrepreneurial activity across European countries today. The VoC literature proposes a more holistic approach to institutions. Rather than focusing on single institutions, this holistic approach to finance, labor, and knowledge institutions identifies four institutional constellations characterizing Europe (Amable 2003; Hall and Soskice 2001; Dilli et al. 2018). The first one is the liberal market economies (LMEs), exemplified with the USA and UK, where institutions support market-based solutions. On the other side of the spectrum are coordinated market economies (CMEs), such as Germany, where institutions provide social security and stimulate coordination among firms, governments, and other agents in the market economy such as the labor unions. A third cluster, the Mediterranean Market Economies (MMEs), composed of Italy, Spain, Greece, and Portugal, are characterized by a larger state and governmental regulation. A last cluster is the Eastern Market Economies (EMEs) that have an institutional setup to attract multinational companies.

In Dilli et al. (2018), we established that these four institutional constellations are also relevant to explain the diversity of entrepreneurship in Europe. For instance, in the Eastern European countries there is little protection of minority investors, high minimum capital requirements, little facilitation of venture capital, and a recovery rate favoring creditors over shareholders. In the UK, there are low minimum capital requirements, institutions that facilitate the availability of venture capital, and institutions that privilege shareholders in case of corporate failure by limiting the chances of creditors to recover their investments. In terms of labor market regulations, the Eastern countries and the UK have weak employment protection contrary to the Mediterranean countries where there are strong regulations against firing employees. The governmental transfers to research and development are much higher in the Northwestern European countries compared to the South and Eastern European countries. These cross-national differences in the combination with these institutional factors explain why fewer people are willing to start a new business in the Northwestern European countries compared to the South and East but those who do tend to engage in high-growth innovative sectors. Herrmann (2020) provides a more in-depth discussion of the relevance of the VoC framework for the entrepreneurship literature and our previous findings on this topic.

To stimulate entrepreneurial activity, the European Commission (2013) has identified more flexible labor market institutions, investment in higher education, and better access to finance via regulatory burden reductions as strategies in the Entrepreneurship 2020 Action Plan. Yet, such one-size-fit-all policy tools are unlikely to be successful in Europe. With the establishment of the European Union, there was an expectation of convergence among the Member States. However, comparative studies on the effect of Europeanization have not found strong empirical evidence for such convergence (See Bürzel 1999 for a review). The VoC literature argues against convergence toward a single institutional model in Europe. According to this school of thought, this is because the institutional arrangements of European countries have evolved differently into complex systems of interdependent and complementary institutions over time, which are difficult to change (Hall and Thelen 2009). Another argument against convergence is rooted in history. The literature on path dependency suggests that the institutional legacies of the past limit the range of current possibilities and/or options in institutional innovation (Nielson et al. 1995, p. 6). Historical conditions are thus important in determining the current-day institutional setup as well as socioeconomic outcomes. In this chapter, the focus will be on the latter: the influence of the past in understanding the current institutional diversity and outcomes for entrepreneurship in the dimensions of finance, knowledge, and labor across Europe.

Newly emerging social science literature demonstrates that the historical setting has set in motion divergent evolutionary paths, leading to the deeply entrenched differences in economic, institutional, social, and political outcomes today (see Nunn, 2009, for a review). For instance, Duranton et al. (2009) show that European regions with historically weak family ties perform better in terms of economic growth, adopt better to sectoral shifts, and have a higher educational attainment today. Alesina et al. (2010) find that stringent labor market regulations persist over time despite being economically inefficient due to their deep roots in the historical family structure. Galor and Ozak (2016) find that pre-industrial agro-climatic characteristics have a culturally embodied impact on the economic behavior of countries such as technology adoption, education, and saving today. In the entrepreneurship literature, the deep historical roots as an explanation for the regional and cross-country differences have started to receive attention too. In the case of Germany, for example, Fritsch and Wyrwich (2017) demonstrate that regions with higher levels of self-employment in the 1920s also have higher levels of new business formation today. Nevertheless, the evidence in this strand of literature is largely based on cross-national comparisons, regressing one point in time in the past on a current outcome.

Historians have criticized such cross-country comparisons as it assumes limited change over time and treats countries as being less advantaged in the institutional and development conditions since they first appeared in history (Frankema and Weijenburg 2012). This is a strong assumption to make, as the evidence from historical studies on the persistence and change in historical conditions is rather mixed. On the one hand, historical studies that focus on informal institutions (i.e., norms and values), such as the family systems, the co-residence patterns, and inheritance practices, argue that these institutions experienced limited change since the Middle Ages (Todd 1985; Reher 1998). On the other hand, there are historical studies showing that formal institutions including democratic rule, tax regulation, and social security spending as well as economic conditions such as globalization and distribution of the economic sectors have changed dramatically over time (Lindert 2004; Broadberry 2010). Considering the VoC framework, the debate on whether countries experience a shift between institutional constellations continues to this date (see Hall and Thelen 2009). For instance, according to Sluyterman (2015), the Netherlands has shown liberal market economy characteristics at the beginning and the end of the twentieth century, whereas from the Second World War up to the eighties, it had characteristics of a coordinated market economy and arguably returned to the liberal market since. According to De Goey and Van Gerwen (2008), this shift can also explain why there were more entrepreneurs in the beginning and at the end of the twentieth century in the Netherlands than in the 1950s.

To be able to distinguish between persistent and more dynamic institutions and to evaluate whether and how the institutional constellations described in the VoC literature have evolved over time, this chapter focuses on the historical trends in financial, knowledge, and labor market institutions. Thus, it aims to provide insight into which institutions are more challenging to alter via policy tools. The starting point of this chapter is to include a historical discussion on those institutions, which we found to be crucial for entrepreneurship in Dilli et al. (2018) and Dilli (2019). In order to provide a discussion at the European level in all three institutional aspects in the given scope of this chapter, the discussion of indicators in each dimension has been limited. Here, the availability of time-series data and historical sources mainly determine the choice of indicators and the time coverage presented.

This means that the indicators of finance, knowledge, and labor presented here do not always directly capture the institutional setup in terms of the rules and regulations but are outcomes that are result of the institutional setup and play a central role in entrepreneurial activity. For instance, in the case of finance, the focus is on banks and family, which remain the largest formal and informal sources of financial resources for entrepreneurs in Europe, respectively (OECD 2013).

For knowledge, I present the historical patterns in tertiary education, and research and development, both of which are contributors to higher entrepreneurial activity, business survival, firm growth, or the firm's return on investment (see Van Der Sluis et al. 2008 for a review). Sanders et al. (2020a, b, c) provide a more qualitative analysis of underlying knowledge institutions (e.g., universities, patent systems, etc.) for these two outcomes for Italy, Germany, and the UK, respectively.

On labor institutions, the discussion will be on three dimensions: the regulation of labor markets, wage-setting institutions, and social security systems that are crucial for entrepreneurial activity (Henrekson 2014; Dilli 2019). In terms of time coverage, the focus is mainly on the twentieth century when it is possible to demonstrate the evolution based on quantitative information. However, when possible, a historical discussion going back to the late Middle Ages is included based on secondary literature; thus, the time coverage varies within each subsection. In the country choice, both historical data availability and the four VoC typologies play a role.

This chapter is structured as follows: first finance, second knowledge, and third labor institutions are discussed in subsections in the following order: first I describe the diversity in current institutions and their relevance for entrepreneurship today, and then I discuss the historical trends in the underlying institutions. The last section concludes with the relevance of the historical analysis of institutions and its implications for the entrepreneurship literature.

2.2 Finance[1]

The availability of financing options is crucial in all stages and for all types of entrepreneurial activity: in seeing an opportunity to start a firm, growing a business, and engaging in innovation (Dilli et al. 2018). Among the various sources of financing, banks remain the largest financial intermediaries in all European countries, although their importance varies significantly across countries (OECD 2013; 2015). The share of the nonbank instruments, such as factoring, crowdfunding, private equity, and venture capital, remains relatively small in Europe in comparison to the USA with the notable exception of the UK. For instance, between 1995 and 2010, total European venture capital investment has been, on average, approximately only one-third of the volume in the USA (OECD 2013). Informal financing tools are an important source of capital for entrepreneurs too (OECD 2013). These informal financing options via investors, such as private individuals/business angels and a network of friends, family, and foolhardy investors, provide financing directly to unquoted companies to which they may or may not have a family connection (Szerb et al. 2007). Again, across Europe, differences are present in relative importance of these informal sources to fund entrepreneurs. For instance, in Dilli and Westerhuis (2018a), using the Global Entrepreneurship Monitor (2011), we show that today business angels invest more in close family and relatives in the Eastern and Mediterranean countries (with the exception of Portugal) than in the Northwestern countries. Nevertheless, such trends provide only a snapshot of the current situation. To a historian, they raise the question when banks started to play such a central role for entrepreneurs in Europe and whether their role has changed over time. Another question is whether, given the large historical differences in the family systems (Todd 1985), family can indeed be an alternative financing tool in all the European countries. Below I discuss the historical evolution of the banking system and family systems to address these questions.

[1] This section is taken from the working paper version of Dilli and Westerhuis (2018a). The section on banks (Section 2.2.1) mainly relies on the input by Gerarda Westerhuis in Dilli and Westerhuis (2018a). For an extended version of the finance section please see: https://projectfires.eu/wp-content/uploads/2018/02/D2.4-REVISED.pdf.

2.2.1 Evolution of the Formal Financial Tools for Entrepreneurs: Banks

The historical roots of the banking system can be traced back to the fourteenth century. Although private banks had long provided a mix of commercial and investment services to their customers, the term "universal bank" is usually reserved for the large incorporated financial institutions that emerged in Europe during the second half of the nineteenth century (Cull et al. 2006). Therefore, I will focus here on the period from the late nineteenth century onwards as this covers the period of the emergence of the diverse modern banking system that characterizes most European countries today.

The size of the banks has been linked with the availability of bank credit for entrepreneurship. Small banks have traditionally been important lenders to small firms because small banks have a comparative advantage in relationship lending. Accordingly, the importance of and access to bank credit fell as banks became larger and banking got more concentrated over time (World Bank 2013). According to this view, small banks are better than large banks at relationship lending that depends on "soft" information. Large banks, in contrast, specialize in transaction lending to more mature firms where less discretion is involved (Black and Strahan 2002, p. 2808). In many European countries, large financial conglomerates have emerged over time that are perceived as less willing to finance SMEs in general and entrepreneurship in particular.

In many European countries, the banking landscape had been much more diverse than it is currently. Small, locally embedded credit institutions played an important role in introducing innovations and providing financing to firms and sectors that were overlooked by the larger financial institutions (Wadhwani 2016, p. 192). In some countries (e.g., the Netherlands, UK), this diversity has almost vanished, whereas in others (e.g., Germany), it continues to play an important role in the financial system. At the end of the nineteenth century, these differences between banking systems across European countries started to emerge. In particular, with the Second Industrial Revolution and the emergence of large-scale firms, the increased demand for capital led to the emergence of large commercial banks (Westerhuis 2016). In many countries, these big banks replaced relationship banking that was present prior to the nineteenth century with impersonal transaction banking. In the UK, many local banks that were typically small, private institutions, and limited by law to no more than six partners, played a crucial role in funding local industries during the first industrial revolution (Cull et al. 2006). During the interwar period, UK banking became more concentrated and less competitive. Provincial banks were taken over by large London-based banks, which preferred higher liquidity ratios. This reduced the supply of funds for the industrial clients, in particular the smaller and younger ones. A similar pattern is also visible in the Netherlands. While prior to the twentieth century, regional banks played an important role in financing (new) businesses, around 1910 a process of concentration set in the Netherlands, which created five big banks that would dominate the scene by 1925 (Jonker 1997). An alternative for their clients was offered via market solutions such as stockbrokers and private investors (Cull et al. 2006). This pattern corresponds well with the LME's institutional structure, which stimulates market-oriented solutions (Hall and Soskice 2001).

In contrast, in Germany, a typical CME, and in Italy and France, classified as MMEs, the banking system remained relatively more fragmented and the state intervened by creating public and semipublic (i.e., cooperatives) lending institutions. These public, semipublic, and regional banks specialized in segments of the market reducing information asymmetries (Carnavali 2005). This type of banking structure lowered assessment and monitoring costs due to long-term relations between lenders and borrowers. The governmental intervention corresponds with the type of institutional structure of the CMEs identified in the VoC literature that stimulates coordination between different agents of the economy. The disadvantage was that these banks were less able to diversify and spread risks (Carnavali 2005).

In Germany, for instance, cooperatives emerged in the nineteenth century in response to the failure of existing lenders to give credit to small retailers and rural populations. The cooperatives were owned and controlled by their members and granted loans to members who might lack access to credit at the large financial institutions (Wadhwani 2016). Around the First World War credit cooperatives together with commercial banks and savings banks formed the core of the German banking system (Deeg 1999). The cooperative model spread across Europe since the second half of the nineteenth century. In Italy, it became a very important part of the financial system as well (Carnevali 2005). In contrast, in the UK and USA, typical LME economies, the credit cooperatives were established relatively late. In these contexts, commercial banks were already providing financial services to the working and rural people, whereas large corporates acquired capital through well-developed capital markets.

In Germany, cooperatives and savings banks[2] developed close links with local business. Although in the literature the focus is often on the big banks from Berlin, in Germany many small business owners, artisans, and shopkeepers banked in local and regional banks (Carnevali 2005, p. 46). These small regional banks met fierce opposition from the commercial banks, and it was this conflict that "shaped the state's response toward competition between different types of banks, ensuring the permanence of segmentation" (Carnevali 2005, p. 196). In Germany, the state played an important role in mediating between different types of banks. It was an active political choice to protect the SMEs and their local economies. In contrast, savings banks in the UK, created in the 1810s, for example, were not allowed to lend for commercial purposes by law.

In the 1950s and 1960s, the long-term finance of small businesses in Germany was made available via savings and cooperative banks, ensured by strong competition and state regulation. Regulation provided incentives for the saving and cooperative banks to grant SMEs long-term credits, where these banks operated in a limited market and their success depended on the economic welfare of their region. In their

[2]Saving banks emerged in the late eighteenth century in order to provide possibilities for working and poor people to save for periods of need due to illness, unemployment, or retirement.

charters, it was stated that pursuing profits was important but only as a means to other goals. Savings banks were mandated with the promotion of the local economy, and cooperative banks had to serve the interests of their members (Carnevali 2005).

In Italy, the banking system was decentralized to strengthen local banks after the Second World War. The government wanted to create local financial channels (decentralized capitalism) to act as a counterbalance to the power of the large private business groups. Decentralization and a segmented banking system were seen as elements that would increase stability, whereas a concentrated banking system was perceived as a factor that would hinder economic growth (Carnevali 2005, p. 177). The diverse financial landscape of the 1930s with various types and sizes of financial intermediaries was defended as a guarantee for the diffusion of credit. As a result, regulations were reshaped in order to reduce banking competition and protect the small- and medium-sized banks from the larger national ones (Carnevali 2005, p. 178). The awareness of policymakers, that SMEs had disadvantages in access to market finance, contributed to the introduction of financial subsidies as part of national industrial policy (Spadavecchia 2005). Of the various countries discussed here, the Italian banking system has been the most regulated and subsidized with the aim to promote the development of small firms. From the mid-1970s, however, the decentralized banking system was increasingly being questioned. As a result, many territorial restrictions were abolished as well as controls over interest rates, leading to the mergers of banks in the 1990s.

In contrast to Germany, industrialization in France occurred in a political context of a unified nation-state, with strong central government. Although large French firms established themselves between 1918 and 1930, SMEs remained a very important part of the economy (Lescure 1999). Due to agreements to fix prices and quotas, there were hardly incentives for firms to merge into bigger conglomerates in this period (Carnevali 2005). Due to active government interference, the banking structure remained more diverse in France than in the UK in the nineteenth century. During the Great Depression of the 1930s, many local and regional banks had to close, and after the Second World War, a process of concentration dominated the banking sector in which the regional and local banks merged into national ones. Four large deposit banks were nationalized after 1945. In 1957, 22 regional banks and 158 local banks were left. The local banks had a strong hold over the local market. The greater role of the state in France was also reflected in the role of public and semipublic banks in stimulating investments after the Second World War (Carnevali 2005).

The process of liberalization and harmonization in Europe that eventually led to the monetary union caused concentration to rise in banking across the Eurozone. This is visible in Fig. 2.1. The (three) firm concentration ratio is the percentage of all banking system assets accounted for by the biggest three banks in a country.

For the majority of CME countries, the combination of a few large commercial banks and a broad base of small, local banks resulted in a C-3 ratio of well above 50% (e.g., Switzerland, Austria, Germany, Netherlands). This also applies to the Nordic CME countries Denmark, Finland, and Sweden. An interesting case is the UK banking system, which was rather less concentrated in 1993 with C-3 ratio of 29% increasing to 56% in 2003. Overall, in the clear majority of the 19 EU countries,

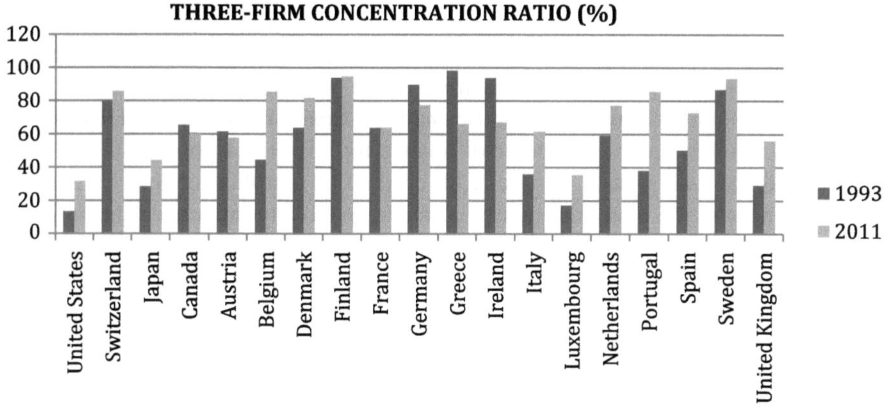

Fig. 2.1 Percentage of all banking system assets by the biggest three banks in a country. *Source* World Bank (2013)

the largest banks dominated the banking industry 20 years ago and continue to do so today.

While historical studies show that prior to the twentieth century, the regional small-sized banks seemed to play a role in funding the small-sized businesses across Europe, and there is still no consensus on the extent to which this diverse banking structure in the cases of France, Italy, or Germany provided advantages in solving finance problems for small businesses. On the one hand, Carnevali (2005) stresses comparative advantages of these regional banks in Italy, France, and Germany after the Second World War compared to the much more consolidated banking system in the UK. On the other hand, the limited historical evidence shows that the number of firms that could take advantage of the banks' combination of investment commercial banking services in Germany was quite small (Cull et al. 2006). According to Cull et al. (2006), instead SMEs mostly relied on local intermediaries and private initiatives, which ranged from notaries to family borrowing in France to the cooperatives in Germany (Cull et al. 2006, p. 3028). In the next section, I evaluate the role private initiatives, in particular family lending, as an alternative source of financing for entrepreneurs and link the current differences in family lending to historical family systems.

2.2.2 *Alternative Source of Finance: The Family*

Historical studies show that entrepreneurs had alternatives to banks as sources of funding (van Zanden et al. 2012; Gelderblom 2011). These historical alternatives were available in the form of retained earnings, family capital, investment from wealthy entrepreneurs, and short-term loans (Westerhuis 2016). However, the availability and type of financial sources differed substantially across Europe. For instance, Cull et al. (2006) show that in the case of UK and the Netherlands domestic capital markets and governmental bonds provided an important source of exchange and finance for businesses, whereas this option was much more limited in the case of the Southern European countries such as Spain and Portugal. Historically, family has also been a crucial source of finance for businesses, though its relevance differed substantially across Europe (Cull et al. 2006). In this section, I argue that the differences in the historical family systems have likely influenced the variation in the family borrowing across Europe and continue to do so today.

Family members are assumed to be important providers of financial resources (Bygrave et al. 2003). This is because financial capital from family members has important advantages such as lower transaction costs (Au and Kwan 2009), favorable interest and payback requirements, and availability when other sources are not available (Steier 2003). Especially when the firm requires more time to provide returns, family may provide a better lending possibility to the entrepreneur than formal financing options (Arregle et al. 2015). Bygrave and Reynolds (2005) argue that the level of social obligations individuals feel toward their family members shape the willingness of the lender to lend money to the family member (supply side) and the willingness of the borrower to borrow from a family member (demand side). One can expect that in contexts where family ties are stronger (family has priority over the individual), both the willingness to lend and borrow from a family member would be higher, and as a result, the level of family lending would be higher.

Demographer Reher (1998), using census data, showed that strong family ties characterize the Mediterranean countries, whereas weaker family ties (the individual has priority over family) characterize the Northwestern European countries. This pattern seems to correspond with the cross-national differences in the European context in terms of lending behavior to family members by business angels today. In the Eastern European and the Mediterranean countries, business angels seem to invest more often in family members than in other European countries despite the unfavorable financial institutional environment. In the Northern European countries, on the other hand, the investment of business angels and borrowing behavior from the family remain limited. Sweden and Belgium, depicted as having weaker family ties, are the exceptions, which outperform the rest of the European countries in terms of their share of business angel investment in family businesses (see Dilli and Westerhuis 2018a for an illustration of these trends). An explanation for these contradictory cases could be attributed to the overall supply of business angels due to the favorable institutional context such as tax cuts for family lending (Au and Ding 2011; OECD 2015).

One of the core explanations as to why Northwestern European countries have much weaker family ties compared to the Eastern and Southern European countries has been linked with the historical differences in the living arrangements of family members, having long-term effects on the norms and values regarding the importance of the family due to the generational transfer of these norms (Reher 1998). According to demographic historians, Hajnal's St. Petersburg–Trieste line separates the Central and Northwestern European territories (Scandinavia, the UK, the Low Countries, much of Germany and Austria) from the Eastern and the Mediterranean in terms of co-residence practices and has been present for centuries (Reher 1998; Todd 1985). For instance, the study of Reher (1998) shows that from at least the late Middle Ages until the second half of the nineteenth century, it was common in rural England and in the Low Countries for young adults to leave their parental households at a young age to work as agricultural servants in other households. On the other hand, in the Southern European societies even though there were servants in both rural and urban settings, it affected only a small part of the young population in rural areas (Reher 1998). These differences in the family systems have arguably been the result of the differences in the agricultural practices, the timing of the Neolithic revolution and geographical factors (Todd 2011).

These historical family arrangements are possibly linked with the long-term development of different forms of (private) financing options for entrepreneurs across European regions. The scarce historical evidence from the late Middle Ages and Early Modern Europe shows that in this period, private lending, even that via the family members, was already formalized in the Low Countries. Van Zanden et al. (2012) demonstrate that in the fifteenth and sixteenth centuries, properties were used as collateral on a large scale, and that interest rates on both small and large loans were relatively low (about 6%). As a result, many households owned financial assets and/or debts, and the degree of financial sophistication was relatively high.

Similarly, Gelderblom and Jonker (2004) show that deposits and bonds were common among businessmen and entrepreneurs as a tool to borrow already in sixteenth century Netherlands. Thus, formal institutions as well as the availability of investors due to deep domestic markets as a result of the international trade at the time stimulated lending both from family and non-family members in this period. This resulted in access to credit for a larger share of the population compared to the Southern European countries. The presence of weak family ties might have created the necessity to regulate the lending behavior more formally in the North. On the other hand, while financial historians show that Italian city-states were crucial financial centers in the fifteenth and sixteenth centuries, wealth was mainly concentrated in the hands of a small group of merchants and family businesses and lending again played a central role. The lack of historical data, however, does not allow us to provide insight into how family lending has changed over time across different European countries.

Nevertheless, past and present cross-country differences in family lending behavior and family funding can provide a feasible alternative to formal financing options especially in the Mediterranean and the Eastern European countries given their strong family ties. This can be done by following the Belgian example. In Belgium, anyone who grants a loan to an entrepreneur as a friend, acquaintance, or family member receives an annual tax discount of 2.5% of the value of the loan. If the enterprise is unable to repay the loan, the lender gets 30% of the amount owed back via a one-off tax credit in the context of the "win-win lending" scheme (OECD 2015). This change in the policy seems to have helped with increasing the availability of finance to entrepreneurs in Belgium, and its implementation might be less costly in the Southern European countries where family members are more willingly to invest in family members. An important implication of weak family systems in the Northwestern European countries is that policies should prioritize targeting improvement of the formal financial institutions rather than family lending. However, as both the case of Belgium and the historical evidence highlight, family lending can still provide an alternative in these countries, even if there might be need for more formal regulation and incentives introduced by the government to support family lending.

A more general conclusion on the financial institutions is that while the banking system has experienced rapid change since the late nineteenth century, family systems as an informal institution persisted over time. Supporting small-scale banks and more formalized private lending options such as equity finance therefore might be a better option to pursue in the CME economies, whereas in the MMEs and EMEs, stimulating informal lending options via friends and family would be easier to implement. Of course, the analysis in this chapter is descriptive in nature and serves only as a first attempt to argue how a historical perspective can potentially help in formulating reform strategies to stimulate entrepreneurship. More in-depth historical analysis is advised when formulating strategies for a specific region or country and general conclusions based on the analysis presented here should be approached with caution.

2.3 Knowledge

The country case studies in Sanders et al. (2020a, b, c) discuss universities and the patent system as the underlying institutions for knowledge creation. In this chapter, I focus instead on outcome variables of these more fundamental institutions of (1) educational attainment in tertiary level and the gender differences therein and (2) research and development, which explain the different levels and types of entrepreneurial activity across Europe (Dilli and Westerhuis 2018b; Dilli et al. 2018). These two indicators can be seen as more direct measures of the knowledge outcomes. I focus on these two measures as they have been commonly used in the VoC literature to capture the knowledge dimension, and there is historical and comparable quantitative data that allows me to evaluate how these two dimensions evolved over time across European countries.

Formal education at the university level is important for entrepreneurial activity. For instance, both the individual entrepreneur's education and the regional and national educational attainment have been shown to be strong drivers of entrepreneurs' decision to start a business and grow their business and the economic sector in which they engage (see Dilli and Westerhuis 2018b for a review of the literature). At the societal level, while the educational level of consumers may shape the demand function for an entrepreneur's venture output, the educational level of employees may affect the entrepreneur's venture productivity and thereby shape his or her supply function (Millán et al. 2014).

Next to formal education, knowledge-driven innovation is frequently considered as the outcome of research and development (R&D) activities and the general concern that firms may underinvest in R&D has resulted in government policies and programs such as favorable fiscal treatment and R&D subsidies (Coad and Rao 2010). In addition to the scientific knowledge generated by the private sector, entrepreneurial ventures may therefore also acquire the necessary scientific knowledge by participating in, or benefitting from, public R&D programs that lead to new commercial opportunities (Dilli et al. 2018, p. 7).

2.3.1 Educational Attainment

The VoC literature highlights differences across industrialized economies in terms of how they organize their educational system. For instance, LMEs stimulate general education, as the flexibility in the labor market and transition between jobs require general skills (as discussed in Herrmann 2020). Figure 2.2 shows the trends in years of education at the tertiary level across a selected number of countries over the twentieth century. The USA, a typical LME, already starts outperforming the rest of the European countries in the beginning of the twentieth century and tertiary education takes off in the second half of the twentieth century.

The next best performers are the UK (another typical LME) and the Netherlands, which show characteristics of an LME in the beginning and the end of twentieth century (Sluyterman 2015). Germany, a coordinated market economy (CME), performs moderately compared to the LMEs, and progress is visible especially from

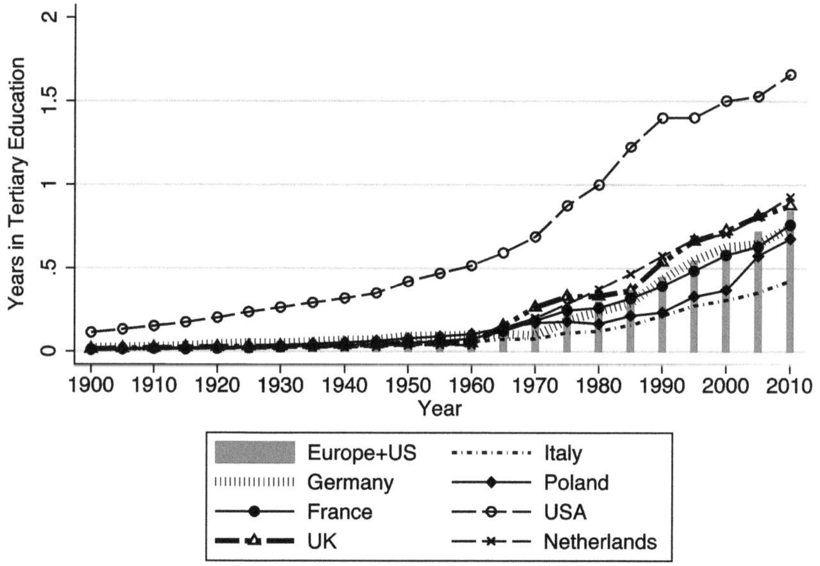

Fig. 2.2 Educational attainment in tertiary level (age group 25–64). *Notes* The figure is based on the Lee and Lee (2016) dataset. The Europe + USA average includes the 19 European countries included in the database

the 1960s onwards. Poland, an Eastern Market Economy, and Italy, a Mediterranean Market Economy, have the lowest attainment in tertiary education among the European countries. Despite the fact that these two countries also witnessed increases in tertiary education since the 1960s, especially in Italy, this progress has been slower compared to the other European countries. The fact that the LME economies perform highest in the tertiary educational attainment compared to the others thus supports the line of reasoning in the VoC framework that the LMEs have a comparative advantage in general education, whereas CMEs focus more on vocational training.[3]

Dilli and Westerhuis (2018b) also looked at the role of gender differences in educational attainment to explain the gender differences in entrepreneurial activity. We showed that women are less likely to engage in all three stages of entrepreneurial activity across Europe (perceived opportunities to start a business, the knowledge intensiveness of the sector in which they start their business, and their growth aspirations), and that education is one of the explanations for this gap. Figure 2.3 displays the ratio of women to men in tertiary education. While a score below 1 indicates women are underrepresented, 1 would indicate gender equality and a value

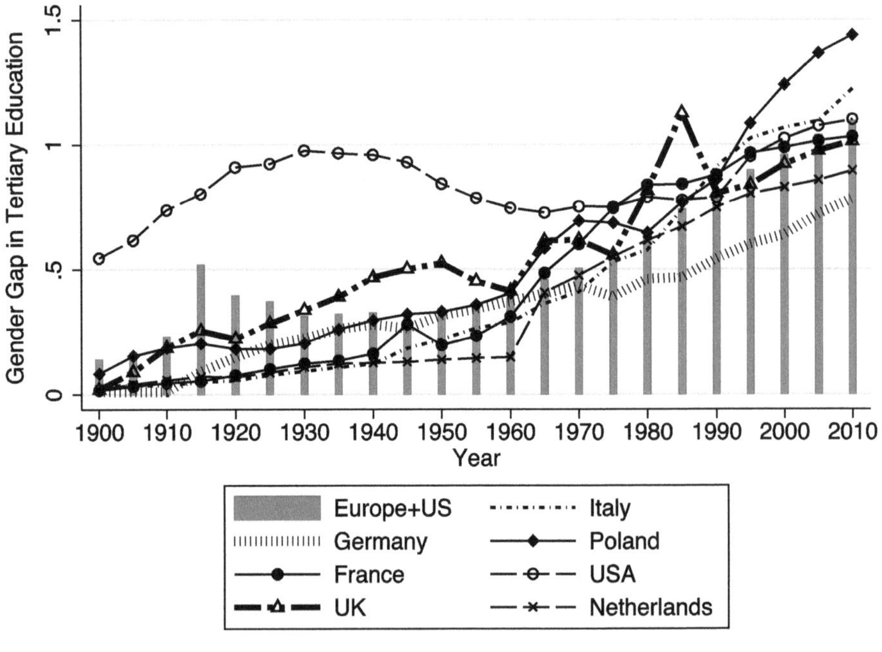

Fig. 2.3 Gender gap in educational attainment in tertiary level (age group 25–64). *Source* Lee and Lee (2016)

[3]An important note here is that the educational attainment at tertiary level compares only cross-country differences in terms of quantity and does not provide information on the quality of education, which is hard to capture historically and across space.

above 1 means women are overrepresented in education. Figure 2.3 shows a slightly different picture than Fig. 2.2 in terms of gender differences in tertiary education.

The USA, an LME economy, is the pioneer in closing the gender gap in tertiary education where equality between men and women is achieved as far back as in the 1940s. However, a reversal is visible between 1940s and 1980s, and in the post-1980 period, the gender gap closes again. The USA context highlights that the progress toward gender equality is not linear (Goldin 1995). The UK, also an LME, witnesses progress toward gender equality by the beginning of the twentieth century. From the 1960 onwards, the gap between men and women at tertiary education really starts to close, and in 1985, equality is reached. In Poland, an EME, the gender gap in tertiary education narrowed in the 1990s and women are even outperforming men since the mid-1990s. A similar trend is visible in Italy. While many of the other European countries also achieved equality in tertiary education during the 1990s, Germany stands out as an exception where the size of the gender gap is largest and only a slow convergence to gender equality is visible from the 1970s onwards.

When the gender differences in field of subjects at the university level are considered, a different picture emerges. This has implications for entrepreneurial activity. In recent years, cross-national differences in entrepreneurship have been attributed to the differences in education, more particularly gender differences in science, technology, engineering, and mathematics (STEM) fields (OECD 2016a). To the extent that entrepreneurial ventures come up with radically new innovations, they are typically based on technological inventions developed by scientifically oriented workforces (Dilli et al. 2018). In Dilli and Westerhuis (2018b), we provided empirical evidence on the evolution of the gender differences in STEM subjects at the tertiary level since 1970s, which showed that the gender gap in science education is negatively correlated with entrepreneurial activity.

In Dilli and Westerhuis (2018b), we demonstrate that there is a clear increase in educational attainment in science subjects in all the four VoC clusters since the 1990s with LME countries having the highest level followed by MMEs, CMEs, and EMEs, respectively. However, despite the increase in the share of the population in science subjects, this did not translate into higher gender equality. Instead, all VoC categories show a decrease in the share of women in science subjects since the mid-1990s. The only exception being the 1970s when women in LMEs became relatively more inclined toward science subjects at the tertiary level. Interestingly, while in the period before the 1990s, the size of the gender gap is largest in CMEs, followed by LMEs and MMEs, and EMEs, a convergence toward gender inequality in science subjects is visible. A sharp decline is particularly visible in EMEs after the collapse of the Soviet Union. An explanation for this increasing gap can be partly due to the change in women's choices to follow careers in other fields such as health and engineering. Thus, we suggest that closing the gender gap in science can be beneficial for knowledge intensive sectors and high-growth aspirational entrepreneurship especially in the institutional environments that are also favorable for women such as in the Nordic CME countries.

2.3.2 Research and Development

The differences across the institutional constellations described in the VoC are also visible in terms of R&D expenditures. Figure 2.4 highlights that the differences among European countries have been present at least since the 1980s. Considering the share of government expenditure in research and development, both Germany and the USA have the largest public investment compared to the other European countries for almost the entire period of 1980 and 2010, followed by France. While the Netherlands and UK show moderate levels of investment in research and development, Italy and Poland have the lowest. In addition, the share of governmental expenditure in research and development remained rather constant over time. A similar trend in terms of cross-country differences is visible when a second indicator of research and development, researchers per capita is considered. While in the UK, the government plays a limited role in supporting research and innovation (in line with the LME typology), it is among the top performers in terms of the number of researchers. This could be attributed to the academic system of the UK that does not only offer sophisticated scientific training, but also attracts high numbers of immigrant scientists (Dilli et al. 2018).

Over time, as the number of researchers has increased substantially across European countries, this progress has been especially limited in the case of Italy and Poland. Overall, the increase in the share of population following science subjects at the tertiary level might be one of the drivers of this general increase over time. Thus, for Poland and Italy, stimulating research and development activity via governmental expenditure and stimulating at the tertiary level to follow science subjects might be tools to support entrepreneurship. Another alternative could also be attracting highly skilled migrants with a science background to increase the number of researchers.

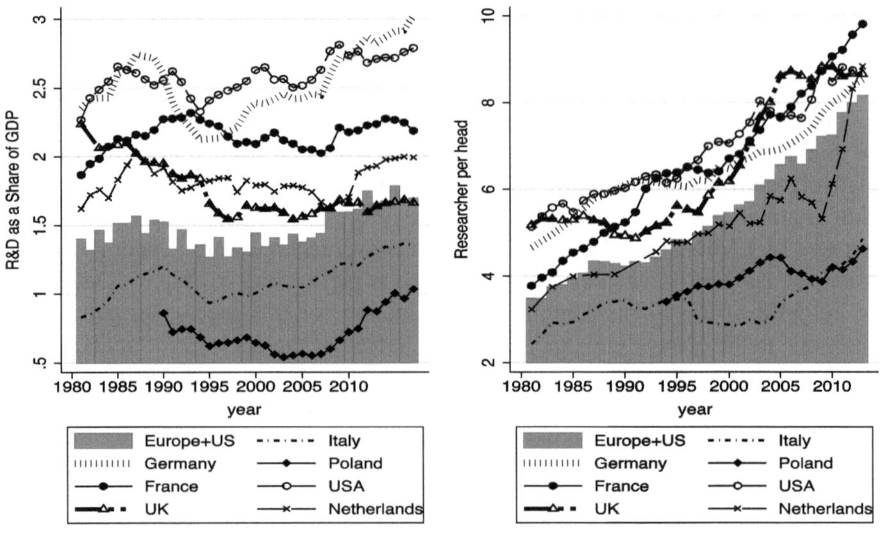

Fig. 2.4 Research and development, 1980–2010. *Source* OECD (2019)

This section illustrated that there have been rapid improvements both in educational attainment and in number of researchers over the second half of the twentieth century. This implies that reforms addressed toward implementation in the field of education, and research might have impact in the short run. However, in pursuing such reforms, it is also important to recognize the differences between CMEs and LMEs in terms of vocational versus general training, as vocational training in the CMEs has also been successful in supporting innovative entrepreneurial activity (Dilli et al. 2018), although arguably, in a more incremental nature (see, e.g., Herrmann 2020).

2.4 Labor Market Institutions

As mentioned in the introduction, the relevant labor market institutions for entrepreneurship are: (1) regulation of labor markets, (2) wage setting institutions, and (3) social security systems (Henrekson 2014; Elert et al. 2019). These institutions were also in focus in the FIRES project (see Dilli 2019, for an empirical test of this link). The flexibility in hiring and firing employees, as well as the extent of the availability of social security, would shape the decision making of entrepreneurs to start and grow their businesses. Centralized wage setting institutions and strong labor unions can discourage entrepreneurship by introducing standard compensation policies for wage labor that closely tie wages to observed characteristics such as seniority and education. Such institutions would discourage innovative entrepreneurship. In terms of social security arrangements, generous unemployment benefit schemes and other social benefits may decrease incentives and increase perceptions of the risk involved in establishing a business (Henrekson 2014; Dilli 2019). But many of these institutions have deep historical roots. The discussion below therefore focuses on the historically evolved differences between the USA and European countries in these three pillars as well as how they have changed over the twentieth century to develop a historical understanding of the cross-national differences in labor market institutions characterizing Europe today.

2.4.1 Labor Market Regulations

Labor market institutions in Europe are less flexible compared to those in the USA (Siebert 1997). For example, the USA stands out as the least regulated country based on indicators for dismissals of individual workers on permanent contracts. The success of the USA in terms of entrepreneurial activity has been attributed to less regulated labor market institutions. Among the European countries, however, there is a large variation in the extent to which labor market regulations are stringent. Similar to the USA context, the UK have fairly unrestrictive individual dismissal regulations. By contrast, regulations in France and Germany are far stricter than the

OECD average (Scarpetta 2014: 3). These differences were also highlighted in the VoC literature. Labor markets have been deregulated with relatively unrestrictive individual dismissal regulations in LME economies such as UK and the USA. Since 1990, EMEs also tend to have more flexible labor market regulations compared to the Nordic countries and the continental European countries, such as the Netherlands, Germany, and Belgium, characterized by a moderate employment protection. In the MMEs, notably France, Italy, and Spain, it is far more difficult to dismiss employees, especially from public service, compared to the other contexts (Dilli 2019). Some of these cross-national differences characterizing Europe today can be traced back in the past of these economies.

The twentieth century witnessed an important move towards flexibility in labor market institutions across Europe. But the extent of this change differs across European countries. This is visible in the study of Aleksynska and Schmidt (2014), which sheds light on the current-day differences in labor market institutions by looking at the origin and evolution of these labor market regulations for a selected number of European countries. Some of the rules on employment protection, such as prohibited grounds for dismissals, have roots going back as far as the late nineteenth century (Aleksynska and Schmidt 2014). Such labor protection laws often emerged to address the social consequences of early industrialization. The issues of equity and equality, dignity and decent incomes, set the scene for emerging national frameworks of regulating work and work relationships. France was the first country to regulate unemployment insurance, fixed-term contracts, and compensation for unfair dismissal in 1890. Greece and Italy pioneered generous notice periods and severance pay. Spain was the first country to explicitly regulate the use and the termination of fixed-term contracts with respective provisions put in place in 1926. These three Mediterranean economies also introduced regulations similar to France on the notice period and regulations on fixed contracts during the 1920s. These economies are known to have more stringent labor market regulations to this day. In Portugal, in contrast to the other Mediterranean economies, many of the rules on unemployment and employment protection were only introduced in the late 1960s and early 1970s, whereas in the UK, the rules on employment protection legislation developed mainly in the second half of the twentieth century (Aleksynska and Schmidt 2014).

In the second half of the century, there is more systematic evidence available on the differences between countries in terms of the employment protection legislation (EPL). This allows me to trace the change in labor market regulations over time in a comparative way. The OECD has developed the EPL index—a commonly used indicator to capture the regulation of the labor markets—based on 21 items such as laws protecting workers with regular contracts, those affecting workers with fixed–term (temporary) contracts or contracts with temporary work agencies, and regulations applying specifically to collective dismissals.[4] A higher score on the

---

[4]More information on the method of OEC in constructing the EPL index and the latest version of the index can be accessed at https://www.oecd.org/els/emp/oecdindicatorsofemploymentprotection.htm.

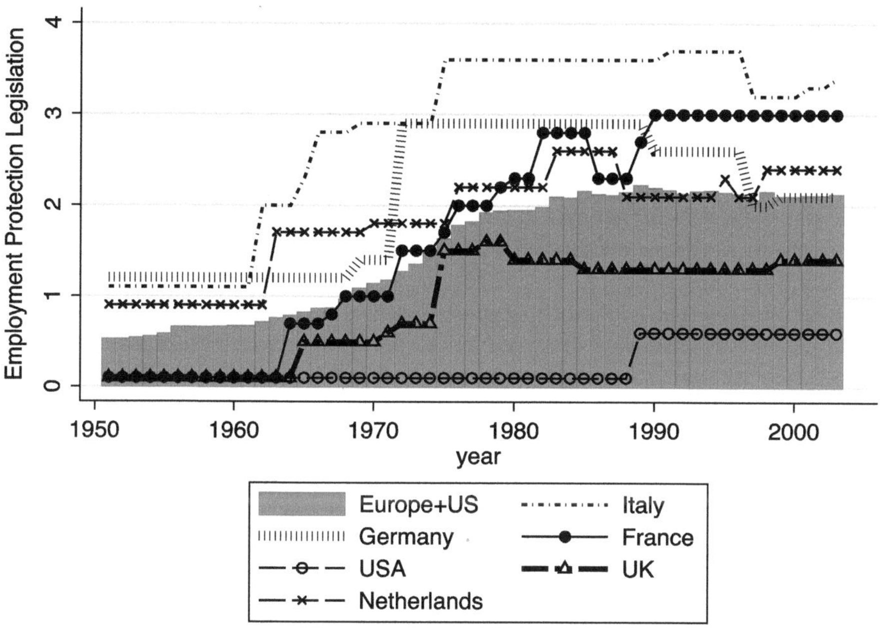

Fig. 2.5 Employment protection legislation (EPL), since 1950. *Source* Allard (2005)

index indicates stricter labor market regulations. Allard (2005) extends this EPL index back to 1950. Using his information, Fig. 2.5 displays the differences across a selected number of European countries and the USA since 1950.

According to Fig. 2.5, in the 1950s, the labor market was relatively unregulated compared to today though the cross-sectional differences between the cluster of countries were already visible in the mid-50s. The typical LME countries, UK and USA, had the lowest employment protection by far throughout this period. Starting from the 1970s onwards, the regulations on employment protection started to become stricter in many countries (e.g., Germany, France). During this period, the EPL increased in the UK as well, though it still remained the least regulated European country. This is because in the 1960s and 1970s, a number of legislations (i.e., the Contracts of Employment Act 1963 and the Industrial Relations Act 1971) were introduced to protect employees against unfair dismissals in the UK. The CMEs Germany and the Netherlands (as well as France, which can either be classified in the Coordinated or in the Mixed Market category) show moderate levels of employment protection. In the early 1970s, however, Germany introduced further legislation to increase employment protection reaching levels similar to Italy.

The late 1970s and beginning of the 1980s witnessed deregulation of the labor market in a number of countries. A deregulation process is visible in the UK, from the late 1970s onwards followed by the Netherlands, and Germany in the late 1980s and early 1990s. In the early 1980s, economic deregulation was the principal labor market policy of the Thatcher government. During the Thatcher government, a significant amount of legislation (i.e., Employment Acts of 1980, 1982, and 1988) was passed, turning back the individual employee rights introduced in the 1960s and 1970s (Capon 2004). In Germany, the major step relaxing the conditions concerning fixed-term employment contracts was the introduction of the Employment Promotion Act (*Beschäftigungsförderungsgesetz*) in 1985 (Schettkat 2002).[5] It is also important to note that in all the European countries, the number of temporary contracts noticeably increased in the 1990s (Amable 2003). Labor market liberalization over the 1990s effectively shows that the bulk of the adjustment was borne by temporary contracts. The decline in employment protection for that group is especially remarkable in Italy. While employment protection for regular contracts seems to have been fairly stable over time, the EPL showed clear reductions for temporary workers over the same period. Nevertheless, the extent of this deregulation process differed substantially across the European societies and is reflected in the cross-national differences in the labor market institutions.

2.4.2 Wage Setting Institutions

In FIRES, in order to capture the wage setting institutions relevant for entrepreneurial activity, we looked at trade union density, the level of wage bargaining (coordination), and governmental intervention in the wage bargaining process (see Dilli 2019 for a discussion on the relevance of these dimensions for different forms of entrepreneurial activity and Sanders et al. 2020a, b, c in this volume for applications). For instance, decentralized and individualized wage setting has been argued to encourage mobility and risk-taking and would therefore support (potential) high-growth firms (Henrekson 2014).

Figure 2.6 shows the cross-national differences in trade union density, defined as the membership as a proportion of all wage and salary earners since 1955 in a selected number of countries (Visser 2013).[6] Figure 2.6 shows that a large variation exists in terms of trade union density between countries.

The low unionization rate of France is remarkably low (an average of 14% for the entire period), given the capability of trade unions to mobilize their members for mass action (e.g., strikes), and their influence on government policy. For instance, in France the government has withdrawn its plans for a new employment contract for young workers in 2006, while in 2010 there were massive demonstrations between September and October protesting against the government's pension reform plans (Fulton 2013). Thus, in terms of union density, France shows much lower levels

[5] The law provided unconditional freedom for the conclusion of fixed-term contracts up to 18 months in duration (Schettkat 2002).

[6] While union density does not reflect the strength of the labor unions (as visible in the case of France which has a very low union density but very strong labor unions in terms of wage bargaining), union density is the only indicator to my knowledge that is available historically over time and across the contexts and to have been commonly linked with entrepreneurship outcomes (see Dilli 2019).

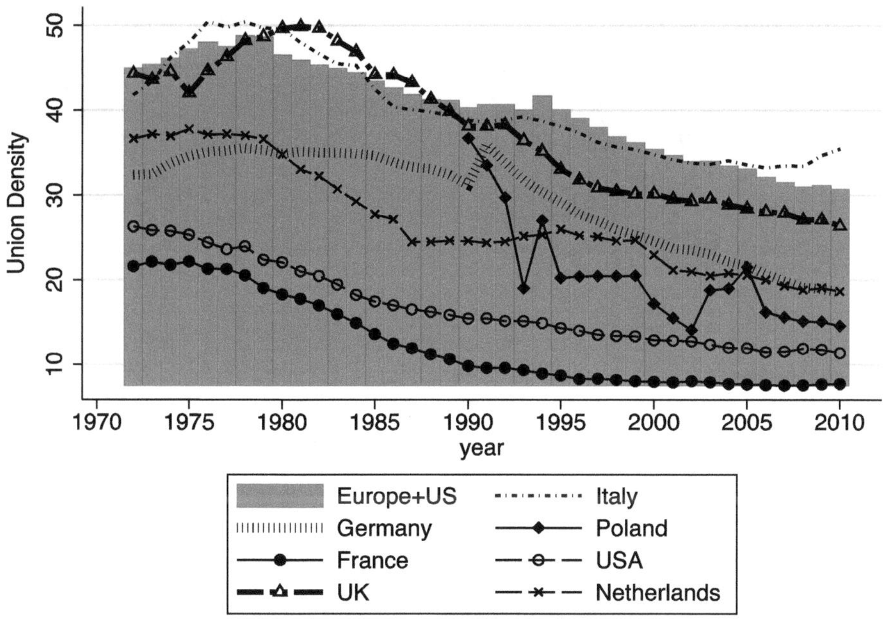

Fig. 2.6 Trade union density, 1970–2010. *Source* Visser (2013)

compared to Germany, for example. The trade unionization in the USA, a liberal market economy, is also one of the lowest in Fig. 2.6, whereas the level of union density in the UK is higher than in the CMEs (e.g., Germany) and the MMEs. The CME and the MME countries are close to the average of overall European in terms of trade union density.

Turning to trends in trade union density over time, during the early postwar period, Western trade union movements grew in membership and achieved an institutionalized role in industrial relations and politics, especially in the CMEs. However, in recent decades, trade unions have seen their membership decline in many countries as they came increasingly under pressure due to social, economic, and political changes. The decline in unionization began in the 1960s in the USA, spread to France after the mid-70s, and was then observed in the Netherlands and the UK (corresponding with the Thatcher years as well) in the late 1970s. With the wave of social protest in the late 1960s, unions targeted social groups such as white-collar, female, and often part-time employees. Some unions were more successful in recruiting members than others. The Italian unions, for instance, enjoyed spectacular post-1968 growth after partially successful attempts to reunite the politically fragmented union movements (Ebbinghaus and Visser 1999). The same period witnessed an increase in unionism in Sweden (see also Visser 2013), but the downward trend continued in other countries. Especially from the mid-90s onwards, there has been a second round of decline in trade unionization observable in many European countries. Arguably, due to the different degrees to which unions were able

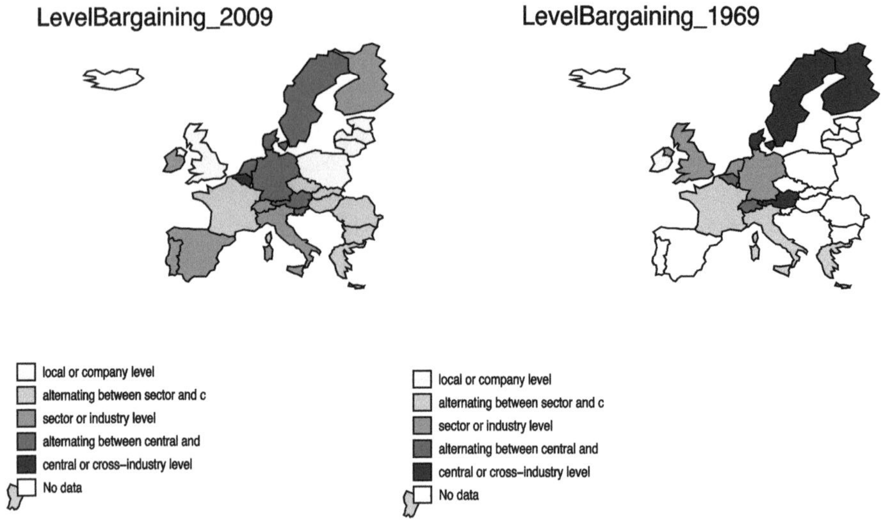

Fig. 2.7 Level of wage bargaining. *Source* Visser (2013)

to maintain coverage in wage bargaining, these changes in trade union density did not lead to a convergence between the European countries and the cross-sectional differences remain rather stable over time.

Figure 2.7 reveals the large variation in terms of centralization of wage bargaining process both between countries and over time. Hall and Soskice (2001) argue that in CMEs, the wage bargaining would be more centralized (i.e., involving governments, businesses and labor unions together and agreements would be made across industries) compared to the liberal market economies. Figure 2.7 shows support for this view. While there was industry-level bargaining in the UK historically, since 1980, there have been no centralizing forces. A similar decentralized wage bargaining system has been in place in the USA. The EMEs show similar patterns to the UK with firm or local level bargaining. In the Scandinavian countries, there has been a shift from a centralized wage arrangement to a more sectorial bargaining model during the 1980s. In Germany, Austria, and Switzerland, industry-level bargaining has been the dominant form. In the Netherlands, until the 1980s, there was a mix between central level negotiations with industry bargaining in which there were frequent government interventions. After the 1980s, the bargaining mostly took place between employers and trade unions though during the 2009–10 recession, the government committed to support financially to reducing temporary working hours (Visser 2013). Among the MMEs, industry-level bargaining seems to be more commonly practiced. While Spain first had central bargaining during the 1970s, it moved to industrial level bargaining during the 1980s. Overall, there seems to be a convergence toward industrial level wage bargaining in Europe since the 1980s, except in Belgium, which counters the trend by moving to a more centralized wage bargaining system over the same period. So, although wage bargaining institutions change over decades, there is no tendency for convergence and the differences between countries in terms of wage bargaining process persist.

2.4.3 Social Security

With regard to social security, we studied the relevance of social spending together with illness, unemployment and pension minimum replacement rates for their relevance for entrepreneurial activity (Dilli 2019). These three show some nuanced differences, but here it will suffice to focus on the historical evolution of social spending with pension minimum replacement rates.

While cross-national differences in terms of social security arrangements are clearly visible today, social security was limited prior to the twentieth century everywhere around the world. During the eighteenth century, there were two forms of tax based social spending, namely poor relief and public schools, which made up at most three percent of GDP in social welfare (Lindert 2004). Still, important differences across societies in terms of social security arrangements are already visible in this period. While the Netherlands and the UK historically led in poverty relief, the USA and Germany led in public schooling. With the extension of suffrage in many countries after the First World War, public spending on welfare started to expand in the world and the modern welfare state emerged with extensive coverage including subsidized healthcare, education, housing, childcare, and old-age pensions emerged (Lindert 2004). The Great Depression of 1929 and economic crisis in the late 1970s were particularly important turning points in the European countries. They gave rise to the role of government in providing security such as in terms of unemployment insurance and introduction of minimum wage laws (Blanchard 2002; Visser 2013); though, a large variation is visible in the national strategies of European countries in terms of government's support in providing security (e.g., Siebert 1997). Despite the general rise in social spending and social security arrangements over the twentieth century, progress toward social welfare regimes has not resulted in a convergence among the European countries.

Figure 2.8 presents the trends in total social spending as the percentage of GDP. While France, Germany, and Italy are characterized with the highest social spending in total, the USA has the lowest followed by the Netherlands and the UK. A significant decline in social spending is visible during the 1980s, followed by an increase during the 1990s almost in most selected European countries. Italy has caught up with the CMEs like Germany, with relatively large social expenditure. Poland, EME, on the other hand shows a moderate level of social spending, which first rose rapidly but declined in the post-Soviet period. Perhaps the most striking decline in total spending is in the case of the Netherlands, where social security reforms in the early 1980s have driven a sustained decline from about 23 to 17% of GDP, eventually even undercutting levels in the USA.

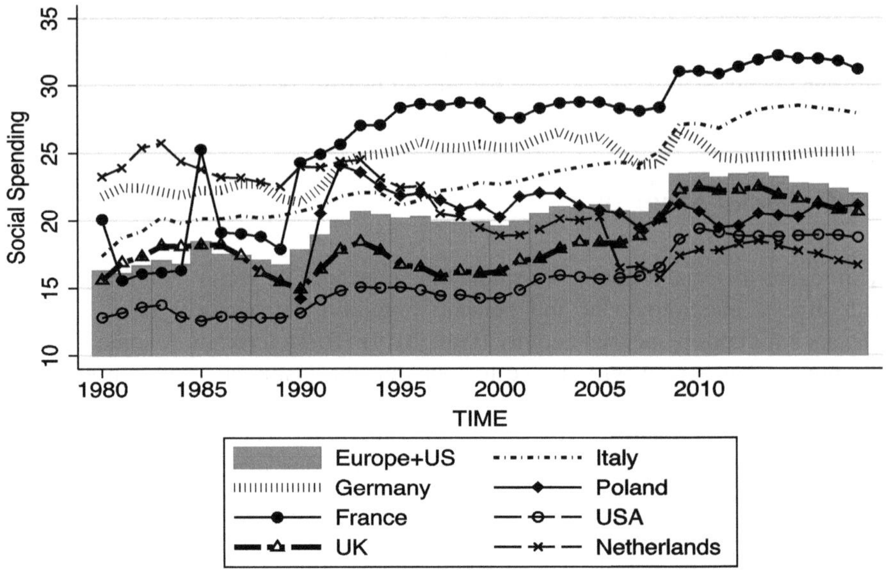

Fig. 2.8 Total social spending, 1980–2012. *Source* OECD (2016b)

Figure 2.9 presents the trends in the minimum pension replacement rates from the 1970s onwards, referring to public pension or equivalent benefit for which a person without working or pension contribution history is entitled. While countries like the Netherlands and France show minimum pension replacement rates high above the European average, the minimum replacement rate in the USA is close to the European average. The USA and the UK, typical LMEs, have lower pension replacement rates than France or the Netherlands, but higher than Germany or Poland. Moreover, some change in the minimum replacement rates[7] is visible in a number of countries. For instance, from the mid-1980s onwards, minimum replacement rates have declined in the Netherlands. On contrary, the same period has witnessed an increase in Italy where the minimum pension replacement rate starts at the lowest level but catches up with countries such as the USA (see also the discussion in Kuitto et al. 2012).

Overall, this section highlights that there have been various changes in the fields of employment protection legislation, centralization of wage bargaining and social security over the twentieth century. Labor market institutions, therefore, do seem rather flexible. Still, despite these changes, the extent to which European countries experienced change has been different from each other and we do not find convergence in labor market institutions. For instance, while an increase in employment protection legislation is visible in many European countries (such as in Germany, Italy, France) up until the 1980s, these regulations became more flexible

[7]This indicator is calculated for a fictive average production worker in manufacturing sector who is 40 years old and has been working for the 20 years preceding the loss of income or the benefit period.

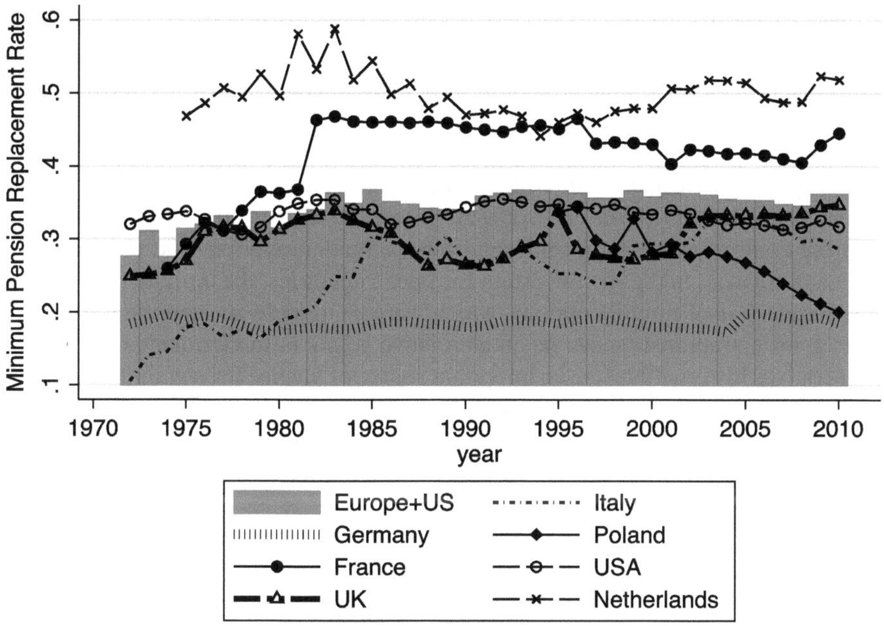

Fig. 2.9 Minimum pension replacement rates, 1971–2011. *Source* Scruggs et al. (2014)

in the case of Germany and Italy after the 1980s. Overall, a convergence toward more industry-level bargaining process is visible in Central European countries. It is therefore important to study the history of labor market institutions and carefully tailor reform proposals to the local and national context.

2.5 Conclusion and Discussion

In the FIRES project, using the Varieties of Capitalism framework, we presented how the different institutional constellations with regard to finance, knowledge, and labor market institutions support different forms of entrepreneurial activity (Dilli et al. 2019; also discussed in Elert et al. 2019 and Herrmann 2020). This chapter provides a long-term perspective on the historical evolution of such institutions. By using a historical perspective, the aim of this chapter is to distinguish between those institutions that change over time versus those that are more resistant to change. This enables us to identify which institutions can be more easily altered versus which are hard to change via policy tools. Overall, while change is visible in all three institutions over the twentieth century, the VoC typology is relevant in understanding the extent and the direction of the institutional change European countries have experienced.

A historical perspective on the financial institutions with a focus on the banking structure in Europe indicates that banks were more diversified in the past than today and provided different possibilities for entrepreneurs to have access to finance. Historically, rather than getting finance from large banks, the challenges in accessing finance were solved in many cases through local and private initiatives. Today in Europe, Eastern and Mediterranean economies face the largest constraints in financial institutions (Dilli et al. 2018). Given the historically strong family ties in these contexts, stimulating informal family funding can provide an alternative source of finance. In the Northwestern European countries, the introduction of more small-scale formal funding options, which were historically an important source of finance for entrepreneurs, can be an alternative solution. In Germany, for instance, cooperatives historically were an important source of finance for entrepreneurs. Such organizational forms can provide alternative sources of formal finance especially in continental European countries. Moreover, platform-based financial intermediation such as through crowdfunding and Fintech are modern-day examples of such institutions.

In terms of knowledge institutions, the LME economies have a clear advantage in tertiary level educational attainment, which stimulates general education compared to occupation and firm specific training in the CMEs. In terms of research and development, the continental European economies are performing as well as the LME economies, but potentially with a slightly different focus. This chapter illustrates that the differences in the knowledge outcomes, which have been highlighted in the VoC framework, have been visible already in the beginning of the twentieth century. The twentieth century also witnessed important progress in closing the gender gap in tertiary education, but the gap remains in STEM education today and presents a challenge for women's involvement in more innovative entrepreneurial activity (Dilli and Westerhuis 2018b). In the case of the UK, the academic environment has managed to attract researchers from abroad. Continental European economies compensate by stimulating research and development via governmental expenditures such as in the case of Germany. This may provide an alternative for contexts where research and development remain limited.

The historical cross-national differences in labor market institutions also change noticeably on the surface, but there is also clear path dependence and deeply rooted elements that clearly persist over time. The LMEs, for instance, always had the least regulated labor market institutions, whereas the tightly regulated labor market institutions have been characteristic for the Mediterranean and the continental economies over the same period. Therefore, from a historical viewpoint, deregulation in labor market institutions to stimulate entrepreneurship would likely face challenges in contexts where labor markets were historically tightly regulated. Overall, the historical analysis shows that elements of the institutional framework in Europe have deep roots that should be carefully considered when contemplating reforms. In line with this conclusion, in Sanders et al. (2020a, b, c), an objective is to let careful historical analysis precede the formulation of reform proposals.

References

Aleksynska M, Schmidt A (2014) A chronology of employment protection legislation in some selected European countries. Working paper. Accessed on 15 Nov 2015. http://www.ilo.org/travail/whatwedo/publications/WCMS_324647/lang–en/index.htm

Alesina A, Giuliano P (2010) The power of the family. J Econ Growth 15(2):93–125

Allard GJ (2005) Measuring job security over time: in search of a historical indicator for EPL (Employment Protection Legislation). SSRN Scholarly Paper. Social Science Research Network, Rochester, NY. Accessed on 17 Dec 2015. http://papers.ssrn.com/abstract=1016327

Amable B (2003) The diversity of modern capitalism. Oxford University Press, Oxford

Arregle JL, Batjargal B, Hitt MA, Webb JW, Miller T, Tsui AS (2015) Family ties in entrepreneurs' social networks and new venture growth. Entrep Theory Pract 39(2):313–344

Au K, Ding ZJ (2011) Institutional influence on love money: informal investment to family, friends, strangers across countries. In: Family business association annual conference, Perth. http://www.fambiz.org.au/wp-content/uploads/Institutional-Influence-on-Love-Money-Informal-Investment-to-Family-Friends-and-Strangersacross-Countries-Professor-Kevin-Au-and-Zhujun-Ding.pdf

Au K, Kwan HK (2009) Start-up capital and Chinese entrepreneurs: the role of family. Entrep Theory Pract 33:889–908

Baumol WJ (1990) Entrepreneurship: productive, unproductive, and destructive. J Polit Econ 98(5):893–921

Black SE, Strahan PE (2002) Entrepreneurship and bank credit availability. J Financ 57(6):2807–2833

Blanchard O (2002) Designing labor market institutions, Working Paper. Accessed on 19 Jan 2016. http://economics.mit.edu/files/664

Broadberry S (ed) (2010) The Cambridge economic history of modern Europe, volume 2: 1870 to the present. Cambridge University Press, New York

Bruton GD, Ahlstrom D, Li HL (2010) Institutional theory and entrepreneurship: where are we now and where do we need to move in the future? Entrep Theory Pract 34(3):421–440

Bürzel TA (1999) Towards convergence in Europe? institutional adaptation to Europeanization in Germany and Spain. J Common Mark Stud 37(4):573–596

Bygrave W, Hay M, Ng E, Reynolds P (2003) Executive forum: a study of informal investing in 29 nations composing the global entrepreneurship monitor. Ventur Cap 5(2):101–116

Bygrave WD, Reynolds PD (2005) Who finances start-ups in the USA? a comprehensive study of informal investors, 1999–2003. Frontiers of Entrepreneurship Research

Capon C (2004) Understanding organizational context: inside and outside organizations. Pearson Education

Carnevali F (2005) Europe's advantage: banks and small firms in Britain, France, Germany, and Italy since 1918. Oxford University Press, Oxford, New York

Coad A, Rao R (2010) R&D and firm growth rate variance. Econ Bull 30(1):702–708

Cull R, Davis LE, Lamoreaux NR, Rosenthal JL (2006) Historical financing of small-and medium-size enterprises. J Bank Finance 30(11):3017–3042

de Goey F, van Gerwen JL (2008) Entrepreneurs in Netherlands (ondernemers in Nederland: varieties in ondernemen. Boom, Amsterdam

Deeg RE (1999) Finance capitalism unveiled: banks and the German political economy. University of Michigan Press, Ann Arbor

Dilli S, Westerhuis G (2018a) A historical perspective on the varieties of institutions, Finance and entrepreneurship. Available at: https://projectfires.eu/wp-content/uploads/2018/05/d2.2-combined-parts-23-n.pdf

Dilli S, Westerhuis G (2018b) How Institutions and gender differences in education shape entrepreneurial activity: a cross-national perspective. Small Bus Econ 51(2): 371–92

Dilli S (2019) The diversity of labor market institutions and entrepreneurship. Socio-Econ Rev. Online first

Dilli S, Elert N, Herrmann AM (2018) Varieties of entrepreneurship: exploring the institutional foundations of different entrepreneurship types through 'varieties-of-capitalism' arguments. Small Bus Econ 51(2):1–28
Duranton G, Andres Rodriguez-Pose A, Sandall R (2009) Family types and the persistence of regional disparities in Europe. Econ Geogr 85(1):23–47
Ebbinghaus B, Visser J (1999) When institutions matter: union growth and decline in Western Europe, 1950–1995. Eur Sociol Rev 15(2):135–158
Elert N, Henrekson M, Sanders M (2019) The entrepreneurial society: a reform strategy for the European union. International studies in Entrepreneurship. Springer, Berlin Heidelberg
European Commission (2013) Entrepreneurship 2020 action plan: reigniting the entrepreneurial spirit in Europe, Brussels, Commission of the European Communities
Frankema E, Van Waijenburg M (2012) Structural impediments to African growth? new evidence from real wages in British Africa, 1880–1965. J Econ Hist 72(4):895–926
Fritsch M, Wyrwich M (2017) The effect of entrepreneurship for economic development—an empirical analysis using regional entrepreneurship culture. J Econ Geogr 17:157–189
Fulton L (2013) Worker representation in Europe. Labour Research Department and ETUI. Produced with the assistance of the SEEurope Network. Accessed on 17 June 2019. http://www.workerparticipation.eu/National-Industrial-Relations/Across-Europe/Trade-Unions2
Galor O, Ozak Ö (2016) The agricultural origins of time preference. Am Econ Rev 106(10):3064–3103
Gelderblom OC (2011) Entrepreneurs in the Dutch golden age. In: Baumol W, Landes D, Mokyr J (eds) The invention of enterprise. Entrepreneurship from ancient Mesopotamia to modern times, Princeton UP, Princeton, pp 156–182 (p 27)
Gelderblom O, Jonker J (2004) Completing a financial revolution: the finance of the Dutch East India trade and the rise of the Amsterdam capital market, 1595–1612. J Econ Hist 64(3):641–672
Global Entrepreneurship Monitor (2011) Global Report. Babson College, Babson Park
Goldin C (1995) Investment in women's human capital and economic development. University of Chicago Press, Chicago
Greif A (2006) Family structure, institutions, and growth: the origins and implications of western corporations. Am Econ Rev 96(2):308–312
Hall PA, Soskice DW (2001) An introduction to varieties of capitalism. In: Hall PA, Soskice DW (eds) Varieties of capitalism—the institutional foundations of comparative advantage. Oxford University Press, Oxford, pp 1–68
Hall PA, Thelen K (2009) Institutional change in varieties of capitalism. Socio-Econ Rev 7(1):7–34
Henrekson M (2014) How labor market institutions affect job creation and productivity growth, IZA World of Labor. http://wol.iza.org/articles/how-labor-market-institutions-affect-job-creation-and-productivity-growth/long
Herrmann A (2020) Chapter 4. On the institutional foundations of the varieties of entrepreneurship in Europe. In: Sanders M, Marx A, Stenkula M (eds) The entrepreneurial society. Springer, Berlin Heidelberg
Jonker J (1997) The alternative road to modernity: banking and currency, 1814–1914. In: Hart MT, Jonker J, Zanden J (eds) A financial history of the Netherlands, Cambridge University Press, Cambridge, pp 94–123
Kuitto K, John D, Düpont N (2012) Welfare policy institutions in the enlarged EU—convergence, divergence or persistence? Greifswald Comparative Politics Working paper No. 1/2012. Accessed on 17 July 2019. https://www.researchgate.net/publication/309291706_Welfare_policy_institutions_in_the_enlarged_EU_-_convergence_divergence_or_persistence
Lee JW, Lee H (2016) Human capital in the long run. J Dev Econ 122:147–169
Lescure M (1999) Small-and medium-size industrial enterprises in France, 1900–1975. In: Odaka K, Sawai M (eds) Small firms, large concerns: the development of small business in comparative perspective. Oxford University Press, Oxford, pp 140–167
Lindert PH (2004) Growing public: social spending and economic growth since the eighteenth century. Cambridge University Press

Millán JM, Congregado E, Román C, van Praag M, van Stel A (2014) The value of an educated population for an individual's entrepreneurship success. Journal of Business Venturing 29(5):612–632

Nielson K, Jessop B, Hausner J (1995) Institutional change in post-socialism. In: Hausner J, Jessop B, Nielsen K (eds) Strategic choice and path-dependency in post-socialism: institutional dynamics in the transformation process. Edward Elgar, Hants, UK

North DC (1990) Institutions, institutional change and economic performance. Cambridge University Press, Cambridge

Nunn N (2009) The importance of history for economic development. Annu Rev Econ 1(1):65–92

OECD (2013) Alternative financing instruments for SMEs and entrepreneurs: the case of mezzanine finance. OECD Publishing, Paris

OECD (2015) Financing SMEs and entrepreneurs 2015 An OECD scoreboard: an OECD scoreboard. OECD Publishing, Paris

OECD (2016a) The missing entrepreneurs 2015 (p. 2015). OECD Publishing, Paris. http://www.oecd-ilibrary.org/content/book/9789264226418-en

OECD (2016b) Total social spending, 1980–2012 (indicator). Accessed on 05 June 2016. https://www.oecd.org/social/expenditure.htm

OECD (2019) Gross domestic spending on R&D (indicator). https://doi.org/10.1787/d8b068b4-en Accessed on 01 July 2019

Reher DS (1998) Family ties in Western Europe: persistent contrasts. Popul Dev Rev 24(2):203–234

Sanders M, Stenkula M, Grilli L, Herrmann AM, Latifi G, Páger B, Szerb L, Terragno Bogliaccini E (2020a) A Reform Strategy for Italy. In: Sanders M, Marx A, Stenkula M (eds) The entrepreneurial society. Springer, Berlin Heidelberg

Sanders M, Stenkula M, Fritsch M, Herrmann AM, Latifi G, Páger B, Szerb L, Terragno Bogliaccini E, Wyrwich M (2020b) A Reform Strategy for Germany. In: Sanders M, Marx A, Stenkula M (eds) The entrepreneurial society. Springer, Berlin Heidelberg

Sanders M, Stenkula M, Dunstan J, Estrin S, Herrmann AM, Páger B, Szerb L, Terragno Bogliaccini E (2020c) A Reform Strategy for the UK. In: Sanders M, Marx A, Stenkula M (eds) The entrepreneurial society. Springer, Berlin Heidelberg

Scarpetta S (2014) Employment protection, IZA World of Labor, pp. 1–10. http://wol.iza.org/articles/employment-protection.pdf

Schettkat R (2002) Regulation in the Dutch and German economies at the root of unemployment? SCEPA working paper series. SCEPA's main areas of research are macroeconomic policy, inequality and poverty, and globalization. Schwartz Center for Economic Policy Analysis (SCEPA), The New School. Accessed on 20 Dec 2015. https://ideas.repec.org/p/epa/cepawp/2002-05.html

Scruggs L, Jahn D, Kuitto K (2014) Comparative welfare entitlements dataset 2. Version 2014–03. University of Connecticut & University of Greiswald

Siebert H (1997) Labor market rigidities: at the root of unemployment in Europe. J Econ Perspect 11(3):37–54

Sluyterman K (ed) (2015) Varieties of capitalism and business history: the Dutch case. Routledge, London and New York

Spadavecchia A (2005) Surviving under the shelter of government subsidies or 'avoiding disaster'? new evidence from Italian industrial districts, 1971–91, Working Papers 5011, Economic History Society

Steier L (2003) Variants of agency contracts in family-financed ventures as a continuum of familial altruistic and market rationalities. J Bus Ventur 18(5):597–618

Szerb L, Terjesen S, Rappai G (2007) Seeding new ventures—greenthumbs and fertile fields: individual and environmental drivers of informal investment. Ventur Cap 9(4):257–284

Todd E (1985) The explanation of ideology: family structures and social system. Basil Blackwell, Oxford

Todd E (2011) L'origine des systèmes familiaux, Tome 1: L'Eurasie. Gallimard, Paris

Van Sluis J, Van Praag M, Vijverberg W (2008) Education and entrepreneurship selection and performance: a review of the empirical literature. J Econ Surv 22(5):795–841
Van Zanden JL, Zuijderduijn J, De Moor T (2012) Small is beautiful: the efficiency of credit markets in the late medieval Holland. Eur Rev Econ Hist 16:3–22
Visser J (2013) Wage bargaining institutions—from Crisis to Crisis. European economy—economic paper. Directorate general economic and financial affairs (DG ECFIN), European Commission. Accessed on 8 Feb 2016. https://ideas.repec.org/p/euf/ecopap/0488.html
Wadhwani RD (2016) Small-scale credit institutions. In: Cassis Y, Grossman RS, Schenk CR (eds) The Oxford handbook of banking and financial history. Oxford University Press, Oxford, pp 191–216
Westerhuis G (2016) Commercial banking: changing interactions between banks, markets, industry and state. In: Cassis Y, Grossman RS, Schenk CR (eds) The Oxford handbook of banking and financial history. Oxford University Press, Oxford, pp 110–163
World Bank (2013) Global financial development database. Accessed on 15 March 2017. http://www.worldbank.org/en/publication/gfdr/data/global-financial-developmentdatabase

Chapter 3
Economic Impact Assessment of Entrepreneurship Policies with the GMR-Europe Model

Attila Varga, László Szerb, Tamás Sebestyén and Norbert Szabó

Abstract This chapter introduces the most recent version of the geographic macro and regional (GMR) Europe model. The model estimates the economic impacts of policies that aim at improving the quality of entrepreneurship ecosystems. As such, GMR-Europe is the first available economic impact assessment model that estimates the effects of entrepreneurship policies on several economic variables like productivity, GDP, employment, and wages. To measure the quality of regional entrepreneurial ecosystems, GMR-Europe integrates the Regional Entrepreneurship and Development Index (REDI) into its structure. In addition to introducing the GMR-Europe

This study was financed by the Financial and Institutional Reforms for an Entrepreneurial Society (FIRES) that has received funding from the EU's Horizon 2020 research and innovation program under grant agreement No. 649378 and by the European Union and Hungary co-financed by the European Social Fund through the project EFOP-3.6.2-16-2017-00017, titled "Sustainable, intelligent and inclusive regional and city models". The research has been conducted as part of the National Excellence in Higher Education Program in Hungary (reference number of the contract: 20765-3/2018/FEKUTSTRAT). The authors of this chapter are indebted to the following colleagues for their invaluable assistance: Gallusz Abaligeti and Dániel Kehl, for their contribution to the empirical calibration of the TFP model equations, Anna Csajkás and Richárd Farkas for their assistance in data collection, data preparation and contribution to estimations and Péter Járosi, whose previous engagement in model development and continuous assistance through this work is an inevitable part of the present model setup. Laszlo Szerb and Attila Varga also gratefully acknowledge support from the National Scientific Research Fund of Hungary (OTKA/NKFI grant no. 120289 titled Entrepreneurship and Competitiveness investigations in Hungary based on the Global Entrepreneurship Monitor surveys 2017–2019). Thanks to Andrea Herrmann for comments on earlier drafts of this chapter.

A. Varga (✉) · L. Szerb · T. Sebestyén · N. Szabó
Regional Innovation and Entrepreneurship Research Center, MTA-PTE Innovation and Economic Growth Research Group, University of Pécs, Pécs, Hungary
e-mail: vargaa@ktk.pte.hu

L. Szerb
e-mail: szerb.laszlo@ktk.pte.hu

T. Sebestyén
e-mail: sebestyent@ktk.pte.hu

N. Szabó
e-mail: szabon@ktk.pte.hu

M. Sanders et al. (eds.), *The Entrepreneurial Society*, International Studies in Entrepreneurship 44, https://doi.org/10.1007/978-3-662-61007-7_3

model, we provide simulations illustrating the capabilities of the model by providing estimates of the economic impacts of policies designed to improve the quality of entrepreneurial ecosystems. The analysis communicates an important message for policymakers demonstrating that the impacts of entrepreneurship policies vary across regions and countries in Europe depending on several territorial features.

Keywords Entrepreneurship policy · Entrepreneurial ecosystems · Economic growth · GMR models · REDI · Regional development

3.1 Introduction

Recently published papers report a positive influence of entrepreneurship on economic growth. Lafuente et al. (2016) emphasize that efficiency at the national level is largely supported by a healthy system of entrepreneurship. This finding gets additional support in a cross-country study of Acs et al. (2017), which concludes that entrepreneurship triggers productivity. Prieger et al. (2016) and Lafuente et al. (2019) test the entrepreneurship-growth nexus and find that national entrepreneurial ecosystems positively and significantly influence economic growth in developing countries. In Szerb et al. (2018), the entrepreneurship ecosystem influences gross value added and employment growth positively in 125 European Union regions.

Despite the fact that evidence on a positive nexus between entrepreneurship and growth is increasing, the extent to which given policy interventions (e.g., the support of entrepreneurial culture or increased financial support to entrepreneurs) affect economic growth is still not known. Furthermore, it is still not clear to what extent entrepreneurship policy is comparable with traditionally applied instruments like R&D or human capital promotion. How would a policy combining entrepreneurship promotion and those traditional instruments affect economic growth? The relevant answers to these queries can only be found by applying specifically constructed economic impact models.

Economic impact estimation provides important information about the likely effects of policy interventions on national or regional economic performance. Policy impacts may be calculated ex-ante (in the design phase) and ex-post (after interventions have been implemented). Economic models are commonly used instruments of impact evaluation. The QUEST (Ratto et al. 2009) and the HERMIN (Bradley 2006) models have been the most frequently used tools of European Cohesion Policy impact assessment, whereas the REMI model (Treyz et al. 1992) is a widely applied instrument of regional policy evaluation in the USA.

However, the economic impact models mentioned above estimate policy impacts either at the macroeconomic (national) or at the regional (sub-national) levels. It is argued that in order to appropriately account for policy effects, economic impact models should represent both (i.e., the regional and the national) dimensions (Varga 2017a). As many development policy interventions are regionally targeted, a suitable economic impact model to estimate their effects should incorporate the regional dimension. Interregional interactions (trade, migration, technology spillovers) are also necessarily involved, as they tend to significantly affect the target region as well as other territories connected to it. Understanding the extent to which some relevant supra-regional units (i.e., the country or the European Union) are affected by regional level interventions may become very relevant in policy design and ex-post policy evaluations. This supports the involvement of the macroeconomic dimension in the model framework. Moreover, interventions at the national and supra-national levels (e.g., monetary or fiscal policies) significantly influence the environment within which regions develop, providing a further argument for the integration of macroeconomic and regional dimensions in development policy impact evaluation models.

With combined multi-regional/macro models, the economic impacts of different development scenarios become comparable at regional and supra-regional levels. Geographic, macro and regional (GMR) models integrate such geographic dimensions. Therefore, in this chapter, we apply the recently extended GMR-Europe model (Varga et al. 2018) in entrepreneurship policy impact estimations.

Nevertheless, at least two major challenges have to be solved in order to successfully estimate the growth effects of entrepreneurship policy with an economic impact model. The first is measuring the changes in the entrepreneurial ecosystem in relation to different interventions that aim to promote it. To date, there exists only one measure of this kind, the recently developed Regional Entrepreneurship and Development Index (REDI) (Szerb et al. 2017). The other challenge is integrating entrepreneurship into an economic impact model to estimate the economic effects of entrepreneurship policy at the relevant spatial scales. To respond to this second challenge, we integrated REDI into the framework of the GMR-Europe policy impact model (Varga et al. 2019). As a result, the most recent version of GMR models became the first available tool to estimate the economic impacts of entrepreneurship policies.

This chapter introduces the REDI in Section Two and the GMR-Europe model in Section Three. For readers who are interested in the technical details of the model, Varga et al. (2018) provide more information. To illustrate the capabilities of the GMR-Europe model in the impact estimations of entrepreneurship policies, we present a counterfactual analysis in the fourth section of this chapter. In these simulations, we assume that the quality of the entrepreneurial ecosystem gets the same relative increase in every NUTS2 region of Europe. The analysis communicates an important message for policymakers demonstrating that the economic impacts of entrepreneurship policies (measured by the change in GDP) vary across regions and countries in Europe depending on several territorial features. The chapter concludes with a summary section.

3.2 Measuring Regional Entrepreneurship Ecosystems: The REDI Model

In order to examine the effect of entrepreneurship on any performance indicators like productivity, economic growth, or development, one needs clear definitions, proper measurement units, and a suitable model which supports the analysis. Currently, there is no agreement among entrepreneurship scholars on any of these preconditions (Landström and Harirchi 2018).

According to Wennekers and Thurik (1999), entrepreneurship is an ill-defined concept, while others view it as eclectic (Audretsch et al. 2015); it is difficult to find even a minimum agreement on how to frame the phenomenon (Shane and Ventakaraman 2000). Yet, a distinctive feature of entrepreneurship is its focus on the individual as opposed to firms or markets. Some identify entrepreneurs based on specific psychological traits (Baum et al. 2014), others associate it with new venture creation (Gartner 1985), and some with its economic and societal effects (Baumol 1996).

Entrepreneurship is used by many different disciplines (Low and MacMillan 1988; Parker 2018). Here, we follow mainly the approach of economics by examining how entrepreneurship affects the economic output from the measurement perspective (Acs et al. 2014). Some believe that entrepreneurial attitudes such as preferences for self-employment, assertiveness toward entrepreneurs and entrepreneurial careers, and perceptions of entrepreneurial skills play an important role in the startup process and, ultimately, in economic growth. However, attitudes are not actions, and the exploration of the mechanism that leads attitudes into action and economic growth has not been unveiled and understood (Autio et al. 2013).

A popular approach is to identify entrepreneurship with some output measures like the startup rate or the Global Entrepreneurship Monitor (GEM) total-early-stage entrepreneurial activity ratio. The drawback of the output view is that it mixes very different measures where all can have varying effects on economic outcomes (Nightingale and Coad 2014; Vivarelli 2013). Moreover, entrepreneurial outputs and their composition vary over development (Naudé 2010; Liñán and Fernandez-Serrano 2014).

Since the seminal work of Baumol (1996), we know that the effect of entrepreneurship is regulated by its context. Framework measures like the World Bank Doing Business or the Index of Economic Freedom aim to quantify the effect of the widely interpreted institutions[1] on entrepreneurship outputs, albeit better institutions are not directly linked to some entrepreneurial actions. While the maturity of the institutions is closely correlated with long-term economic development, their predictive power on growth or productivity is only partially understood (Acs et al. 2014). Besides, institutions are geographically bounded and place-based; many of them are effective and worth measuring in a smaller territorial unit than a country (Qian et al. 2013).

[1] We interpret institutions as formal and informal institutions that shape entrepreneurial attitudes of the population, the abilities of the entrepreneurs, and aspirations of startups.

In the 2010s, a new research direction, the entrepreneurship ecosystem (EE) approach emerged focusing on the systemic (framework) conditions that lead to the occurrence of potentially high impact entrepreneurial output—so-called fast-growing gazelles (Malecki 2018; Stam 2015). While EE is still in a very early stage of development as a scientific concept, its approach is useful for examining the economic effect of entrepreneurship (Alvedalemn and Boschma 2017). Szerb et al. (2018) characterize the basic features of EE as (1) the clear distinction of entrepreneurial environment and entrepreneurial outputs, whereby (2) the performance of the EE depends on the systemic interaction between institutions and various players, (3) agglomeration economies, networking, and spillover effects are the basic features and mechanisms of the ecosystems, and (4) ecosystems are very different resulting from a path-dependent development process with forward and backward linkages.

There is an agreement among advocates of EE that each entrepreneurial ecosystem is unique, and the replication of successful examples is not possible. Some even believe that EEs are so unique that it is impossible to measure them. Consequently, EEs should be examined by individual case studies and their development strategy should be unique, place-, and case-based (Spigel 2017). Partially contradicting to this approach, we believe that there are some common elements of EEs and that a common measurement can be a useful tool for tailor-made policy recommendations. At present, there exists only one tool, the Regional Entrepreneurship and Development Index (REDI), which provides a measure of EE for a mix of 125 NUTS1 and NUTS2 European Union regions (Szerb et al. 2017). REDI is a regional version of the well-known Global Entrepreneurship Index (GEI) defining the system of entrepreneurship (SE) as "… the dynamic, institutionally embedded interaction between entrepreneurial attitudes, ability, and aspirations, by individuals, which drives the allocation of resources through the creation and operation of new ventures" (Acs et al. 2014, p. 119). REDI is a measure of a very complex and multidimensional quality of the entrepreneurship ecosystem. As compared to GEI, REDI is not simply a more precise, but also a more appropriate measure of EE because it incorporates a different set of institutional variables reflecting the regional forces of agglomeration, connectivity, and clustering that interact with individual entrepreneurial features.

In what follows, we provide an outline of the REDI index. For more details on the technical aspects of REDI construction, we refer to a detailed technical report (Szerb et al. 2017). The composition of REDI follows the common composite indicator building methodology with three exceptions (Joint Research Centre of the European Commission 2008). First, the construction of some variables includes some agglomeration effects. Second, we use the equalization of the averages methodology to equalize the marginal effects of the potential policy steps. Third, we use the penalty for bottleneck method to identify the optimal combination of the fourteen pillars. We follow a six-level index-building methodology starting from (1) 60 sub-indicators, then (2) creating 44 indicators, followed by (3) calculating 28 variables, (4) 14 pillars, (5) three sub-indices, and finally (6) the single REDI super-index (for details see Szerb et al. 2017).

The three sub-indices of attitudes (ATT), abilities (ABT), and aspiration (ASP) constitute the entrepreneurship super-index, which is called REDI. All three sub-indices contain four or five pillars, which can be interpreted as quasi-independent building blocks of this entrepreneurship index. Each of the 14 pillars is the result of the multiplication of an individual variable and an associated institutional variable. In this case, institutional variables can be viewed as particular (region level) weights of the individual variables. Table 3.1 provides a detailed picture of the sub-indices.

Unlike other EE approaches, REDI clearly defines how the different elements are interrelated. REDI elements can have an additive (indicator level) or a multiplicative (variable level) influence on the system performance. The novelty of this method is that it portrays the entrepreneurial disparities among EU regions and provides country and regional level, tailor-made public policy suggestions to improve the level of entrepreneurship and optimize resource allocation over the different pillars of entrepreneurship.

Entrepreneurship is defined as the interaction of entrepreneurial attitudes, abilities, and aspirations. The penalty for bottleneck (PFB) methodology is developed for measuring and quantifying these interactions (Rappai and Szerb 2011). A bottleneck is defined as the worst performing element, the weakest link, or binding constraint in the system. With respect to entrepreneurship, we define a bottleneck as a shortage, or the lowest level of a particular entrepreneurial pillar as compared to other pillars. The sub-indices are composed of four or five components, defined as pillars that should be adjusted in a way that takes this notion of balance into account. After normalizing the scores of all the pillars, the value of each pillar in a region is penalized by linking it to the score of the pillar with the weakest performance in that region. This simulates the notion of a bottleneck, and if the weakest pillar were improved, the particular sub-index and ultimately the whole REDI would likewise show a material improvement. On the contrary, improving a relatively high pillar value will presumably enhance only the value of the pillar itself and cause a much smaller increase of the whole REDI. Summarizing the REDI technique intuitively, it is an index that combines information from many variables at the individual and regional level, assumes that institutions complement individual action (multiplicative), while for the total score the least performing elements weight more than the best ones, and finally a well-balanced ecosystem without bottlenecks scores higher.

This notion of bottlenecks is important for policy purposes. Our model suggests that attitudes, ability, and aspiration interact, and if they are out of balance, productive entrepreneurship is inhibited. REDI has the capacity to demonstrate how resource allocation can be optimized along the 14 pillars to improve the REDI score and, ultimately, the regional entrepreneurship system performance. Moreover, the systemic combination of the pillars influences the effectiveness of the ecosystem. An improvement in the weakest pillar would produce an increase in the overall REDI score. An EE with a homogeneous pillar configuration is viewed to be optimal (Szerb et al. 2017). The Appendix provides a concise description of the REDI methodology. Tables 3.2 and 3.3 below provide regional REDI values and country REDI scores based on population-weighted average REDI scores.

Table 3.1 Structure of the Regional Entrepreneurship and Development Index

	Sub-indices	Pillars	Variables (*individual*/**institutional**)
Regional Entrepreneurship and Development Index	Entrepreneurial **Attitudes** Sub-index	Opportunity perception	*Opportunity recognition*
			Market agglomeration
		Startup skills	*Skill perception*
			Quality of education
		Risk acceptance	*Risk perception*
			Business risk
		Networking	*Know entrepreneurs*
			Social capital
		Cultural support	*Carrier status*
			Open society
	Entrepreneurial **Abilities** Sub-index	Opportunity startup	*Opportunity motivation*
			Business environment
		Technology Adoption	*Technology level*
			Absorptive capacity
		Human capital	*Educational level*
			Education and training
		Competition	*Competitors*
			Business strategy
	Entrepreneurial **Aspiration** Sub-index	Product innovation	*New product*
			Technology transfer
		Process innovation	*New technology*
			Technology Development
		High growth	*Gazelle*
			Clustering
		Internationalization	*Export*
			Connectivity
		Risk capital	*Informal investment*
			Financial Institutions

Source Authors' own compilation

Table 3.3 shows, perhaps surprisingly, that Ireland leads, but the top ten comprise all the usual suspects in North-western Europe. This table, however, also hides significant regional variation within these countries. As Table 3.2 shows, with some interesting exceptions, the best performing entrepreneurial ecosystems in Europe are typically found in densely populated urban centers in the North and North-western parts of Europe. Stockholm, Helsinki, London, Paris, Amsterdam, and Berlin are all

Table 3.2 REDI values and ranks in the 125 EU regions (2012–2014)

Rank	Region name	REDI	Rank	Region name	REDI	Rank	Region name	REDI
1	Stockholm	78.3	43	North West (UK)	50.4	85	Illes Balears	34.3
2	Hovedstaden	76.6	44	Région wallonne	50.3	86	Region Pólnocno-Zachodni	34.2
3	London	75.5	45	Niedersachsen	50.3	87	Region Pólnocny	33.7
4	Southern and Eastern	71.3	46	Zahodna Slovenija	50.0	88	Centro (IT)	33.5
5	Île de France	70.8	47	Schleswig-Holstein	49.8	89	Nord-Ovest	33.5
6	Helsinki-Uusimaa	70.0	48	Westösterreich	49.0	90	Andalucía	33.2
7	South East (UK)	69.6	49	Länsi-Suomi	48.9	91	Lithuania	32.8
8	Hamburg	69.5	50	Sjalland	48.4	92	Cantabria	32.7
9	Sydsverige	65.8	51	Lisboa	48.1	93	Centro (PT)	32.7
10	West-Nederland	63.5	52	Südösterreich	47.6	94	Nord-Est	32.6
11	Bruxelles/Brussels	63.2	53	Ouest (FR)	46.6	95	Aragón	31.9
12	Berlin	62.4	54	Nord-Pas-de-Calais	46.4	96	Region Wschodni	31.8
13	South West (UK)	62.3	55	Småland med öarna	45.6	97	Közép-Magyarország	31.1
14	Baden-Württemberg	62.0	56	Est (FR)	45.5	98	Principado de Asturias	30.3
15	Syddanmark	61.6	57	Norra Mellansverige	45.5	99	Macroregiunea trei	29.9
16	Bayern	60.6	58	Méditerranée	45.4	100	Galicia	29.5
17	Scotland	60.5	59	Estonia	45.3	101	Región de Murcia	29.3
18	Border, Midland and Western	60.4	60	Rheinland-Pfalz	44.6	102	Canarias (ES)	29.2
19	Östra Mellansverige	59.9	61	North East (UK)	44.3	103	Attiki	28.3
20	Västsverige	59.8	62	Bratislavsky kraj	44.2	104	La Rioja	28.2
21	Hessen	58.9	63	Bassin Parisien	44.1	105	Západné Slovensko	26.7

(continued)

Table 3.2 (continued)

Rank	Region name	REDI	Rank	Region name	REDI	Rank	Region name	REDI
22	East of England	58.7	64	Pohjois-ja Ita-Suomi	43.2	106	Isole	26.7
23	Center-Est (FR)	58.5	65	Vzhodna Slovenija	43.0	107	Stredné Slovensko	26.5
24	Midtjylland	58.2	66	Region Centralny	43.0	108	Extremadura	26.1
25	East Midlands (UK)	57.9	67	Thüringen	41.1	109	Macroregiunea unu	26.1
26	Zuid-Nederland	57.6	68	Cataluna	40.9	110	Vychodné Slovensko	26.0
27	Bremen	57.1	69	Region Poludniowy	40.5	111	Sud	25.7
28	Ostösterreich	56.9	70	Mecklenburg-Vorpommern	40.2	112	Kontinentalna Hrvatska	25.6
29	Saarland	56.7	71	Mellersta Norrland	39.9	113	Castilla-la Mancha	24.7
30	Nordjylland	56.5	72	País Vasco	38.8	114	Jadranska Hrvatska	23.5
31	Noord-Nederland	55.3	73	Czech Republic	38.8	115	Macroregiunea patru	22.3
32	Northern Ireland (UK)	55.0	74	Sachsen-Anhalt	38.2	116	Voreia Ellada	22.0
33	Nordrhein-Westfalen	54.8	75	Sud-Ouest (FR)	37.6	117	Nyugat-Dunántúl	21.7
34	Övre Norrland	54.8	76	Alentejo	37.1	118	Macroregiunea doi	21.4
35	West Midlands (UK)	54.0	77	Latvia	36.7	119	Nisia Aigaiou, Kriti	21.3
36	Etelä-Suomi	52.4	78	Region Poludniowo-Zachodni	36.7	120	Kentriki Ellada	20.0
37	Oost-Nederland	51.8	79	Comunidad Foral de Navarra	36.2	121	Dél-Dunántúl	19.8
38	Yorkshire and The Humber	51.8	80	Algarve	35.4	122	Észak-Magyarország	18.9
39	Vlaams Gewest	51.3	81	Brandenburg	35.1	123	Közép-Dunántúl	18.8
40	Comunidad de Madrid	51.1	82	Comunidad Valenciana	34.9	124	Észak-Alföld	18.2
41	Sachsen	50.5	83	Castilla y León	34.6	125	Dél-Alföld	17.7
42	Wales	50.4	84	Norte	34.3			

Source Authors' own compilation

Table 3.3 Country-level REDI values and ranks in the 24 countries (2012–2014) (Based on population-weighted REDI scores)

Ranking	Country	REDI 2012–2014 average
1.	Ireland	64.3
2.	Denmark	59.0
3.	Sweden	58.2
4.	United Kingdom	56.0
5.	Netherlands	56.0
6.	Finland	52.5
7.	Germany	51.1
8.	Austria	50.2
9.	Belgium	49.1
10.	France	7.6
11.	Slovenia	44.3
12.	Estonia	42.3
13.	Portugal	36.3
14.	Czech Republic	36.2
15.	Poland	34.4
16.	Spain	34.1
17.	Latvia	33.5
18.	Italy	30.0
19.	Lithuania	29.9
20.	Slovakia	25.4
21.	Croatia	23.1
22.	Romania	22.0
23.	Greece	21.8
24.	Hungary	20.7
	EU average	42.5

Source Authors' own compilation

in the top ten of European regions. But the countries scoring high in Table 3.3 also have regions in the middle range of the regional ranking.

3.3 Integrating Entrepreneurship in the GMR-Europe Policy Impact Model

The GMR-Europe model is capable of estimating the economic impacts of entrepreneurship policy. These policies promote entrepreneurial activity which can contribute to a region's innovative capacity, eventually leading to technological and economic development. Economic impact models like the GMR-Europe are then able to track the widespread effects of the initial interventions. The key link through which entrepreneurship is integrated into the GMR-Europe model is the REDI introduced above. Entrepreneurship policies are assumed to affect the REDI in separate regions, while the changes in REDI set in motion the GMR-Europe model simulating the likely effects of such an exogenous improvement in the regional entrepreneurial ecosystems.

3.3.1 General Features of GMR Models

Models frequently applied in development policy analysis are neither geographic nor regional. They either follow the tradition of macro econometric modeling (like the HERMIN model—ESRI 2002), the tradition of macro Computable General Equilibrium (CGE) modeling (like the ECOMOD model—Bayar 2007), or the most recently developed Dynamic Stochastic General Equilibrium (DSGE) approach (QUEST III—Ratto et al. 2009). They also bear the common attribute of national-level spatial aggregation. The novel feature of the GMR approach is that it incorporates geographic effects (e.g., agglomeration, interregional trade, migration) while both macro and regional impacts of policies are simulated.

Geography plays a critical role in the effectiveness of development policies for at least four major reasons. First, interventions are implemented at a certain point in space, and their impacts might spill over to proximate locations to a considerable extent. Second, the initial impacts could be significantly amplified or reduced by short-run (static) agglomeration effects. Third, cumulative long-run processes, resulting from labor and capital migration, may further amplify or reduce the initial impacts in the region resulting in a change of the spatial structure of the economy (dynamic agglomeration effects). Fourth, as a consequence of the above effects, different spatial patterns of interventions might result in significantly different growth and convergence/divergence patterns.

"Regions" are spatial reference points in the GMR approach. They are subnational spatial units ideally at that level of geographic aggregation which is appropriate to capture proximity relations in innovation. Besides intraregional interactions, the model captures interregional connections such as knowledge flows expanding over regional borders (scientific networking or spatially mediated spillovers), interregional trade, and migration of production factors.

The "macro" level is also important when the impact of policies is modeled: fiscal and monetary policy, national regulations, or various international effects are all potentially relevant factors when calculating these impacts. As a result, the model system simulates the effects of policy interventions both at the regional and macroeconomic level. Depending on the question of interest, the macroeconomic level in the GMR-Europe model can be considered as national economies, the whole coverage of EU countries within the model, or both. With this approach, different scenarios can be compared on the basis of their impacts on economic growth and interregional convergence.

The GMR framework is rooted in different traditions of economics (Varga 2006). While modeling the spatial patterns of knowledge flows and the role of agglomeration in knowledge transfers, it incorporates insights and methodologies developed in the geography of innovation field (e.g., Anselin et al. 1997; Varga 2000). Interregional trade and migration linkages and dynamic agglomeration effects are modeled with an empirical general equilibrium model in the tradition of new economic geography (e.g., Krugman 1991; Fujita et al. 1999). Specific macroeconomic theories are followed while modeling macro level impacts.

GMR models reflect the challenges of incorporating regional, geographic, and macroeconomic dimensions in development policy impact modeling by structuring the system around the mutual interactions of three sub-models: the Total Factor Productivity (TFP), Spatial Computable General Equilibrium (SCGE), and macroeconomic (MACRO) model blocks. Following this approach, the macroeconomic block of GMR-Europe calculates policy impacts at the aggregated (international, EU) level while the 181 NUTS2-level regional blocks provide results at the regional level.

Some policy interventions, such as changes in international trade, tax regulations, or income subsidies, can be modeled in the macroeconomic block via policy shocks affecting specific macroeconomic variables. However, many other policy instruments apply to the regional level, stimulating the regional base of economic growth such as investment support, infrastructure building, human capital development, R&D subsidies, promotion of (intra- and interregional) knowledge flows, and entrepreneurship, which is the main focus of this chapter. These interventions are modeled in the regional model blocks and interact endogenously with the macroeconomic part. In the following sub-section, we zoom in on the mechanisms of these latter policies.

3.3.2 *GMR Model Blocks*

The GMR framework is built around three interconnected model blocks: the TFP block which is responsible for simulating changes in regional productivity levels, the SCGE block which ensures a cross-regional equilibrium and provides estimations for region-level economic variables like output and employment, and finally the MACRO block which provides the dynamics of economic variables and simulates aggregate level effects of policy interventions.

3.3.2.1 The TFP Model Block

TFP is one of the most important variables in GMR-Europe. It represents the main point through which different aspects of innovation, and innovation policy interventions in particular, interact with other parts of the model. The TFP block serves as the point in the GMR system where different driving factors behind innovation, especially entrepreneurial activity, are modeled. Then, in line with the traditions in economic modeling, the impact of these factors is implemented in the MACRO and

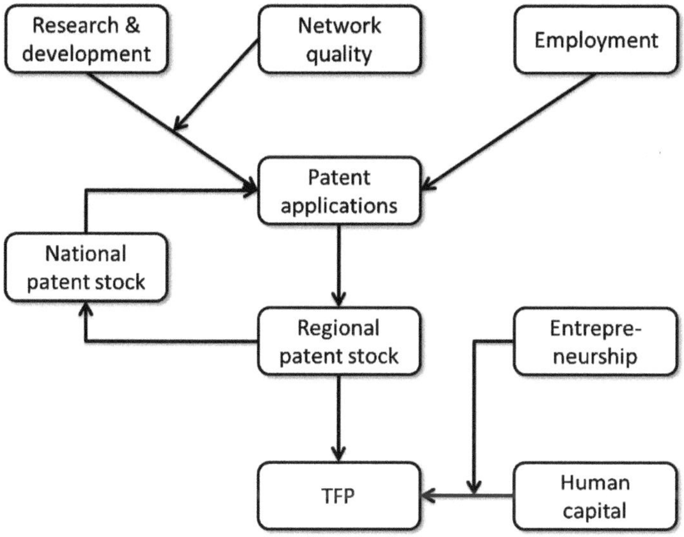

Fig. 3.1 Schematic structure of the TFP block. *Source* Authors' own compilation

SCGE blocks through one technology variable, generally referred to as total factor productivity, or TFP.

Figure 3.1 illustrates the setup of the TFP block in GMR-Europe. TFP is the final variable which transfers impacts generated in the TFP block over to the other parts of the model, namely the SCGE block and the MACRO block. However, the main role of the TFP block is to provide a sophisticated background for determining TFP and implement innovation-oriented policy interventions, including those targeting entrepreneurship.

The TFP block is based on the knowledge production function approach, where new knowledge, represented by patent applications in our model setup, is produced using knowledge production factors, namely R&D efforts and labor (employment), as well as already existing knowledge which is represented by national patent stock (knowledge creation and TFP are directly modeled at the regional level). In addition to this standard approach, we also include the role of knowledge available through interregional networks, using the Ego Network Quality index (Sebestyén and Varga 2013) which is assumed to affect the productivity of R&D in knowledge creation (better network positions lead to higher knowledge output for the same amount of inputs). New knowledge, in this case patent applications at the regional level, then feeds back into knowledge creation in a dynamic way by building up the national patent stock.

TFP is primarily linked to the regional knowledge levels in the model, but two additional forces are assumed to determine regional TFP. First, the level of human capital in the region affects TFP and second, a focal element of this setup of the GMR model, we added the entrepreneurial environment measured by REDI to the model.

We assumed REDI to have a positive influence on TFP via enhancing the contribution of human capital to TFP. This formulation is inspired by the knowledge spillover theory of entrepreneurship (Acs et al. 2009). As entrepreneurs transfer knowledge to economic applications, a better entrepreneurial climate in a region intensifies new firm formation and helps to better exploit the knowledge embodied in human capital, which eventually leads to increasing total factor productivity. This is the point where the REDI feeds into the GMR-Europe model; productive entrepreneurship is measured by the REDI, and policy interventions that improve the entrepreneurial ecosystem are assumed to affect this variable which then sets in motion the TFP block, inducing changes in regional productivity levels as well as economic activity in the targeted region and elsewhere.

The TFP block consists of econometrically estimated equations. First, the patent equation describes how certain variables depicted in Fig. 3.1 affect regional patenting:

$$\begin{aligned}\log\left(\mathrm{PAT}_{t,r}\right) = \alpha + \beta_1 \log\left(\mathrm{PATSCKN}_{t-1,N}\right) + \beta_2 \log\left(\mathrm{EMP}_{t-1,r}\right) \\ + \beta_3 \log\left(\mathrm{RD\_TOTAL}_{t-1,r}\right) \\ + \beta_4 \log\left(\mathrm{RD\_TOTAL}_{t-1,r}\right) \log\left(\mathrm{ENQFP}_{t-1,r}\right) + \varepsilon_{t,r}^{\mathrm{PAT}} \qquad (3.1)\end{aligned}$$

Patents on the left-hand side are measured by EPO patent applications (PAT), national patent stock is the cumulative number of patents at the country level (PATSCKN), research and development efforts are proxied with R&D expenditures (RD_TOTAL), employment is captured by the total level of employment in the region (EMP), and network quality is measured with the ENQ index (Sebestyén and Varga 2013), calculated over the network of Framework Program partnerships between regions (ENQFP). The patent equation (Eq. 3.1) potentially contains endogeneity through network formation, employment, and R&D as these factors may be shaped by patenting in a region just as well as shaping it. We designed the equations with a one period (year) lag in order to overcome this problem to a certain extent.

Second, the TFP equation describes how certain variables (as shown in Fig. 3.1) affect regional productivity:

$$\begin{aligned}\log\left(\mathrm{TFP}_{t,r}\right) = \alpha + \beta_1 \log\left(\mathrm{PATSCKR}_{t-1,r}\right) + \beta_2 \log\left(\mathrm{HUMCAP}_{t-1,r}\right) \\ + \beta_3 \log\left(\mathrm{HUMCAP}_{t-1,r}\right)\mathrm{REDI}_{t-1,r} + \varepsilon_{t,r}^{\mathrm{TFP}} \qquad (3.2)\end{aligned}$$

In this equation, accumulated knowledge is measured by the cumulative number of patents in the region (PATSCKR), while the level of human capital at the regional level is proxied by the population (between age 25 and 64) with tertiary education attainment (HUMCAP). To model the influence of entrepreneurship on TFP, human capital interacts with the quality of the entrepreneurial ecosystem in the equation.[2]

[2] It could be argued that a reasonable alternative of the TFP equation would be a specification where REDI interacts with the regional patent stock. However, there is a very important distinction between the two forms of knowledge (human capital and accumulated knowledge stock) in the Romerian knowledge production function framework, and this distinction is followed in our specifications

The quality of the entrepreneurial ecosystem is measured by the REDI.[3] The TFP on the left-hand side is estimated using a standard production function approach with capital and labor.

After estimating the two equations of the TFP block, we have a system of equations which is able to simulate the effects of different interventions affecting research and development, human capital, networking, or the entrepreneurial climate on regional TFP. One drawback of this system is that the estimated coefficients which drive these impacts are common across all regions in the model, reflecting average tendencies in the sample of regions. However, one may argue that due to the large differences in the development level as well as the sociocultural and institutional context of European regions, mechanisms through which different interventions affect regional productivities differ largely across regions. We control for these differences in two ways. First, in both equations, the interaction terms render the respective marginal effects of R&D, human capital, network quality, and entrepreneurship development level region-specific. Second, we augment this heterogeneity with a specific calibration process through which region-specific parameters are calculated through an optimization process to improve model fit. This second method is discussed briefly below.

Given the observed data, we fit linear trends on these data points for all variables, except regional and national patent stocks (the former is directly given by the patent equation and the latter is calculated by summing up regional patent stocks in every period). After trend fitting, we extrapolate the trend for out-of-sample years. These trends constitute the baseline of the TFP block. After extrapolating trend values for all variables in the TFP block, we perform the regressions on these data points as well. Coefficients estimated on the historical data and coefficients estimated on the trend data closely approximate each other.

The coefficients estimated on the trend data constitute the basis of region-specific parameter calibrations in the next step. The aim of the calibration is to find region-specific values for selected parameters, which improve the overall fit of the model. After a careful selection procedure among several model versions, three coefficients of the TFP block, namely the constant term and the coefficient of employment in the patent equation (parameters α and β_2) and the constant term in the TFP equation

---

of the equations in the TFP block (Romer 1990). The stock of patents represents accumulated knowledge that is available in the region for *potential* economic applications, whereas human capital refers to knowledge which is *actually* present in the region being embodied in qualified labor. Therefore, the stock of knowledge plays a passive role in technology development, whereas human capital is the one that contributes actively to regional productivity improvements. In our formulation of the TFP equation, this role is enhanced by the quality of the regional entrepreneurial ecosystem. With a higher quality of this ecosystem, the same level of human capital contributes to a more intensive increase in TFP via more active involvement of human capital in new firm formation.

[3]As described in Sect. 3.2, the REDI is a complex index that accounts for several features of the entrepreneurial ecosystem. Due to this complexity, some of the variables that appear in the GMR model also play a role in the REDI. However, these variables are interactive with several others, and throughout the pillar system, the correlation of the REDI super-index with any single component variable is small.

(parameter α), are calibrated.[4] As a result of this calibration process, we are presented with region-specific parameter values for the listed three parameters of the TFP block which improve the fit of the TFP block equations and retain the average tendencies represented by the trend-based estimation. In this way, we obtain region-specific mechanisms built in the TFP block with respect to the effects of right-hand side variables on patenting activity and the productivity of the regions.

3.3.2.2 The SCGE Model Block[5]

The SCGE model block draws on regional productivity changes and then simulates the likely impacts of these changes on regional economic variables like output, prices, wages, and employment. SCGE models add the spatial dimension to the (usually a-spatial) CGE models. Economic units are regions, which are interconnected by trade flows and migration. The most important feature of this block is that it takes into account interactions across regions through the trade of goods and services as well as the mobility of production factors. Also, transportation costs are explicitly accounted for and positive and/or negative agglomeration effects are also part of the model structure.

The model distinguishes between short-run and long-run equilibria. In the short run, markets are in equilibrium within and across all regions. However, this does not necessarily mean that the whole regional system has reached a balanced situation. In the long run, differences in utility levels across regions induce labor migration, followed by the migration of capital, leading to a long-run spatial equilibrium where interregional utility differences are eliminated. Although possible in principle, this equilibrium is hardly reached within the applied simulation horizon, leaving considerable gaps in utility levels in the simulated outcomes.

3.3.2.3 The MACRO Model Block

The macroeconomic block of the GMR approach serves two purposes. First, this is the point, where aggregate relationships and policies, such as exchange rate toward the rest of the world, inflation, monetary, and fiscal policy, can be handled. Second,

---

[4]This results in an optimization procedure where the objective function is the sum of the following five elements: (1) Mean average percentage error of the regional patent application variable (average percentage deviation of simulated $\text{PAT}_{i,t}$ values from the trend values). (2) Mean average percentage error of the TFP variable (average percentage deviation of simulated $\text{TFP}_{i,t}$ values from the trend values). (3) Mean average percentage error of the average calibrated region-specific constant terms in the patent equation (average percentage deviation of calibrated constant terms from the trend-based estimated values). (4) Mean average percentage error of the average calibrated region-specific coefficient of employment in the patent equation (average percentage deviation of calibrated coefficients from the trend-based estimated values). (5) Mean average percentage error of the average calibrated region-specific constant terms in the TFP equation (average percentage deviation of calibrated constant terms from the trend-based estimated values).

[5]This section reiterates a short passage that was published in Varga et al. (2018).

it provides dynamics to the otherwise static SCGE block. In the latter, regional productivity, labor, and capital stocks are exogenous. The TFP block provides the dynamics of regional productivity levels, but in order to account for the possible employment and investment effects of the simulated policies, we need to provide dynamics for labor and capital stocks of the regions. This is performed by the MACRO block, which provides an aggregate estimation of the likely employment and capital stock impacts of the simulated policies, and are then broken down to the regions in function of the regional productivity growth rates.

The macroeconomic block of GMR-Europe calculates policy impacts at the EU and national level while the 181-region NUTS2-level TFP and SCGE blocks provide results at the regional level. The model calculates the policy impacts on various economic variables such as GDP, employment, investment, prices at the regional, national, and aggregate European levels.

The macroeconomic block is a standard, large-scale Dynamic, Stochastic, General Equilibrium (DSGE) model. We apply the QUEST III model developed by the European Commission for the Euro area and re-estimated it with additional countries to cover the same set of regions as those represented in the other two model blocks. Therefore, the set of countries include the Euro-countries and some Eastern European countries that are not part of the monetary union. The description of the original model can be found in Ratto et al. (2009), while the re-estimated version is described in Varga et al. (2018).

3.3.3 Impact Mechanisms in the GMR Model

The three mutually connected model blocks are depicted in Fig. 3.2. Without interventions, the TFP growth rate is assumed to follow an exogenous and identical steady state growth rate in every region, and the economy grows on a balanced growth path primarily driven by the MACRO block. If any exogenous shocks are fed into the model, it leaves this balanced growth path, and we can examine how the policy-induced shocks affect the path of the economy compared to the steady state path.

Given its setup, the GMR-Europe model is able to handle several types of policy interventions, as shown on the left-hand side of Fig. 3.2. Different macroeconomic policies, such as inflation targeting, other aspects of monetary policy, general fiscal expansion, and different tax-related policies, are applied at the macro level, directly affecting the MACRO block, while their effects spill over to other model parts as well. Other policies apply at the regional level. These may include investment support or public infrastructure development, which directly affects the (private or public) capital stock in specific regions. Through the interconnected model setup, these interventions then affect economic activity in other regions as well. Finally, there are policies which directly affect the TFP block. These are interventions which have an effect on regional productivity, like supporting education, R&D, network formation,

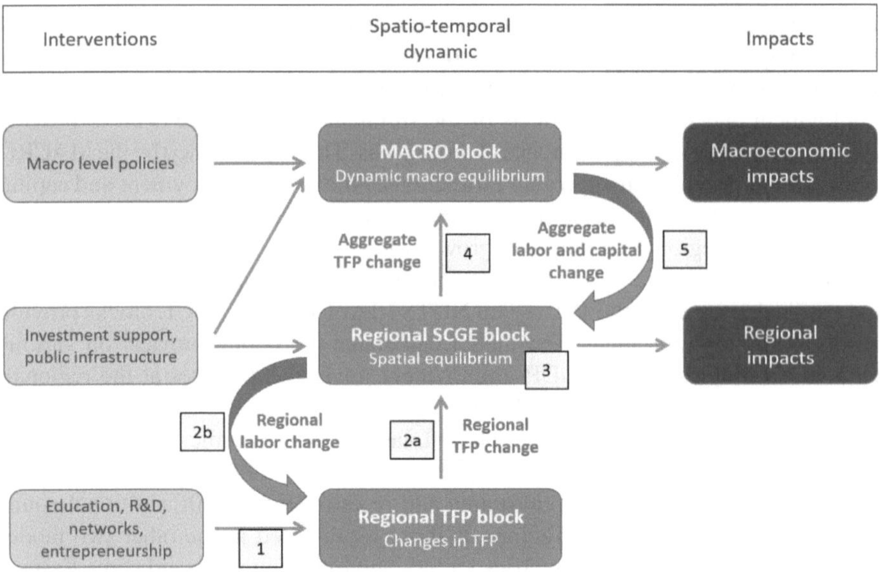

Fig. 3.2 Regional and macroeconomic impacts of the main policy variables in the GMR-Europe model. Numbers refer to the steps of the impact mechanism of policy interventions. *Source* Authors' own compilation

or entrepreneurial activity. These interventions affect regional TFP as described in Fig. 3.1, and then these effects spill over to other parts of the model.

As the present chapter focuses on policy interventions related to entrepreneurial activity, we provide a more detailed account of the policies affecting regional TFP. The following steps, augmented by the numbers in Fig. 3.2, help keeping track of the adjustment process initiated by policy interventions targeting entrepreneurship, R&D, education, or network formation, all affecting regional TFP in the first place.

1. Resulting from R&D, entrepreneurship- and network-related interventions as well as human capital and physical infrastructure investments (which increase public capital and eventually impact the level of TPF as well), regional Total Factor Productivity changes/increases (link 1 in the figure);
2. Changing TFP induces changes in quantities and prices of output and production factors in the short run (link 2a) while in the long run (following the mechanisms described above) the impact on in-migration of production factors implies further changes in TFP not only in the region where the interventions happen but also in regions which are connected by trade and factor migration (link 2b);
3. Induced by the increasing productivity, private investments increase expanding regional private capital which causes further changes in regional variables (output, prices, wages, prices, TFP, etc.) in the SCGE model block. The impact of private investment support affects the MACRO model also via increased private capital (link 3, within the SCGE block);

4. For every year, changes in TFP are aggregated to the national level, which increases TFP in the MACRO model as time-specific shocks (link 4). The macroeconomic model calculates the changes in all affected variables at the national level;
5. Changes in employment and investment calculated in the MACRO block are distributed over the regions following the spatial pattern of TFP impacts (link 5);
6. The SCGE model runs again with the new employment and capital values to calculate short-run and long-run equilibrium values of the affected variables (links 3, 2a, and 2b are used again);
7. The process described in steps 5 and 6 continues until aggregate values of regional variables calculated in the SCGE model get sufficiently close (less than 10^{-10} percentage deviation) to their corresponding values calculated in the MACRO model. This solution ensures consistent simulation results across the different model blocks. Also, our experience shows that convergence is always achieved and within a very limited number of iterations.

3.4 Policy Simulations

The following simulations illustrate the potential use of the GMR-Europe model in evaluating reforms which aim to strengthen the entrepreneurial society. In principle, it would be possible to simulate the effects of a differentiated and tailored strategy to improve regional entrepreneurial ecosystems as, for example, presented in Chaps. 5–7 in this volume (Sanders et al. 2020a, b, c). In this chapter, the aim is to illustrate how our model setup works, and we therefore focus on how a common shock to the REDI score would be transmitted in the GMR framework. Results show that there are differences in the extent to which an equi-proportional increase in the REDI scores affects regional productivities. Moreover, the dynamic feedback mechanisms within the model generate diverse paths for regional output levels in response to such a shock.

3.4.1 Simulation Setup

In the simulation presented below, we track the effects of an exogenous increase in the REDI in all regions. More formally, we follow the strategy below:

1. We take the baseline REDI scores of the model. The base year is 2012, and the baseline of the TFP block goes along empirically fitted trends from 2012 to 2031, which means that in the baseline model runs, the REDI score of every region proceeds along a trend line derived from the observed data;

2. For every region, we then calculate the average of the baseline REDI scores over the simulation years (2012–2031) and define 1% of these average scores as a policy intervention (technically an exogenous shock to the model);
3. This 1% improvement is applied to the REDI in every region in a way that the REDI is increased from its baseline value to a 5% higher value through the first 5 years of the simulation (2012–2016). Note that after five years the value of the REDI does not change meaning that the annual improvements in REDI result in a permanent positive effect on the quality of EE in every NUTS2 region;
4. Every region receives this 1% annual improvement in the REDI, and we trace their effect on regional TFP and GDP levels as well as aggregate country-level versions of these variables.

Of course, focusing on the REDI provides a bird-eye view on entrepreneurial policies. We can interpret the idea behind these simulations as follows: What is the economic impact of a five percent improvement of the entrepreneurial climate/ecosystem in each region over a five-year period? We use this counterfactual simulation as a first approximation and for illustrative purposes, but emphasize that the detailed structure of the REDI allows the model to account for more detailed approaches in this respect. Overall, these simulations reflect the potential effects of policies which are capable of improving the entrepreneurial ecosystem of a region by adjusting either of the pillars behind the REDI. It is important to underline that the equality of the shocks (in percentage terms) implies regional divergence in our simulations. The impact of a REDI shock depends most importantly on the size of the REDI (i.e., the development level of the regional entrepreneurial ecosystem) and on the size of human capital in the region. Therefore, many highly entrepreneurial regions with strong human capital gain more from the shock than their less developed counterparts. One should realize that the same percentage increase in the REDI score cannot be the consequence of regionally balanced policy interventions, and, indeed, the improvement of the quality of the ecosystem in more entrepreneurial places probably requires more effort than in less developed regions.

3.4.2 Simulation Results

Although the model is capable of tracking many regional and aggregate level variables, we focus on the effect of the REDI improvement on total factor productivity (TFP) and GDP. In both cases, we present the percentage deviation of the simulated TFP/GDP values after the applied interventions from their baseline levels. As a result, the diagrams reflect the percentage impact of these policies, or, to what extent would TFP and GDP be higher/lower as a result of the policy intervention, compared to the no intervention (business as usual) case.

In Fig. 3.3, we summarize the country-level results of the simulations. On the left-hand side, the country-level impacts are shown for TFP, while on the right-hand side the time averages of the GDP impacts are depicted for countries. The

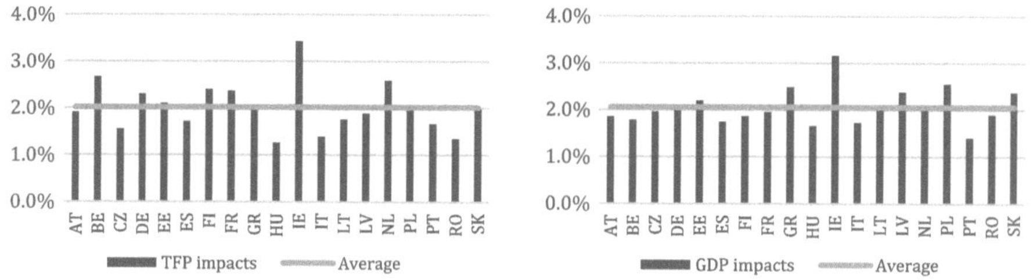

Fig. 3.3 Country-level impacts of 1% annual shocks over a five-year period to REDI on TFP and GDP. *Source* Authors' own compilation

horizontal lines show the EU-average impacts. The graphic shows that a 1% annual improvement in the entrepreneurial climate over 5 years in every region leads to a 2% increase in TFP and productivity on average (EU level). The GDP impact is slightly higher, but the productivity and GDP effects go hand in hand. This is not surprising, as in the simulations, the shock has its effect through enhancing regional productivity. Figure 3.3 also shows that the positive development in the entrepreneurial environment of regions positively affects the productivity levels in all countries. However, there are differences in the magnitude of this effect. While Ireland benefits the most from this policy, Hungary seems to be performing worst in this respect. This corresponds with the initial ranking of regions and countries in Tables 3.2 and 3.3.

In the dynamic analysis of policy impacts, we zoom in on the mechanisms in the case of four countries representing the four types of capitalism: Ireland (a Liberal Market Economy), Germany (a Coordinated Market Economy), Hungary (an Eastern Market Economy), and Italy (a Mediterranean Market Economy). Although, GDP impacts follow the TFP impacts quite closely, as seen from Fig. 3.4, there are considerable qualitative differences in the time path of the effects. In some countries, although the overall effect of the policy is positive, after the "lifting" power of the policy (first 5 years) phases out, the impacts tend to decrease compared to the peak year. This effect is due to the complex mechanisms within the GMR model where

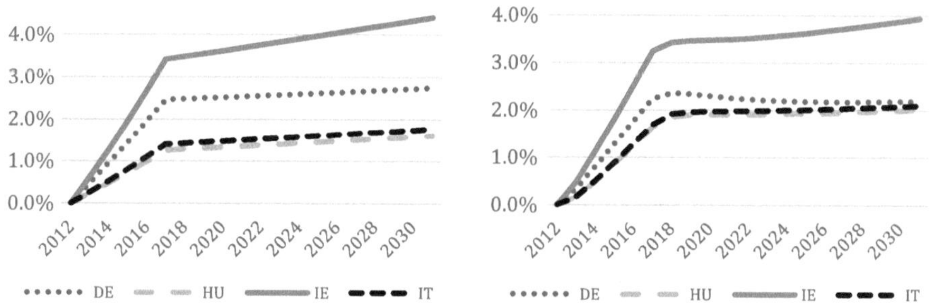

Fig. 3.4 Dynamics of impacts of annual 1% shocks over a five-year period to REDI on TFP and GDP in the selected countries. *Source* Authors' own compilation

productivity growth and the resulting economic development affect and feed back to that of other regions through trade and factor mobility. These feedback mechanisms may result in out-migration or capital flight which negatively affects the growth of some regions.

In order to better understand the impact mechanism behind these results, it is useful to distinguish all steps of the mechanism. First, the impact of the initial REDI improvement has a one-year lag on TFP and GDP changes. Thus, interventions between 2012 and 2016 have direct productivity and economic effects between 2013 and 2017. Second, the initial level of entrepreneurship is a defining factor in the changes in productivity since the same increase of the REDI index in entrepreneurially developed regions means a much higher absolute change in the REDI and a similarly higher productivity change as a consequence. Third, the direct short-run GDP and TFP impacts are heavily dependent on the level of human capital endowment in regions. Regions with higher levels of human capital are capable of taking more productivity and economic advantage from a higher-quality entrepreneurial ecosystem. If the levels of entrepreneurship and human capital stock are large in a region, the short-run economic impacts are large as well. In Fig. 3.4, this means that the slope of the curves is higher than the EU average during the 5 years of the interventions. Fourth, some other aspects, such as investment, have to be considered in the long run. The direct impacts of REDI last until 2017 since after 2016 there is no further improvement in the entrepreneurial ecosystem. However, economic impacts are still observed in years that follow. We especially experience further increase of growth in 2018. This indirect impact is caused by the increased capital stock due to the additional investment that is possible as a result of increased income and saving caused by the positive effects of entrepreneurship development policy, since there is a two-year time lag between REDI changes and the effects of investment decisions. As a result of improvements in the entrepreneurial ecosystem, income changes in the next period and as a result of this change in income investment will increase, resulting in a larger capital stock available for production two years later. Finally, human capital accumulation also affects the results in the long run (after the interventions), as it follows different trends in the regions.

After 2018, the path of GDP and TFP changes less rapidly. In many countries, these paths are stabilizing to a long-run growth path. However, some countries are able to further increase their growth rate even in the long run, while others lose some of the initial gains of entrepreneurship policy. The long-run growth paths are influenced by many factors, but productivity is still a key variable in this process which is heavily influenced by the changes in human capital stock. Countries that are characterized by a high rate of human capital accumulation can grow faster in the long run than the average. In contrast, low human capital accumulation reduces the growth rate in the long run, and those countries might face a slowing growth path. These effects are further influenced by interregional migration and changes in trade as well.

In addition, the interplay between the growth and substitution effects of TFP improvement might play a role in regional GDP impacts. In cases when demand for output does not increase, firms might use less inputs resulting from productivity improvement. As a result of that some regions might lose some of their employment in the long run. Thus, even if a region experiences an improvement in TFP, it does not necessarily mean that the region will grow faster than others with less impressive TFP growth.

As shown in Fig. 3.4, Ireland is capable of benefitting most from the REDI improvements, in terms of TFP and GDP. Ireland is characterized by the highest level of REDI among the countries in the model, thus in absolute terms, the Irish shock will be the largest as well. This is accompanied by a relatively high level (significantly higher than average) of human capital. These two factors and the description of the impact mechanism above can explain why Ireland's TFP and GDP increase so much under the five years of the intervention. In the long run, Ireland has one of the highest rates of human capital accumulation, which drives the long-run impacts after the interventions. All these factors contribute to the predicted success of entrepreneurship development policy in Ireland.

Germany also gains much from the improvement of the REDI scores. The initial levels of REDI and human capital are somewhat smaller than in case of Ireland. Thus the growth of productivity and GDP under the first 5 years is lower but still above the other two less developed countries. In the long run, we have shown that human capital accumulation drives economic growth. The German path clearly illustrates that slow human capital accumulation is not enough to maintain the initial economic impacts of the shock.

At the same time, Italy and Hungary have similar, lower-level growth paths. Although Italy has a higher level of initial REDI, this advantage is partially compensated by the higher average regional human capital stock in Hungary. As a consequence, in the first five years, Italy grows only slightly faster than Hungary. In the long run, both the Hungarian and Italian paths approach the German growth path due to the higher level of human capital accumulation. Again, the Italian accumulation is slightly higher than the Hungarian one, so a small gap can be found in the long-run economic development paths of these countries.

Migration also contributes to the determination of these growth paths. While Germany is capable of attracting new labor force in the short run due to its high growth potential in the first five years, Hungary and Italy lose some of their labor forces. This effect, however, is weakened significantly in the long run when the German growth advantage disappears, and Hungary and Italy catch up. As mentioned before, Ireland has the highest level of capital accumulation, thus economic and productivity impacts are further increased in the long run which, as a consequence, generates more immigration strengthening the positive effects.

At the regional level, the same impact mechanism drives the economic effects, but in that case the differences are more pronounced since the national impacts can be interpreted as a weighted average of the regional effects. Thus, by looking at the regional impacts, one can have a much more detailed picture of the spatial effects of entrepreneurship policies. Figure 3.5 shows the regional breakdown of the simulated impacts. As can be seen, GDP impacts (on the right-hand side) follow the productivity impacts (on the left-hand side), but there are considerable differences between regions. In most of the cases, we see that central, more developed regions

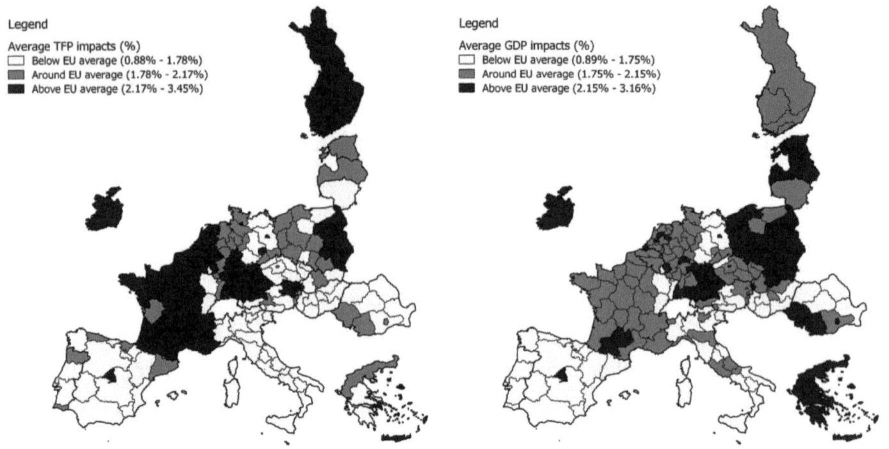

Fig. 3.5 Regional impacts of 1% annual REDI shocks over a five-year period on regional TFP and GDP levels. *Source* Authors' own compilation

(Ireland, southern Germany, northern regions, capital cities, French regions) gain more from the improvement in REDI. The complex interaction mechanisms in the GMR model are visible at the regional level, marked by significant differences in regional impacts and especially in favor of central regions. Due to their economic weight, these regions are able to attract production factors in the long run, eventually implying improvements in less developed regions. However, we can also see that in the long run, improving the entrepreneurial ecosystem can be successful in less developed regions, as some Polish, Greek, and some parts of Romania are able to catch up.

Turning our attention to the regions of the four selected countries, we can identify strong regional differences in the effectiveness of entrepreneurship policies. First, since Ireland consists only of one region in our model, we cannot give a more detailed analysis of spatial economic impacts. As described previously, entrepreneurship policy is extremely effective in Ireland both in the short and the long run.

In Germany, we see that the less developed, eastern part gains the least in economic and productivity improvement. This is due to the fact that the majority of these regions are characterized by low initial REDI scores and low human capital accumulation. Even in the slowly growing areas, central places like Berlin are capable of growing around the EU average thanks to the concentration of human capital and entrepreneurial activities (REDI).

The southern, more developed part of the country is mainly characterized by a developed entrepreneurship ecosystem (high REDI) and with some variation, and exceptions, the majority of regions has high level and accumulation of human capital (in some regions only one of these factors are given), which makes them very successful in terms of economic impacts. However, some regions are not able to translate all of the productivity changes into GDP growth since other factors play a significant role. For example, in Stuttgart, productivity improvements might substitute for labor which can mitigate the growth potential to some extent.

Regions in the countries located in the East of the EU are more diverse. In general, they all excel at some determining factors of the policy, but they do not excel in all of them which means that they are not able to generate exceptionally high productivity and economic growth. In some cases, judging the factors behind regional growth changes can be straightforward since all the influencing factors contribute to growth in the same direction. In Hungary, which has a highly concentrated spatial structure, Budapest is characterized by the highest level of both human capital and REDI. As a consequence, this region is the most potent in terms of the short-run impacts. In the long run, both human capital accumulation and the substitution effect must be considered. In the case of Budapest, accumulation is also the highest in the country which increases the growth path of Budapest in the long run. This growth is only slightly reduced by the substitution effect described above. Still our result suggests that the TFP effect is slightly below the EU average, while the GDP effect is around the EU average. Outside the capital, however, due to the lack of foundations, we see only limited potential of entrepreneurial development policies.

Finally, Italy has a traditionally divided spatial economic structure. We find again that the core regions can benefit the most from entrepreneurial policies. This concerns mainly northern Italian regions (like Lombardy and the capital with some neighboring regions). If we look behind these results, we can state that northern, developed regions benefit from both the high level of human capital and entrepreneurship, while regions around the capital are less developed in terms of entrepreneurship, but still concentrate a high stock of human capital. Compared to EU averages, however, these nationally high values are not high enough to provide the basis for significant economic growth at the EU level. Our simulations also show that southern regions that are far from the capital have a low chance of benefitting significantly from these policies due to their low level of development, both in terms of entrepreneurship and human capital.

3.5 Conclusions

Policy interventions and their impacts have always been in the center of interest. Over the decades, economists have developed various tools to estimate the ex-ante impact as well as to evaluate the ex-post effects of policy interventions. Simple econometric regression models are able to test the significance of a policy instrument based on the *ceteris paribus* assumption. However, these uniform suggestions neglect the likely diverse effects of policy interventions as well as the potential complex impact of a particular policy element on other influential factors. Simultaneous regressions could handle the complex effect of closely related factors. However, the one-size-fits-all policy recommendations remain an open issue.

Many entrepreneurship scholars believe that improving the entrepreneurial ecosystem contributes positively to economic growth, development, job creation, and productivity. However, empirical studies report contradicting impacts depending on the definition of entrepreneurship, the level of development, the unit of analysis, and modeling strategy, just to mention the most important factors. Most of these studies rely on regression-based methodologies by assuming a universal and homogenous impact of entrepreneurship policies. In this chapter, we used the REDI to simulate the impact of improving the entrepreneurship ecosystem of regions in 24 countries of the European Union. REDI is a composite indicator that combines the individual and the institutional factors of entrepreneurship into fourteen pillars and three sub-indices. Two analytical tools, the average equalization and the penalty for bottleneck techniques serve to identify region-based bottlenecks in the entrepreneurial ecosystem.

We have incorporated REDI into the recently extended GMR-Europe model to test the effects of improving the entrepreneurial ecosystem on TFP and GDP levels. Unlike regression-based methods, GMR-Europe builds on spatial patterns of dynamic agglomeration and spillover effects. GMR-Europe has three parts, the Total Factor Productivity (TFP), the Spatial Computable General Equilibrium (SCGE), and the macroeconomic (MACRO) model blocks. REDI, our measure for entrepreneurial ecosystem quality, is the part of the TFP block influencing regional productivity through interaction with human capital. The TFP block is able to simulate region-specific impacts of policy interventions like R&D support, development in human capital, entrepreneurship, or innovation networks on regional productivity. The macroeconomic block calculates policy impacts at the overall EU and national levels, while the 181-region NUTS2-level TFP and SCGE blocks provide results at the regional level. The model calculates the impact on various economic variables such as GDP, employment or prices at the regional, national, and aggregate European levels.

This chapter zoomed in on the impacts of improving the entrepreneurial ecosystem at the regional level. Our simulations were based on a 1% annual improvement of the REDI score in every region over a five-year period. The impacts of these improvements were tracked on regional and aggregate TFP and GDP levels. On average, a 1% annual improvement over the five-year period leads to an average 2% increase both in GDP and in TFP, while GDP impact is slightly larger. However, the magnitude of the impact varies significantly across countries while regional impacts are even more dispersed. In part because of the way we set up our simulation, but these differences are also due to the complex mechanisms within the GMR model where productivity growth and the resulting economic development affect and feed back to other regions through trade and factor mobility. These feedback mechanisms may result in out-migration or capital outflows that can have negative effects on the growth of some regions. Our simulation results suggest that it is the more developed, central regions that benefit the most from REDI improvements, such as policy interventions targeting the entrepreneurial ecosystem.

Like any other simulation exercise, our analysis has its limitations. First, we have not yet explored the full richness of the REDI in our simulation. To illustrate how policy analysis could work with the combination of REDI and GMR modeling, we chose to implement a uniform exogenous 1% annual shock to REDI in all regions. Future research could easily go into more detail and simulate more specific and realistic interventions. REDI-based policy recommendations are built on the so-called system failure improvement that is an analogy to classical public policy aiming to correct market failures. That is, policymakers could target policies at improving the weakest link in the regional ecosystem, giving them endogenous REDI improvements that can then be simulated as was shown. In Chaps. 5–7 in this volume (Sanders et al. 2020a, b, c), we illustrate how REDI can be used to diagnose and inform a reform strategy for Italy, Germany, and the UK, respectively. The GMR simulations in this chapter have shown that such tailored reforms are likely to cause heterogeneous effects across regions. A limitation of the REDI is that the interventions that can be studied under the proposed framework remain limited to those that affect aspects of the ecosystem represented in the REDI. We believe the processes and mechanisms in the GMR are important to consider, and the present model setup can generate testable hypotheses. Future research could rigorously and empirically test the assumed structures and specifications in the REDI-extended GMR model.

Appendix: The REDI Calculation Method

In constructing the index, we followed eight steps:

1. ***The selection of variables***: We start with the variables that come directly from the original sources for each region involved in the analysis. The variables can be at the individual level (personal or business) that are coming from the GEM Adult Population Survey or the institutional/environmental level that are coming from various other sources. Altogether, we have data for a mix of 125 NUTS1 and NUTS2 regions.

2. ***The construction of the pillars***: We calculate all pillars from the variables using the interaction variable method, that is, by multiplying the individual variable with the proper institutional variable. This results in pillar values for all the 125 EU regions.

$$z_{i,j} = \mathrm{IND}_{i,j} * \mathrm{INS}_{i,j} \tag{3.3}$$

   for all $j = 1, \ldots, k$, the number of individual and institutional variables
   $\mathrm{IND}_{i,j}$ is the original score value for region i and variable j individual variable
   $\mathrm{INS}_{i,j}$ is the original score value for region i and variable j institutional variable
   $z_{i,j}$ is the original pillar value for region i and pillar j.

3. ***Normalization***: Pillars values were first normalized to a range from 0 to 1 by using the distance methodology:

$$x_{i,j} = \frac{z_{i,j}}{\max z_{i,j}} \tag{3.4}$$

for all $j = 1, \ldots, k$, the number of pillars
where $x_{i,j}$ is the normalized score value for region i and pillar j
$z_{i,j}$ is the pillar value for region i and pillar j
max $z_{i,j}$ is the maximum value for pillar j.

4. ***Capping***: All index building is based on a benchmarking principle. In our case, we selected the 95-percentile score adjustment meaning that any observed values higher than the 95-percentile are lowered to the 95-percentile.

5. ***Average pillar adjustment***: The different averages of the normalized values of the pillars imply that reaching the same pillar values requires different efforts and inputs. Since we want to apply REDI for public policy purposes, the additional inputs for the marginal improvement of the pillar values should be the same for all pillars. Therefore, we need a transformation to equalize the average values of the components. Equation 3.5 shows the calculation of the average value of pillar:

$$\bar{x}_j = \frac{\sum_{i=1}^{n} x_{i,j}}{n} \tag{3.5}$$

We want to transform the $x_{i,j}$ values such that the potential minimum value is 0 and the maximum value is 1:

$$y_{i,j} = x_{i,j}^{k} \tag{3.6}$$

where k is the "strength of adjustment," the kth moment of X_j is exactly the needed average, $\bar{y}_j$. We have to find the root of the following equation for

$$\sum_{i=1}^{n} x_{i,j}^{k} - n\bar{y}_j = 0 \tag{3.7}$$

It can be seen, based on previous conditions and derivatives, that the function is decreasing and convex, meaning it can be quickly solved using the well-known Newton–Raphson method with an initial guess of 0. After obtaining k, the computations are straightforward. Note that if

$$\begin{aligned} \bar{x}_j &< \bar{y}_j \; k < 1 \\ \bar{x}_j &= \bar{y}_j \; k = 1 \\ \bar{x}_j &> \bar{y}_j \; k > 1 \end{aligned}$$

that is k be thought of as the strength (and direction) of adjustment.

6. ***Penalizing***: After these transformations, the penalty for bottleneck (PFB) methodology was used to create pillar adjusted PFB values. We define our penalty function as follows:

$$h_{(i),j} = \min y_{(i),j} + \left(1 - e^{-(y_{(i)j} - \min y_{(i),j})}\right) \quad (3.8)$$

where $h_{i,j}$ is the modified, post-penalty value of pillar j in region i
$y_{i,j}$ is the normalized value of index component j in region i
$y_{\min}$ is the lowest value of $y_{i,j}$ for region i
$i = 1, \ldots n =$ the number of regions
$j = 1, \ldots, m =$ the number of pillars.

The penalizing feature reflects the belief that the entrepreneurial performance of each region is mainly determined by its weakest component(s), and all other pillars with higher values cannot exploit their full potential because of the existence of bottleneck in their system of entrepreneurship.

7. ***Sub-index calculation***: The pillars are the basic building blocks of the sub-index. There are three: entrepreneurial attitudes, entrepreneurial abilities, and entrepreneurial aspirations. The value of a sub-index for any region is the penalty weighted average of its average equalized pillars for that sub-index multiplied by 100. The maximum value of the sub-indices is 100 and the potential minimum is 0, both of which reflect the relative position of a region in a particular sub-index.

$$\mathrm{ATT}_i = 100 \sum_{j=1}^{5} h_{i,j} \quad (3.9a)$$

$$\mathrm{ABT}_i = 100 \sum_{j=6}^{9} h_{i,j} \quad (3.9b)$$

$$\mathrm{ASP}_i = 100 \sum_{j=10}^{14} h_{i,j} \quad (3.9c)$$

where $h_{i,j}$ is the modified, post-penalty value of pillar j in region i
$i = 1, \ldots, n =$ the number of regions
$j = 1, \ldots, 14 =$ the number of pillars.

8. ***REDI score calculation***: The super-index, the REDI, is the simple average of the three sub-indices. Since 100 represents the theoretically available limit, the GEDI points can also be interpreted as a measure of the efficiency of the entrepreneurship inputs

$$\mathrm{REDI}_i = \frac{1}{3}(\mathrm{ATT}_i + \mathrm{ABT}_i + \mathrm{ASP}_i) \quad (3.10)$$

where REDI_i is the Regional Entrepreneurship and Development Index score of region i
$i = 1, 2, \ldots, n =$ the number of regions.

From the policy perspective, REDI methodology has two key features. The first is the average equalization methodology (Point 5) that is designed to equalize the marginal effects of the additional inputs over the average of 14 pillars while keeping all the values in the [0,1] range. This means that after transformation, below average (0.49) pillar values increased (Opportunity Perception, Networking, Technology Absorption, Human Capital and Finance) and all the other pillar values decreased. Consequently, improving the originally below average pillar value requires a smaller absolute increase of additional inputs as compared to the originally higher average pillar value where a larger increase is necessary for the same marginal improvement.

References

Acs ZJ, Audretsch DB, Braunerhjelm P, Carlsson B (2009) The knowledge spillover theory of entrepreneurship. Small Bus Econ 32:15–30

Acs ZJ, Autio E, Szerb L (2014) National systems of entrepreneurship: measurement issues and policy implications. Res Policy 43:476–494. https://doi.org/10.1016/j.respol.2013.08.016

Acs Z, Estrin S, Mickiewicz T, Szerb L (2017) Institutions, entrepreneurship and growth: the role of national entrepreneurial ecosystems. Small Bus Econ (Forthcoming)

Alvedalen J, Boschma R (2017) A critical review of entrepreneurial ecosystems research: towards a future research agenda. Eur Plan Stud 25:887–903. https://doi.org/10.1080/09654313.2017.1299694

Anselin L, Varga A, Acs Z (1997) Local geographic spillovers between university research and high technology innovations. J Urban Econ. 42(3):422–448

Audretsch DB, Kuratko DF, Link AN (2015) Making sense of the elusive paradigm of entrepreneurship. Small Bus Econ 45(4):703–712

Autio E, Pathak S, Wennberg K (2013) Consequences of cultural practices for entrepreneurial behaviors. J Int Bus Stud 44(4):334–362

Baum JR, Frese M, Baron RA (2014) Born to be an entrepreneur? Revisiting the personality approach to entrepreneurship. In: The psychology of entrepreneurship. Psychology Press, pp 73–98

Baumol WJ (1996) Entrepreneurship: productive, unproductive, and destructive. J Bus Ventur 11(1):3–22

Bayar A (2007) Simulation of R&D investment scenarios and calibration of the impact on a set of multi-country models. European Commission DG JRC Institute for Prospective Technological Studies (IPTS)

Bradley J (2006) Evaluating the impact of european union cohesion policy in less-developed countries and regions. Reg Stud 40:189–199

ESRI (2002) An examination of the ex-post macroeconomic impacts of CSF 1994–1999 on Objective 1 countries and regions

Fujita M, Krugman PR, Venables AJ (1999) The spatial economy: cities, regions and international trade. Wiley Online Library

Gartner WB (1985) A conceptual framework for describing the phenomenon of new venture creation. Acad Manag Rev 10(4):696–706

Joint Research Centre-European Commission (2008) Handbook on constructing composite indicators: methodology and user guide. OECD publishing

Krugman P (1991) Increasing returns and economic geography. J Polit Econ 99(3):483–499. https://doi.org/10.2307/2937739

Lafuente E, Szerb L, Acs ZJ (2016) Country level efficiency and national systems of entrepreneurship: a data envelopment analysis approach. J Technol Transfer 41(6):1260–1283
Lafuente E, Acs Z, Sanders M, Szerb L (2019) The global technology frontier: productivity growth and the relevance of Kirznerian and Schumpeterian entrepreneurship. Small Bus Econ 1–26. Online https://doi.org/10.1007/s11187-019-00140-1
Landström H, Harirchi G (2018) The social structure of entrepreneurship as a scientific field. Res Policy 47(3):650–662
Liñán F, Fernandez-Serrano J (2014) National culture, entrepreneurship and economic development: different patterns across the European Union. Small Bus Econ 42(4):685–701
Low MB, MacMillan IC (1988) Entrepreneurship: past research and future challenges. J Manag 14(2):139–161
Malecki EJ (2018) Entrepreneurship and entrepreneurial ecosystems. Geography Compass. Online access, pp 1–21. https://doi.org/10.1111/gec3.12359
Naudé W (2010) Entrepreneurship, developing countries, and development economics: new approaches and insights. Small Bus Econ 34(1):1
Nightingale P, Coad A (2014) Muppets and gazelles: political and methodological biases in entrepreneurship research. Ind Corp Change 23:113–143. https://doi.org/10.1093/icc/dtt057
Parker SC (2018) The economics of entrepreneurship. Cambridge University Press
Prieger JE, Bampoky C, Blanco LR, Liu A (2016) Economic growth and the optimal level of entrepreneurship. World Dev 82:95–109
Qian H, Acs ZJ, Stough RR (2013) Regional systems of entrepreneurship: the nexus of human capital, knowledge and new firm formation. J Econ Geogr 13:559–587. https://doi.org/10.1093/jeg/lbs009
Rappai G, Szerb L (2011) Összetett indexek készítése új módon: a szűk keresztmetszetekért történő büntetés módszere. PTE KRTI Műhelytenulmányok 2011/1
Ratto M, Roeger W, in't Veld J (2009) QUEST III: an estimated open-economy DSGE model of the euro area with fiscal and monetary policy. Econ Model 26:222–233
Romer P (1990) Endogenous technological change. J Polit Econ 98:71–102
Sanders M, Stenkula M, Grilli L, Herrmann AM, Latifi G, Páger B, Szerb L, Terragno Bogliaccini E (2020a) A Reform Strategy for Italy. In: Sanders M, Marx A, Stenkula M (eds) The entrepreneurial society. Springer, Berlin Heidelberg
Sanders M, Stenkula M, Fritsch M, Herrmann AM, Latifi G, Páger B, Szerb L, Terragno Bogliaccini E, Wyrwich M (2020b) A Reform Strategy for Germany. In: Sanders M, Marx A, Stenkula M (eds) The entrepreneurial society. Springer, Berlin Heidelberg
Sanders M, Stenkula M, Dunstan J, Estrin S, Herrmann AM, Páger B, Szerb L, Terragno Bogliaccini E (2020c) A Reform Strategy for the UK. In: Sanders M, Marx A, Stenkula M (eds) The entrepreneurial society. Springer, Berlin Heidelberg
Schalk H, Varga A (2004) The economic effects of EU community support framework interventions. An Ex-ante Impact Analysis with EcoRET, A Macroeconomic Model For Hungary. Center of Applied Economic Research Münster (CAWM), University of Münster
Sebestyén T, Varga A (2013) Research productivity and the quality of interregional knowledge networks. Ann Reg Sci 51:155–189
Shane S, Venkataraman S (2000) The promise of entrepreneurship as a field of research. Acad Manag Rev 25(1):217–226
Spigel B (2017) The relational organization of entrepreneurial ecosystems. Entrepreneurship Theory Pract 41(1):49–72
Stam E (2015) Entrepreneurial ecosystems and regional policy: a sympathetic critique. Eur Plan Stud 23:1759–1769. https://doi.org/10.1080/09654313.2015.1061484
Szerb L, Vörös Zs, Komlósi É, Acs ZJ, Páger B, Ortega-Argilés R, Abaligeti G (2017) The new regional entrepreneurship and development index: structure, data and description of methodology. Unpublished manuscript

Szerb LE, Lafuente K Horváth, Páger B (2018) The relevance of quantity and quality entrepreneurship for regional performance: the moderating role of the entrepreneurial ecosystem. Reg Stud . https://doi.org/10.1080/00343404.2018.1510481
Treyz G, Rickman D, Shao G (1992) The REMI economic-demographic forecasting and simulation model. Int Reg Sci Rev 14:221–253
Varga A (2000) Local academic knowledge transfers and the concentration of economic activity. J Reg Sci 40(2):289–309
Varga A (2006) The spatial dimension of innovation and growth: empirical research methodology and policy analysis. Eur Plan Stud 14(9):1171–1186. https://doi.org/10.1080/09654310600933298
Varga A (2007) GMR-Hungary: a complex macro-regional model for the analysis of development policy impacts on the Hungarian economy. PTE KTK KRTI Working Papers (2007/4)
Varga A (2017a) Geographical macro and regional impact modeling. In: Jackson R, Schaeffer P (eds) Regional research frontiers, advances in spatial science, vol 2, pp 49–58. https://doi.org/10.1007/978-3-319-50590-9_3
Varga A (2017b) Place-based, spatially blind, or both? Challenges in estimating the impacts of modern development policies: the case of the GMR policy impact modeling approach. Int Reg Sci Rev 40:12–37. https://doi.org/10.1177/0160017615571587
Varga A, Baypinar M (2016) Economic impact assessment of alternative European neighborhood policy (ENP) options with the application of the GMR-Turkey model. Ann Reg Sci 56:153–176
Varga A, Sebestyén T, Szabó N, Szerb L (2018) Economic Impact assessment of Entrepreneurship policies with the GMR-Europe Model. FIRES Project Report D4.6, 2018.04.06
Varga A, Sebestyén T, Szabó N, Szerb L (2019) Estimating the economic impacts of knowledge network and entrepreneurship development in smart specialization policy. Reg Stud. https://doi.org/10.1080/00343404.2018.1527026
Vivarelli M (2013) Is entrepreneurship necessarily good? Microeconomic evidence from developed and developing countries. Ind Corp Change 22:1453–1495. https://doi.org/10.1093/icc/dtt005
Wennekers S, Thurik R (1999) Linking entrepreneurship and economic growth. Small Bus Econ 13(1):27–56

Chapter 4
On the Institutional Foundations of the Varieties of Entrepreneurship in Europe

Andrea M. Herrmann

Abstract For decades, research into the link between national institutions and entrepreneurship has been characterized by three shortcomings: First, clear-cut concepts of institutions are rare. Second, a parsimonious understanding of how a few core institutions influence entrepreneurship is missing. Third, scholars often ignore that incrementally innovative ventures constitute a distinct (and under-researched) type of entrepreneurship next to the (over-researched) form of radically innovative, high-growth or high-tech entrepreneurship. This chapter seeks to illustrate how the application of the "Varieties-of-Capitalism" (VoC) reasoning does not only enable focused rather than eclectic analyses of institutional influences on entrepreneurship but also reveals the institutionally induced equifinality of the varieties of entrepreneurship across Europe. These insights invite future entrepreneurship research to move away from the ideology that displays radically innovative entrepreneurship as, by far, the most desirable form of entrepreneurship. This finding also invites policymakers to target entrepreneurial support measures more specifically to their economy's institutional environment.

Keywords Entrepreneurship · Varieties-of-Capitalism · National institutions · Institutional complementarities

---

This chapter summarizes some of the core findings of Work Package 5 of the FIRES research project (https://projectfires.eu), which received funding from the European Union's Horizon 2020 research and innovation program under grant agreement No 649378. The theoretical foundations for this work package published earlier in Herrmann (2019) were reiterated—largely verbatim—in Sects. 4.1 and 4.2. While Sects. 4.1 and 4.2 are therefore no original work, the remainder of the chapter is original work to the extent that it provides a systematic overview over how this argument is based on a set of papers that have been published or are under review, in (Dilli et al. 2018; Held et al. 2018; Held et al. 2018a, b; Held 2019). I thank Selin Dilli for comments on earlier drafts of this chapter.

A. M. Herrmann (✉)
Innovation Studies, Copernicus Institute of Sustainable Development, Utrecht University, Utrecht, The Netherlands
e-mail: A.M.Herrmann@uu.nl

M. Sanders et al. (eds.), *The Entrepreneurial Society*, International Studies in Entrepreneurship 44, https://doi.org/10.1007/978-3-662-61007-7_4

4.1 Introduction

Over the past two decades, the Varieties-of-Capitalism (VoC) literature, going back to the work of Hall and Soskice (2001a), has become a widely applied framework in the political sciences, in political economy and economic sociology alike. In a nutshell, the VoC literature illustrates that different national institutions governing labor and financial markets as well as inter-organizational collaborations facilitate different types of corporate innovation. While the VoC framework has been developed mostly through studies of incumbent firms, its reasoning is also applicable to new ventures. National institutions are likely to lead also new ventures to develop business ideas of different innovativeness. To put it differently, given that incumbent firms were found to compete on different types of innovations and thus, in different market segments between countries, it is reasonable to assume that many firms have chosen these competitive strategies from their inception as new ventures.

However, until the beginning of the H2020 project *Financial and Institutional Reforms for an Entrepreneurial Society in Europe* (FIRES), the VoC framework has hardly been applied in entrepreneurship research (for exceptions, see Ebner 2010; van der Walt 2010).[1] To be clear, the entrepreneurship literature illustrates that entrepreneurs are driven by different motives and reasons, and have diverse aspirations and growth ambitions (for example, Cooper and Artz 1995; Wiklund et al. 2003). Accordingly, the literature acknowledges that different forms of entrepreneurship exist, ranging from solo self-employment over small family businesses to high-growth gazelle ventures (see also Delmar et al. 2003; Henrekson and Stenkula 2016; Vivarelli 2013). The Global Entrepreneurship Monitor, by far the most comprehensive dataset on entrepreneurship forms across the world, also shows that entrepreneurship takes different forms between countries. However, systematic research into institutional reasons, as laid out by the VoC literature, for how and why entrepreneurship between countries may differ in its innovation focus remained underdeveloped until the start of the FIRES project.

This research gap has arguably (see Herrmann 2019) persisted because of a strong focus on radically innovative—that is "technology-intensive" (OECD 1998), "R&D-intensive" (Schreyer 2000), or "knowledge-intensive" (Delmar et al. 2003)—ventures. This focus can be theoretically motivated by their high-growth potential and empirically because these ventures have been shown to generate a disproportionately high share of employment (see also Amat and Perramon 2010; Davidson and Segerstrom 1998; Hölzl 2009; OECD 2002; Shane 2009). Radically innovative ventures typically develop goods and services based on new technologies, leading to strong corporate growth on the one hand and a higher risk of failure on the other. Examples of such radically innovative ventures have emerged particularly frequently in Silicon Valley which, in turn, has led to an idolization of this radically innovative,

[1] The reason why the VoC framework has hardly been applied in business and management research today seems straightforward: The core proponents of the VoC arguments, as well as their followers, are political scientists (Peter Hall, Kathleen Thelen), political economists (David Soskice), and sociologists (Wolfgang Streeck) rather than business and management scholars.

"Silicon Valley" entrepreneurship. Newspapers have reported with high frequency about the heroic efforts and outstanding success of Silicon Valley entrepreneurs, and even mainstream movies have been made about the start-up stories of Apple and Facebook. Because attention and impact have accrued to studies of extraordinary rather than every-day phenomena, scientific research has paid inordinate attention to the funding and other needs, along with the impact of radically innovative ventures (see, for example, Henrekson and Johansson 2010; Shane 2009). And as a consequence, policymakers across Europe explicitly or implicitly aim to facilitate high-growth ("Silicon Valley") entrepreneurship (Commission 2010; OECD 2002; see also Hölzl 2009; Mason and Brown 2013).

This focus on radically innovative entrepreneurship is problematic for various reasons. First, it conveys the impression that less innovative types of entrepreneurship are second-best as they grow less rapidly (see, for example, Amat and Perramon 2010; Davidson and Segerstrom 1998; Hölzl 2009; OECD 1998, 2002; Schreyer 2000). This reasoning is flawed as recent studies show that high employment growth is not only generated by highly innovative start-ups but also by more established firms of at least five years (Anyadike-Danes et al. 2009) and with an average age of 25 years (Acs et al. 2008a). Furthermore, a recent study of the German ministry of economic affairs finds that "high-growth ventures can also shrink again as well. A high-growth venture (…) is thus no guarantee for sustained employment growth but constitutes a temporary phenomenon" (BMWi 2012, p. 42; see also Daunfeldt and Halvarsson 2015). Second, the focus on radically innovative entrepreneurship is also problematic because it neglects the comparative institutional advantages that continental European economies offer to incrementally innovative start-up firms. As laid out in detail below, the institutional environment of regulated economies makes it easier for entrepreneurs to establish incrementally rather than radically innovative ventures. Third, incrementally innovative ventures grow at a lower but more sustainable rate than their radically innovative counterparts (Herrmann 2008, Chap. 5). If successful, radically innovative ventures typically yield higher returns than incrementally innovative ventures. But the chances of becoming successful are decisively lower for radically than for incrementally innovative ventures. Last but not least, radically innovative ventures occur much less frequently than their incrementally innovative counterparts, even in the USA. While most new ventures are not innovative across economies, among those that are, incremental innovation is the rule and radical innovation is the exception (see Baumol 2002, 2004; Henrekson and Sanadaji 2014, p. 1760; Nightingale and Coad 2014).

In several studies, whose most important results are reported in Sect. 4.3 of this chapter, we show how a core set of distinct national institutions facilitates the development of different types of entrepreneurial innovation across Europe. These studies do not only explain why radically innovative ventures develop more frequently in Anglo-Saxon economies. They also illustrate why incrementally innovative ventures are more common in Northern Europe, while new ventures reproducing goods and services at lower costs are particularly frequent in Southern and Eastern European economies. Importantly, the insights gained from these studies may motivate future research to move away from its focus on radically innovative entrepreneurship as the most desirable entrepreneurship type. Overall, the studies below (see Sect. 4.3) thus illustrate how a better understanding of the varieties of entrepreneurship in Europe can lead to a more balanced understanding of the possibilities and needs—or rather the difficulties and needless efforts—to equally foster radically innovative entrepreneurship in Continental Europe.

To illustrate how the VoC reasoning offers a more balanced understanding of the link between distinct national institutions and different types of entrepreneurial innovativeness, I first review the core arguments of the VoC literature on a country's institutional foundations in Sect. 4.2. Section 4.3 then provides an overview of four FIRES studies that show how different institutional frameworks induce different types of entrepreneurial venturing across Europe. Section 4.4 illustrates the implications that result for researchers and policymakers from these findings.

4.2 Theoretical Foundations

Importantly, the VoC arguments on how a distinct set of institutions support different types of corporate innovativeness have, until the start of the FIRES project, been empirically tested on the basis of *incumbent firms* (Hall and Soskice 2001a; Hancké et al. 2007; Casper 2007; Herrmann 2008). We therefore begin with the question of whether these arguments are equally applicable to *nascent ventures*. To answer this question, we first develop a theoretical framework that could explain which institutions are core to the development of (different types of) entrepreneurship, and why.

Starting with the work of Stinchcombe (1965), the entrepreneurship literature investigating how institutions influence entrepreneurship gained momentum in the early 1990s. Its contributors arrived at the conclusion that institutions "matter" because they structure economic payoffs which influence entrepreneurial efforts and activities (Calcagno and Sobel 2014; Baumol 1990; Murphy et al. 1990; Sobel 2008). While the literature agrees that both formal and informal institutions incentivize individual behavior (North 1990), thereby influencing the extent and character of an economy's entrepreneurial activity (Acs et al. 2008b; Stenholm et al. 2013; Urbano and Alvarez 2014), it also—often implicitly—focuses on the institutional drivers of *radically innovative entrepreneurship*. The formal institutions were found to be beneficial for "productive," "high-growth" entrepreneurship and include law and order, contract enforcement, competition policy, trade policies, tax codes, social insurance systems, employment protection legislation, capital market regulation, as well as the protection of private property (Bjørnskov and Foss 2013; Hall and Jones 1999; Henrekson and Johansson 2009). Informal institutions supporting growth-oriented entrepreneurship include individualism, social capital, trust, and power distance (Hechavarria and Reynolds 2009; Taylor and Wilson 2012). In short, the literature suggests that differences in entrepreneurship between countries or regions can, *inter alia*, be explained by a broad diversity of institutions (Case and Harris 2012; Stam 2014; World Economic Forum 2013).

This literature on institutions and entrepreneurship suffers from three problems. First, a clear-cut concept of institutions is missing. Second, a parsimonious understanding of whether and how a few core institutions facilitate different types of entrepreneurship is not provided. Third, the literature focuses on explaining how different types of institutions foster "high-growth" or "high-impact" entrepreneurship (Davidsson and Henrekson 2002; Henrekson 2005; Henrekson and Johansson 2009). While this leads to a focus on "technology-intensive" (OECD 1998), "R&D-intensive" (Schreyer 2000), or "knowledge-intensive" (Delmar et al. 2003) ventures, incrementally innovative ventures, their needs, and institutional drivers tend to be overlooked.

The VoC literature makes it possible to address these three problems. First, taking the perspective of historical institutionalism and in line with North (1990, p. 3), the VoC literature clearly defines institutions as "... formalized rules that may be enforced by calling upon a third party" (Streeck and Thelen 2005, p. 10). Institutions thus are the written or verbally agreed rules of the game which lead to a systematic behavior of actors—individuals and organizations, such as entrepreneurs and their ventures. Compared to rational-choice institutionalism, the VoC literature thus takes a broader perspective, including informal institutions that develop on the basis of less formal agreements than written rules (such as laws or contracts). At the same time, the VoC literature, in line with Ostrom (1990), focuses on those institutions that provide capacities for deliberation, the exchange of information, monitoring, and the enforcement of agreements (Hall and Soskice 2001a, pp. 9–12). In this regard, the VoC literature has a more focused understanding than sociological institutionalism: While shared understandings (such as norms, values, and culture) provide the basis for the development of (informal) institutions, the latter "... must be reaffirmed periodically by appropriate historical experience" (Hall and Soskice 2001a, p. 14), in order to remain viable as rules upon which third parties can be called.[2]

Second, the VoC literature offers a parsimonious theoretical framework to identify a core of institutions which influence any business activity (Hall and Soskice 2001b). To this end, the VoC literature draws on the insights of economic theory (Milgrom and Roberts 1992; Teece and Pisano 1998; Williamson 1985), as well as the resource-dependence view (Pfeffer and Salancik 1978), which illustrate that three types of resources are essential for any business to operate: labor, finance, and know-how. These resources are considered as most important because firms can only secure them after solving a collective action problem with external economic actors, namely their workforces, financiers, and R&D partners. Institutions channeling the resources between firms and their workforces, financiers, and R&D partners can therefore offer comparative advantages and are thus considered to be economically most influential. Accordingly, the VoC literature illustrates how education-related together with labor-market institutions, finance-related institutions, and institutions governing inter-organizational collaborations are shaped differently between countries, and it explains how these institutional constellations together lead to different,

[2]For a more in-depth understanding of how different schools of thought differ from each other in their understanding of institutions, see (Koelble 1995; Hall and Taylor 1996).

complementary institutional environments on the one hand and to different types of corporate behavior on the other.

Third, based on these theoretical considerations, the VoC literature convincingly argues that incrementally innovative firms are institutionally supported by a regulated environment. To illustrate this point, the VoC literature (Hall and Soskice 2001a) compares the regulated institutional environment of the Northern European countries, the so-called "Coordinated Market Economies" (CMEs), to the deregulated institutional environment of the Anglo-Saxon countries, or the "Liberal Market Economies" (LMEs). In doing so, the VoC scholars often illustrate their reasoning at the examples of Germany, which they consider the most typical CME, and the UK or USA, which are considered particularly typical LMEs. Later contributors to the VoC literature questioned the dichotomous distinction between CMEs and LMEs as they identified additional, particularly typical institutional constellations of country groups, most notably Mediterranean Market Economies (MMEs) and Eastern Market Economies (EMEs) (for example Amable 2003; Hancké et al. 2007; Schneider and Paunescu 2012).

Based on these distinctions, I here summarize our FIRES studies which illustrate that radically innovative entrepreneurship is facilitated by a deregulated institutional environment (that is typical for Anglo-Saxon economies), whereas regulated institutional constellations (typical of Northern European countries) facilitate incrementally innovative forms of entrepreneurship. The over-regulated or rapidly liberalized institutional environment of Southern and Eastern European economies, respectively, facilitate reproductive entrepreneurship based on the imitation of existing business ideas. Applying the VoC reasoning to new ventures explains why high-growth, radically innovative entrepreneurship develops particularly frequently in the deregulated institutional environments of LMEs, including the Anglo-Saxon economics such as the USA, UK, and Ireland.

Beginning with *labor*, the VoC literature highlights the free-riding problem related to the training of specifically skilled workforces (Dencker et al. 2009; Hall and Soskice 2001b). Given that the education and training system of LMEs tends not to be coordinated via a country-wide dialog between the social partners, sophisticated industry-wide job classifications that could serve as a basis for training workforces do not exist. Workforces therefore acquire a versatile skill set which they can use in different work environments. Upon completion of education trajectories, the flexible labor-market institutions of LMEs further strengthen the general skills of workforces. Short notice periods, dismissal without substantial reasons, and weak work councils imply that workforces are faced with hire-and-fire at short notice and change jobs frequently. Workers therefore acquire general skills that are useful for, and thus adequately rewarded by, all firms needing a certain business function. Importantly, such general skills imply that workers are particularly imaginative (thanks to the different work environments they have seen in different firms) and flexible as they are used to adapt to new corporate environments. Radically innovative firms, in turn, do not only require the capacity to imagine completely new business ideas but are also characterized by rapid changes. Flexible workforces with general skills are thus particularly well equipped to develop radical innovations. In sum, the flexible education and labor-market institutions of LMEs thus facilitate the development of radically innovative ventures as they equip workforces with general skills (see also Herrmann and Peine 2011).

In addition to labor-market institutions, also those institutions governing the access to venture *finance* facilitate the development of radically innovative ventures in LMEs. The VoC literature shows that institutions differ in how they address the principal-agent problem related to the provision of shareholder capital (Hall and Soskice 2001b; Kenyon and Vitols 2004; Vitols 2001). To be willing to invest, shareholders need to be assured that their funds are used in the most efficient way by the firm's management. In LMEs, supervisory boards overlooking the activities and decisions of the management board of directors do not exist. While shareholders directly elect corporate managers, they have little or no systematic insight into, or control over, managerial investment decisions via a supervisory board. Consequently, managers have unilateral power to take major strategic and financial decisions, while shareholders can monitor the soundness of managerial decisions only through the development of equity prices at the stock market. This, in turn, drives managers to maximize returns on investment by engaging in high-risk, radical innovation projects. Radically innovative start-ups are therefore a particularly attractive investment option for venture capitalists. Venture capital investments into start-up firms are furthermore facilitated by the private pension systems of LMEs, which imply that comparatively high sums destined to build up future pensions are invested *inter alia* in venture capital firms. Accordingly, the pension and corporate governance systems of LMEs facilitate the development of radically innovative ventures.

The VoC literature furthermore highlights how solutions to hold-up problems, related to inter-organizational development of *know-how*, facilitates the emergence of radically innovative ventures (Hall and Soskice 2001b; Tate 2001; Teubner 2001). Start-up firms often engage in R&D collaborations with other organizations, such as research labs, universities, or suppliers, in order to jointly develop new products or services (Lundvall 1992; Tate 2001, pp. 444–446). But such joint developments also bear the risk of hold-up. The latter occurs whenever two or more actors try to appropriate the intellectual property (IP) developed by their cooperation partner(s) without having contributed proportionally to the knowledge development (see Klein 1996; Rogerson 1992, p. 777). Institutions governing inter-firm collaborations influence the ways in which companies can protect themselves against such IP drift or theft, depending on how institutions facilitate the enforcement of R&D contracts between collaboration partners (Tate 2001; Teubner 2001). In LMEs, the case-by-case decisions of lay juries or judges make the outcome of lawsuits unpredictable. Consequently, start-up firms often shy away from approaching courts to have the contractual obligations of their R&D collaboration partners enforced. This, in turn, does not only discourage firms to engage in large-scale R&D cooperation where the risk of hold-up is simply higher, but it also stimulates fierce competition between potential collaboration partners, which is at the basis of radical innovation.

While these VoC arguments explain why radically innovative ventures occur with particular frequency in the Anglo-Saxon LMEs (most notably in the USA and the UK), the VoC literature also explains why the regulated institutional environment of the Northern European CMEs (in particular, that of Germany) facilitates the development of incrementally innovative ventures.

With regard to *labor skills*, the VoC literature highlights how workforces in CMEs tend to acquire company-specific rather than general skills (Hall and Soskice 2001b). The acquisition of company-specific skills is essentially induced by regulated labor-market institutions which prohibit the hiring-and-firing of employees at will. Unless they fall under exempt regulations, such as start-up companies of less than 10 employees, ventures can only dismiss employees for limited reasons, after respecting specific notice periods and involving the ventures' work councils. Often, temporary forms of employment can also be strongly protected with the intention to gear them toward permanent employment (Dencker et al. 2009). Given that these institutions tie employees to the same firm for a long time period, employees in CMEs tend to have in-depth firm-specific knowledge and long-standing relationships with their firms' suppliers. Such firm-specific skills enable workforces in CMEs to autonomously propose and develop improvements which translate into incremental innovations and high-quality products. At the same time, given their focus on just one (or a few) corporate environments, workforces with firm-specific skills lack the imaginative capacity and adaptiveness arising from frequent job changes. While workforces with firm-specific skills are thus less likely to come up with radically innovative ideas, they are particularly well equipped for developing incremental innovations (Herrmann and Peine 2011).

In addition, the pension and corporate governance systems of CMEs, institutionalizing the access of ventures to *finance*, tend to facilitate the development of incrementally innovative ventures (Hall and Soskice 2001b; Kenyon and Vitols 2004; Vitols 2001). Venture capital tends to be scarce in CMEs especially when the public pension system is a pay-as-you-go scheme. In these systems, such as in Germany, the pension provisions paid in by the current working population are directly redistributed by the state to the retirees and not invested into profit-yielding projects, let alone venture capital funds.

Once limited liability ventures reach a certain size, a supervisory board typically needs to be established including employees as well as shareholder representatives. Given that the supervisory board needs to agree to major strategic investment decisions of the board of directors, managers have no unilateral decision-making power. On the one hand, this makes it difficult to rapidly invest into, or divest from, new business units, which is often necessary for radical innovations. On the other hand, shareholders with insights into, and a say about, how their funds are to be used are typically less interested in maximizing returns on investment in the short run. This is particularly true whenever members of supervisory boards represent large corporate stakeholders, such as the firm's "house banks" or suppliers. In these cases, the board members are often reluctant to agree that "their" venture engages in high-risk projects (even if these promise high returns) because radically innovative businesses are also more likely to fail. Supervisory board members thus tend to have a preference for the firm to engage in incrementally innovative projects because the latter typically have more stable and predictable (albeit lower) returns in the long run.

Furthermore, the hold-up problem related to joint *know-how* development with R&D partners is overcome by the code-based legal system of CMEs in general and Germany in particular (Hall and Soskice 2001b; Tate 2001; Teubner 2001). Because of the clearly defined conditions for IP infringements, the outcome of lawsuits is better predictable. Contractual obligations of R&D collaborations can therefore be enforced in a straightforward manner, which limits the risks of uncompensated IP appropriation by a collaboration partner. Additionally, if supported by the fairly reliable and efficient legal system, start-up firms in CMEs have a higher propensity to engage in R&D collaborations on a large scale (Herrmann 2008, Chap. 4). This, in turn, facilitates incremental product improvements rather than radical innovations.

Given that they are either all deregulated (LMEs) or regulated (CMEs), the institutions governing labor, financial, and supplier–producer relations in LMEs and CMEs are complementary, which implies that "… the presence (or efficiency) of one [institution] increases the returns from (or efficiency) of the other" (Hall and Soskice 2001b, p. 17). For example, the complementary availability of generally skilled workforces and easily accessible venture capital makes it disproportionately easier for nascent ventures to be radically innovative than this would be the case if the skill sets of national workforces had been geared toward firm-specific skills—even if venture capital was available—and the other way around.

Importantly, the institutional environment in Mediterranean and Eastern European economies are often not complementary. Consequently, nascent ventures typically lack the types or combinations of labor skills and financial resources that facilitate radical or incremental innovation. This, in turn, can explain why a particularly high share of new ventures in these economies is focused on reproducing goods or services at lower costs rather than developing radical or incremental innovations.

Due to their recent histories of extensive state intervention, firms in Mediterranean Market Economies (MMEs) have built specific capabilities of non-market coordination in the sphere of corporate finance. Given that venture capital from national investors is hardly available and that external shareholders are not well protected, venture funding is often provided by family members, friends, and acquaintances of the entrepreneur (Herrmann 2008, Chap. 3). While new ventures thus have access to small funding amounts, they have difficulties in acquiring larger funds from institutional investors which, in turn, are needed for developing incrementally or radically innovative products.

While MMEs are characterized by moderate levels of social protection and high public expenditure for poverty alleviation and pensions, national expenditures for education are limited. Together with a fragmented social dialog and stifling labor-market regulation, which makes dismissals of employees close to impossible, new ventures are reluctant to hire employees (Hall and Soskice 2001b). The human resources of new ventures are thus often very limited which, in turn, makes any kind of innovation difficult and rather leads firms to focus on the reproduction of products and services, which does not require a broader skill basis.

Together with a fragmented and unreliable judicial system that makes recourse to legal action in case of IP conflicts difficult, this gives firms in MMEs a comparative advantage in low-cost reproduction—with the exception of some niche markets, such as furniture or fashion, where, for example, Italian firms compete on incremental innovations and design (Molina and Rhodes 2007).

Contrary to CMEs, employers in Eastern Market Economies (EMEs) are not willing to bear the additional costs of on-the-job training for inexperienced young workers. This, in turn, leads to a shortage of specifically skilled labor in EME ventures. But given that labor markets were rapidly deregulated in EMEs (with the exception of Slovenia) after the fall of the wall, workforces are comparatively mobile which, like in the LMEs, facilitates the acquisition of general skills.

Regarding financial markets, foreign direct investment is among the most important sources of capital. Domestic bank lending, the second most important source of finance, is dominated by transnational companies (Hancké et al. 2007; Nölke and Vliegenthart 2009).

Together with a less reliable judicial system, this gives EMEs a comparative institutional advantage in the assembly and production of relatively complex and durable consumer goods. These comparative advantages are based on national institutions which combine low labor costs and a skilled population with substantial knowledge of medium-level technologies and the availability of foreign direct investment.

To conclude, the institutional environment of LMEs can be expected to facilitate the development of radically innovative ventures, CME institutions lead entrepreneurs to rather set up incrementally innovative ventures, whereas the institutional framework of MMEs and EMEs facilitates, slightly different types of, reproductive entrepreneurship.

4.3 Empirical Evidence

To test the empirical applicability of these theoretical arguments, we proceeded in three steps. In the first step (Dilli et al. 2018, pp. 293–309), we assessed whether the entrepreneurship-related institutions of the EU member states indeed form distinct institutional families. To this end, we operationalized the environment of overall 21 Western economies with regard to those labor-, finance-, and R&D-related institutions that, according to the VoC literature, are most influential on entrepreneurial innovativeness (Dilli et al. 2018, pp. 301–304). For each country, we determined the availability of workforces with general entrepreneurial skills on the basis of overall six OECD and GEM indicators.[3] We furthermore measured the availability of venture finance by institutional investors with the help of four Eurostat and World

[3] To measure the extent of highly and generally skilled workforces, these indicators report (for each country): (i) the share of population with tertiary education, (ii) the percentage of researchers, and (iii) the amount of R&D transfers to entrepreneurial ventures, as well as (iv) the stringency of regular employment protection legislation, (v) the stringency of temporary employment protection, and (vi) the social spending on start-up incentives.

Bank indicators.[4] Finally, we identified the reliability of supplier–producer collaborations on the basis of five World Bank indicators.[5] This data was available for 20 EU countries as well as the USA.[6]

Having operationalized the institutional environment of these 21 countries, we wondered whether countries cluster into distinct groups on the basis of these institutions. In other words, which countries resemble—and respectively differ from—each other with regard to their entrepreneurship-relevant institutions? To answer this question, we run cluster analyses on the basis of all 15 aforementioned institutional indicators, which were measured at the country level and, depending on data availability, as the average of the 2004–2014 time span.[7] The results of these cluster analyses are depicted in Fig. 4.1.

We find that the clustering corresponds remarkably well to the institutional families identified in the VoC literature. Accordingly, we find that countries form distinct families with regard to their finance-, labor-, and R&D-related institutions governing entrepreneurship. Importantly, the institutions we studied go far beyond the classical VoC institutions, as they influence the ease or difficulty with which entrepreneurial ventures, rather than incumbent firms, can acquire different types of finance, labor, and know-how. This makes it surprising that the country groups we identify are basically identical to the ones discussed in the VoC literature.

In line with the VoC literature, we called the different varieties of entrepreneurial capitalism which we identified LMEs, CMEs, MMEs, and EMEs. LMEs include the Anglo-Saxon economies (Ireland, the UK, and the USA) with permissive financial-market institutions and deregulated labor markets comprising scientific education systems teaching workforces general skills, as well as reliable legal systems governing inter-firm collaborations. In contrast, CMEs (including Austria, Germany, the Netherlands, Switzerland, Belgium, Norway, Denmark, Sweden, and Finland) are characterized by less permissive financial-market institutions, well-regulated labor markets based on vocational education systems that teach specific skills to workforces, and reliable legal systems supporting inter-firm collaborations. MMEs

[4]These indicators capture the influence of institutional investors on nascent ventures by reporting the extent (i) of protection of minority interests, (ii) of minimum capital requirements, (iii) of venture capital investments, and (iv) of recovery rates in case of venture failure.

[5]These indicators measure the reliability of legal procedures in case of lawsuits related to supplier–producer collaborations by capturing the extent (i) of enforcing contracts, (ii) of judicial independence, (iii) of impartial courts, (iv) of the protection of property rights, and (v) of the integrity of the legal system.

[6]More precisely, the countries covered include Austria, Belgium, Czech Republic, Denmark, Finland, France, Germany, Hungary, Ireland, Italy, the Netherlands, Norway, Poland, Portugal, Slovakia, Slovenia, Spain, Sweden, Switzerland, the UK, and the USA.

[7]In order to identify possible changes that may have taken place in the countries' institutional environments over time, we also split our data into two groups: the periods of 2004–2009 and of 2009–2014, respectively. Importantly, though our separate analyses for these two time periods revealed that no major institutional changes have taken place, the results are very similar between the two periods. We therefore used the average of the 2004–2014 time span in the analyses and results presented below.

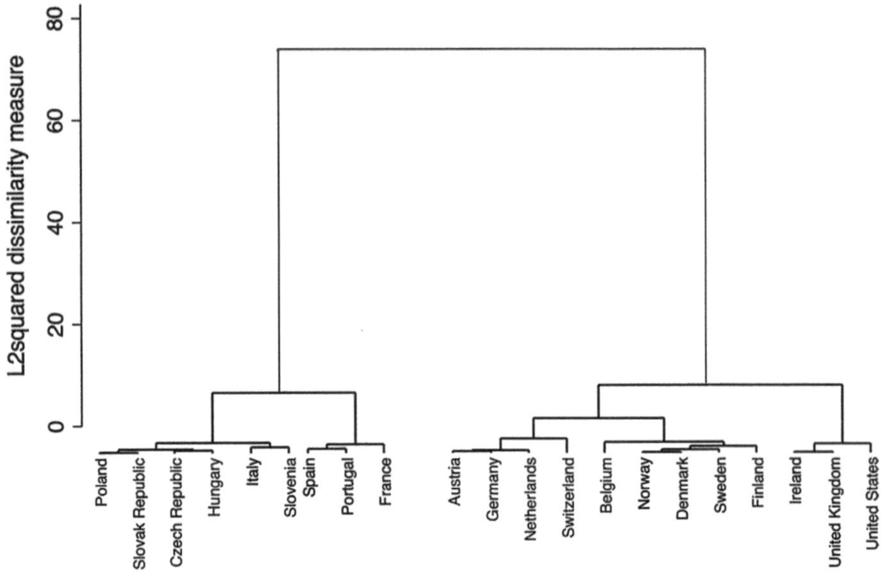

Fig. 4.1 Country families with similar entrepreneurship-relevant institutions. *Source* Dilli et al. (2018)

(including Italy, Spain, Portugal, and France), in turn, are characterized by constraining financial and labor-market institutions including education systems that mostly teach basic skills to workforces, and, with the exception of France, less reliable legal systems that make inter-firm collaborations difficult. Finally, EMEs (including Poland, the Slovak Republic, the Czech Republic, Hungary, and Slovenia) are characterized by constraining financial-market institutions, well-regulated labor markets based on education systems that mostly teach basic skills, and unreliable legal systems that hamper inter-firm collaborations. In short, varieties-of-capitalism similar to the ones described in the VoC literature for established firms can be identified for nascent ventures with regard to those national institutions governing entrepreneurship.

We assessed the impact of these distinct varieties of entrepreneurship-related institutions on entrepreneurship in the second step (Dilli et al. 2018, pp. 309–320). Based on the VoC reasoning about the impact of institutions on entrepreneurial innovativeness, we would expect to find an above-average share of radically innovative ventures in LMEs, an elevated proportion of incrementally innovative ventures in CMEs, and a plurality of imitative ventures in MMEs and EMEs. We assessed these hypotheses on the basis of several regression analyses. Taking the technology intensity of industries as indicator of entrepreneurial innovativeness, these analyses tested whether specific types of entrepreneurship (e.g., venture creation in technology-intense or, respectively, in less technology-intense industries) are particularly frequent in LMEs, CMEs, MMEs, and EMEs, respectively.

Overall, our regression analyses lend support to the idea that the institutional constellations of LMEs, CMEs, MMEs, and EMEs support different types of entrepreneurship (Dilli et al. 2018, pp. 309–314). While these analyses can only establish correlations, not causalities, it is noteworthy that entrepreneurs in LMEs outperform their counterparts in other economies in the extent to which they found radically innovative, high-tech ventures which also grow fast. Entrepreneurs in CMEs often develop incrementally innovative ventures. That is, they create more high- and medium-tech ventures than entrepreneurs in EMEs and MMEs but also more low-tech ventures than their counterparts in LMEs, whereby these ventures are overall characterized by lower but sustainable growth. In contrast, entrepreneurs in EMEs specialize in less innovative product imitations. Accordingly, they are outperformed by entrepreneurs in both LMEs and CMEs in setting up high-tech ventures. However, EME entrepreneurs are decisively better in setting up medium- and low-tech ventures than their counterparts in CMEs and MMEs alike. Importantly, though, these ventures show little growth. Finally, innovative entrepreneurship is least developed in MMEs. Accordingly, MME entrepreneurs hardly set up any high-tech or medium-tech ventures compared to their counterparts in all other economies. At the same time, entrepreneurs in MMEs do outperform entrepreneurs in all other economies in the extent to which they set up low-tech ventures, whereby these ventures hardly show any growth.

Having established that distinct institutional constellations correlate with different types of entrepreneurship across Europe, we asked in a third step whether, and if so how, venture creation processes differ between countries. To this end, we collected a unique dataset of venture creation activities. More concretely, this dataset traces—on a monthly basis—the activities that nascent ventures undertake during their start-up period in order (1) to build up the necessary human resources, (2) to acquire funding, and (3) to develop product-related know-how. Based on optimal matching techniques, we analyzed—with a specific focus on country-specific differences—how ventures approach any of these three components of the start-up process. In short, our findings are presented below:

(1) Beginning with human resources, two separate studies (Held 2019; Held et al. 2018) investigate how labor-market institutions influence the composition of start-up teams in nascent ventures. The influence of the institutional setting comes particularly to the fore in the first study, which analyzes the circumstances in which part-time entrepreneurs, who worked for the nascent venture less than 30 h per week, transition to full-time entrepreneurship (Held 2019). Interestingly, and in line with the expectations of the VoC literature, Held finds that part-time entrepreneurs in CMEs, such as Germany, are significantly less likely to transition to full-time entrepreneurship than those in LMEs, such as the UK and the USA, presumably because, in case of venture failure, it is particularly difficult in CMEs to regain a responsible position as a well-paid and well-insured employee. The study highlights that national labor-market institutions do not only elicit the emergence of a dominant type of entrepreneurship (Dilli et al. 2018) but also specific entry choices by the entrepreneur herself.

Having analyzed the entry processes of individual entrepreneurs, we investigate team formation processes at the venture level in an additional study (Held et al. 2018). To this end, we employ a definition of the venture team that goes beyond the founders involved in the creation of the venture and encompasses employees and external service providers. As a result of this broader conceptualization of team formation (in line with Cardon and Stevens 2004; Koch et al. 2013), our study discerns overall seven distinct approaches toward team formation. More concretely, the study does not only describe these seven-team formation processes with regard to the founder team but also uncovers the existence of distinct approaches to the hiring of employees and service providers. It furthermore shows that significant interaction takes place between the approaches to these three components of the venture team. While an additionality effect exists between founder team size and the hiring of employees, we observe substitution effects between the hiring of employees and service providers. Interestingly, the reliance on service providers is especially prevalent among nascent ventures in coordinated market economies. This finding is in line with the expectation of the VoC literature that entrepreneurs in CMEs are more reluctant to hire employees because dismissal at short notice is difficult which, in turn, elicits only low venture growth (Dilli et al. 2018). As such, our findings confirm that the VoC reasoning, originally developed in the context of established firms (Estevez-Abe et al. 2001; Hall and Soskice 2001b), also applies to nascent ventures—at least with regards to aspects of the team formation.

(2) In another study (Held et al. 2018a), we find that nascent ventures follow one of seven distinct processes of funding acquisition. The majority of ventures follows one of the two processes that fit the expectations formulated in the financial bootstrapping literature: these nascent ventures rely almost exclusively on the funding of their founders (Winborg and Landström 2001), but a small yet significant number of ventures deviates from this process. These ventures acquire funding from other sources than their founders. The type of funding a venture acquires correlates with various venture characteristics such as the type of good that it develops, the product's novelty, venture size, industry, as well as its institutional context. With regard to the latter, we find that ventures in countries with a higher stock market capitalization, such as the UK and the USA, are less likely to seek debt finance. This, in turn, lends empirical support to the VoC idea that the availability of institutional (venture) capital influences the financial sources into which ventures tap to finance their endeavors.
(3) Finally, we find in a third study that nascent ventures in LMEs are less likely to engage in R&D collaborations with external partners, such as universities and laboratories, than nascent ventures in CMEs (Held et al. 2018b). This, in turn, supports the VoC idea presented above that nascent ventures are more careful to engage in external R&D collaborations whenever the institutions governing inter-firm collaborations make the outcome of lawsuits in case of disagreement of the collaborating partners less predictable.

Taken together, these studies lend support to the theoretical arguments that a distinct set of national finance-, labor-, and R&D-related institutions correlates with the development of different types of entrepreneurial innovativeness across the European Union. While the deregulated institutional environment of Anglo-Saxon economies implies that an above-average share of radically innovative ventures is founded in LMEs, an elevated proportion of incrementally innovative ventures is set up in CMEs, while a plurality of imitative ventures is founded in MMEs and EMEs.

4.4 Implications for Entrepreneurship Research and Policymaking

In light of this empirical evidence supporting the VoC argument that distinct institutional constellations facilitate different types of entrepreneurship, which implications arise for entrepreneurship research and policymaking?

As we have argued elsewhere (Herrmann 2019; Dilli et al. 2018), entrepreneurship research would first of all benefit from assuming a more parsimonious approach toward investigating the link between institutions and entrepreneurship. The work of Dilli (forthcoming) offers a useful example in this regard. One of the major insights resulting from the VoC framework is that economic actors in different institutional environments need to behave differently in order to achieve the same outcome. And as a corollary, if economic actors across national institutions behave alike, this behavior tends to result in different outcomes. To give an example, ventures that go public in order to raise funds for increasing their R&D activities are likely to become radically innovative in the USA and incrementally innovative in Germany. Germany's corporate governance and education systems as well as the regulated labor market imply that the resources for radical innovations are less available and, hence, more expensive. This makes radically innovative entrepreneurship in Germany considerably more difficult while facilitating incrementally innovative entrepreneurship. Germany's entrepreneurs thus need to behave differently from their USA and UK counterparts if they want to achieve the same outcomes. Meanwhile, start-ups in the UK have difficulties recruiting and retaining specifically skilled workers to grow their businesses into export champions, as this arguably requires a disciplined and loyal workforce that is harder to attain in LMEs. If British and German founders behave alike, they will achieve different outcomes, while different behaviors are required to achieve the same outcome. Research into such questions of institutionally induced equifinality can offer a novel approach to investigating the link between institutions, entrepreneurial behavior, and outcomes.

The entrepreneurship literature can furthermore benefit from the finding that entrepreneurship types diffused in one institutional environment do not serve as a role model for entrepreneurship in other institutional environments. To put it bluntly, Silicon Valley cannot be a role model for the Continental European economies because of their institutional differences. But neither is Baden-Württemberg, known for its incrementally innovative firms, a suitable role model for the Midlands. Such insights force the entrepreneurship literature to acknowledge that different institutional constellations allow for different types of entrepreneurship to flourish.

This also has important implications for policymaking. The VoC framework highlights that institutional constellations which are at the same time conducive to radically innovative, high-tech entrepreneurship and incrementally innovative, medium-tech entrepreneurship do not exist and may in fact be impossible to create. Policymakers are therefore faced with a trade-off and the question about which entrepreneurship type to facilitate. Of course, as laid out in the final chapters of this volume (Sanders et al. 2020a, b, c), policymakers can design individual policy measures to stimulate those types of entrepreneurship that are currently less supported by their national institutional environment. But historically grown institutional complementarities imply that one has to make a choice whether to support radical, incremental, or imitative innovation.

Policymakers should be aware of these trade-offs and carefully consider the interplay of institutions. While labor protection has a negative impact on the development of radically innovative, high-tech entrepreneurship, it stimulates the development of incrementally innovative, medium-tech entrepreneurship. Germany, for example, is characterized by a lively start-up scene in this area (see Dilli et al. 2018; Herrmann 2019; Pahnke and Welter 2019). Finally, one should keep in mind that the regulation or deregulation of labor and financial markets has broader societal implications that may be undesirable. To give just some examples: strong wage inequalities and increasing disparities between the rich and the poor, as well as systematic underinsurance against the risks of disability, old-age poverty, and illness that seem to come with LMEs' deregulated labor markets. Similarly, high capital market volatility and risky investments go hand in hand with deregulated financial markets. From the above research, one can conclude that a one-size-fits-all institutional constellation that stimulates radically and incrementally innovative and imitative entrepreneurship while facilitating social cohesion does not exist and cannot be created. There is no blueprint. The best policymakers can hope to do is experiment with small improvements, carefully assessing their policies' impacts as they go along.

References

Acs ZJ, Desai S, Hessels J (2008b) Entrepreneurship, economic development, and institutions. Small Bus Econ 31(3):219–234

Amable B (2003) The diversity of modern capitalism. Oxford University Press, Oxford

Amat O, Perramon J (2010) Gazelle companies: growth drivers and an evolution analysis. Universitat Pompeu Fabra, Working Paper 1244

Anyadike-Danes M, Bonner K, Hart K, Mason C (2009) Measuring business growth: high-growth firms and their contribution to employment in the UK. NESTA, London

Baumol WJ (1990) Entrepreneurship: productive, unproductive, and destructive. J Polit Econ 98(5):893–921

Baumol WJ (2002) Entrepreneurship, innovation and growth: the David-Goliath symbiosis. J Entrepreneurial Fin 7(2):1–10
Baumol WJ (2004) Entrepreneurial enterprises, large established firms and other components of the free-market growth machine. Small Bus Econ 23(1):9–21
Bjørnskov C, Foss NJ (2013) How strategic entrepreneurship and the institutional context drive economic growth. Strateg Entrepreneurship J 7(1):50–69
BMWi (2012). Studie über schnell wachsende Jungunternehmen (Gazellen). Bundesministerium für Wirtschaft und Technologie, Berlin
Calcagno PT, Sobel RS (2014) Regulatory costs on entrepreneurship and establishment employment size. Small Bus Econ 42(3):541–559
Cardon MS, Stevens CE (2004) Managing human resources in small organizations: what do we know? Hum Resour Manag Rev 14:295–323
Case S, Harris D (2012) The startup uprising: eighteen months of the startup America Parternship. Ewing Marion Kauffman Foundation, pp 1–49
Casper S (2007) Creating Silicon Valley in Europe: public policy towards new technology industries. Oxford University Press, Oxford
Commission E (2010) Europe 2020: a strategy for smart, sustainable and inclusive growth: communication from the commission. European Commission, Brussels
Cooper AC, Artz KW (1995) Determinants of satisfaction for entrepreneurs. J Bus Ventur 10(6):439–457
Daunfeldt S-O, Halvarsson D (2015) Are high-growth firms one-hit wonders? Evidence from Sweden. Small Bus Econ 44(2):361–383
Davidson C, Segerstrom P (1998) R&D subsidies and economic growth. RAND J Econ 29(3):548–577
Davidsson P, Henrekson M (2002) Determinants of the prevalance of start-ups and high-growth firms. Small Bus Econ 19(2):81–104
Delmar F, Davidsson P, Gartner WB (2003) Arriving at the high-growth firm. J Bus Ventur 18(2):189–216
Dencker JC, Gruber M, Shah SK (2009) Individual and opportunity factors influencing job creation in new firms. Acad Manag J 52(6):1125–1147
Dilli S (forthcoming) The diversity of labor market institutions and entrepreneurship. Socio-Econ Rev
Dilli S, Elert N, Herrmann AM (2018) Varieties of entrepreneurship: exploring the institutional foundations of different entrepreneurship types through 'Varieties-of-Capitalism' arguments. Small Bus Econ 51(2):293–320
Ebner A (2010) Varieties of capitalism and the limits of entrepreneurship policy: institutional reform in Germany's coordinated market economy. J Ind Competition Trade 10(3–4):319–341
Estevez-Abe M, Iversen T, Soskice DW (2001) Social protection and the formation of skills: a reinterpretation of the welfare state. Varieties of capitalism—the institutional foundations of comparative advantage. Oxford, Oxford University Press, pp 145–183
Hall RE, Jones CI (1999) Why do some countries produce so much more output per worker than others? Q J Econ 114(1):83–116
Hall P, Soskice DW (2001a) Varieties of capitalism. Oxford University Press, Oxford
Hall PA, Soskice DW (2001b) An introduction to varieties of capitalism. Varieties of capitalism—the institutional foundations of comparative advantage. In Hall PA, Soskice DW (eds) Oxford University Press, Oxford, pp 1–68
Hall P, Taylor RCR (1996) Political science and the three new institutionalisms (and the subsequent debate between the authors and Hay and Wincott in Political Studies, 1998, 46, 951–962). Polit Stud 44:936–957
Hancké B, Rhodes M, Thatcher M (eds) (2007) Beyond varieties of capitalism. Oxford University Press, Oxford
Hechavarria DM, Reynolds PD (2009) Cultural norms & business start-ups: the impact of national values on opportunity and necessity entrepreneurs. Int Entrepreneurship Manag J 5(4):417–437

Held L (2019) Part-time entrepreneurship: the role of institutions, venture and individual characteristics in entry and transition choices. Unravelling the patterns in venture creation processes. Ph.D. thesis. Utrecht University, Utrecht, pp 25–55

Held L, Herrmann AM, van Mossel A (2018) Team formation processes in new ventures. Small Bus Econ 51(2):441–464

Held L, Herrmann AM, Polzin F (2018a) Follow the money: the funding acquisition process of nascent ventures. Horizon 2020 Project on "Financial and Institutional Reforms for an Entrepreneurial Society" (FIRES), Workpackage 5, Deliverable 5.1; currently under review. Available in Held L (2019) Unravelling the patterns in venture creation processes. Ph.D. thesis. Utrecht University, Utrecht, pp 91–122

Held L, Herrmann AM, Storz C (2018b) Whom do nascent ventures search for? Variance of linkage formation activities during new roduct development processes. Horizon 2020 Project on "Financial and Institutional Reforms for an Entrepreneurial Society" (FIRES), Workpackage 5, Deliverable 5.1; currently under review. Available in Held L (2019) Unravelling the patterns in venture creation processes. Ph.D. thesis. Utrecht University, Utrecht, pp 123–150

Henrekson M (2005) Entrepreneurship: a weak link in the welfare state? Ind Corp Change 14(3):437–467

Henrekson M, Johansson D (2009) Competencies and institutions fostering high-growth firms. Found Trends Entrepreneurship 5(1):1–80

Henrekson M, Johansson D (2010) Gazelles as job creators: a survey and interpretation of the evidence. Small Bus Econ 35(2):227–244

Henrekson M, Sanadaji T (2014) Small business activity does not measure entrepreneurship. PNAS 111(5):1760–1765

Henrekson M, Stenkula M (2016) Understanding entrepreneurship – definition, function, and policy. Lund, Studentlitteratur

Herrmann AM (2008) One political economy, one competitive strategy? Comparing pharmaceutical firms in Germany, Italy, and the UK. Oxford University Press, Oxford

Herrmann AM (2019) A plea for varieties of entrepreneurship. Small Bus Econ 52(2):331–343

Herrmann AM, Peine A (2011) When 'national innovation system' meet 'varieties of capitalism' arguments on labour qualifications: on the skill types and scientific knowledge needed for radical and incremental product innovations. Res Policy 40(5):687–701

Hölzl W (2009) Is the R&D behaviour of fast-growing SMEs different? Evidence from CIS III data for 16 countries. Small Bus Econ 33(1):59–75

Kenyon T, Vitols S (2004) Corporate governance in Germany and the United States: key challenges for the transatlantic business community. AICGS Policy Report. American Institute for Contemporary German Studies, Washington

Klein B (1996) Why hold-ups: the self-enforcing range of contractual relationships. Econ Inquiry XXXIV(July):444–463

Koch A, Späth J, Strotmann H (2013) The role of employees for post-entry firm growth. Small Bus Econ 41(3):733–755

Koelble TA (1995) The new institutionalism in political science and sociology. Comp Polit 27(2):231–243

Lundvall B-A (1992) National systems of innovation—towards a theory of innovation and interactive learning. Pinter Publishers, London

Mason C, Brown R (2013) Creating good public policy to support high-growth firms. Small Bus Econ 40(2):211–225

Milgrom PR, Roberts J (1992) Economics, organization and management. Prentice Hall, Englewood Cliffs

Molina O, Rhodes M (2007) The political economy of adjustment in mixed market economies: a study of Spain and Italy. In: Hancké B, Rhodes M, Thatcher M (eds) Beyond varieties of capitalism. Oxford University Press, Oxford, pp 223–252

Murphy KM, Shleifer A, Vishny RW (1990) The allocation of talent: implications for growth. Q J Econ 106(2):503–530

Nightingale P, Coad A (2014) Muppets and gazelles: political and methodological biases in entrepreneurship research. Ind Corp Change 23(1):113–143
Nölke A, Vliegenthart A (2009) Enlarging the varieties of capitalism: the emergence of dependent market economies in East Central Europe. World Polit 61(4):670–702
North DC (1990) Institutions, institutional change and economic performance. Cambridge University Press, Cambridge
OECD (1998) Technology, productivity and job creation. Best policy practices. OECD Publishing, Paris
OECD (2002) High-growth SMEs and employment. Organisation for Economic Co-operation and Development, Paris
Ostrom E (1990) Governing the commons: the evolution of institutions for collective action. Cambridge University Press, New York
Pahnke A, Welter F (2019) The German Mittelstand: Antithesis to the Silicon Valley entrepreneurship model? Small Bus Econ 52(2):345–358
Acs Z, Parsons, W., Spencer Tracy LJ (2008a) High-impact firms: gazelles revisited. Study prepared for the U.S. Small Business Administration, Office of Advocacy, Washington D.C.
Pfeffer J, Salancik GR (1978) The external control of organizations: a resource dependence perspective. Harper and Row, New York, NY
Rogerson WP (1992) Contractual solutions to the hold-up problem. Rev Econ Stud (59):777–794
Schneider MR, Paunescu M (2012) Changing varieties of capitalism and revealed comparative advantages from 1990 to 2005: a test of the Hall and Soskice claims. Socio-Econ Rev 10(4):731–753
Schreyer P (2000) High-growth firms and employment. OECD Publishing, Paris
Shane S (2009) Why encouraging more people to become entrepreneurs is bad public policy. Small Bus Econ 33(2):141–149
Sobel RS (2008) Testing Baumol: institutional quality and the productivity of entrepreneurship. J Bus Ventur 23(6):641–655
Sanders M, Stenkula M, Grilli L, Herrmann A, Latifi G, Pager B, Szerb L, Terragno BE (2020a) A reform strategy for Italy. In: Marx A, Sanders M, Stenkula M (eds) The entrepreneurial society. Reform strategies for Italy, Germany and the UK. Springer, Berlin
Sanders M, Stenkula M, Dunstan J, Estrin S, Herrmann A, Pager B, Szerb L, Terragno BE (2020b) A reform strategy for the UK. In: Marx A, Sanders M, Stenkula M (eds) The entrepreneurial society. Reform strategies for Italy, Germany and the UK. Springer, Berlin
Sanders M, Stenkula M, Fritsch M, Herrmann A, Latifi G, Pager B, Szerb L, Terragno BE, Wyrwich M (2020c) A reform strategy for Germany. In: Marx A, Sanders M, Stenkula M (eds) The entrepreneurial society. Reform strategies for Italy, Germany and the UK. Springer, Berlin
Stam E (2014) The Dutch entrepreneurial ecosystem. SSRN Electron J
Stenholm P, Acs ZJ, Wuebker R (2013) Exploring country-level institutional arrangements on the rate and type of entrepreneurial activity. J Bus Ventur 28(1):176–193
Stinchcombe AL (1965) Social structure and organizations. In: March JG (ed) Handbook of organizations. Rand McNally, Chicago, pp 142–193
Streeck W, Thelen K (2005) Introduction: institutional change in advanced political economies. In: Streeck W, Thelen K (eds) Beyond continuity: institutional change in advanced political economies. Oxford University Press, Oxford, pp 1–39
Tate J (2001) National varieties of standardization. In: Hall PA, Soskice DW (eds) Varieties of capitalism—the institutional foundations of comparative advantage. Oxford University Press, Oxford, pp 442–473
Taylor MZ, Wilson S (2012) Does culture still matter? The effects of individualism on national innovation rates. J Bus Ventur 27(2):234–247
Teece DJ, Pisano G (1998) The dynamic capabilities of firms. In: Dosi G, Teece DJ, Chytry J (eds) Oxford University Press, Oxford, pp 193–212

Teubner G (2001) Legal irritants: how unifying law ends up in new divergences. In: Hall PA, Soskice DW (eds) Varieties of capitalism—the Institutional foundations of comparative advantage. Oxford University Press, Oxford, pp 417–441

Urbano D, Alvarez C (2014) Institutional dimensions and entrepreneurial activity: an international study. Small Bus Econ 42(4):703–716

van der Walt J (2010) Entrepreneurship and the varieties of capitalism paradigm. Working Paper No. 10-10, Mercatus Center at George Mason University

Vitols S (2001) Varieties of corporate governance: comparing Germany and the UK. In: Hall PA, Soskice DW (eds) Varieties of capitalism—the institutional foundations of comparative advantage. Oxford University Press, Oxford, pp 337–360

Vivarelli M (2013) Is entrepreneurship necessarily good? Microeconomic evidence from developed and developing countries. Ind Corp Change 22(6):1453–1495

Wiklund J, Davidsson P, Delmar F (2003) What do they think and feel about growth? An expectancy-value approach to small business managers' attitudes toward growth. Entrepreneurship Theory Pract 27(3):247–270

Williamson OE (1985) The economic institutions of capitalism: firms, markets, relational contracting. Free Press, New York

Winborg J, Landström H (2001) Financial bootstrapping in small businesses: examining small business managers' resource acquisition behaviors. J Bus Ventur 16(3):235–254

World Economic Forum (2013) Entrepreneurial ecosystems around the globe and company growth dynamics. World Economic Forum, Davos

Chapter 5
Towards an Entrepreneurial Society: What Can the European Union Contribute?

Axel Marx

Abstract The European Union (EU) is a political system involving multiple levels of governance. Changing the institutional environment responsible for the quality of the entrepreneurial ecosystem will require changes on multiple levels. However, each level is not of equal importance. For some policy areas, the EU level is the most important level of policy-making, and for other policy areas other levels of governance are more important. This chapter will make clear that several institutions which might be reformed in the context of creating a more entrepreneurial society fall under the 'shared' or 'supporting' competence category of EU policy-making. This implies that the centre of gravity for institutional reform remains firmly on the level of the EU Member States or on the level of sub-national regions. The chapter shows that fostering entrepreneurship will require a multi-level approach with a strong focus on the level of EU Member States.

Keywords Entrepreneurship policy · European Union · Multi-level governance · Subsidiarity

JEL Classifications L26 · L5

5.1 Introduction

The European Union (EU) is a political system involving multiple levels of governance. Changing the institutional environment responsible for the quality of the entrepreneurial ecosystem will require changes on multiple levels. However, each level is not of equal importance. For some policy areas, such as trade policy the EU level is the most important level of policy-making since the EU has an 'exclusive'

The author thanks Philip De Man, Ward Munters and Andrei Suse-Gavril for research assistance. This chapter is based on joint FIRES reports. Thanks to Mark Sanders, Mikael Stenkula, László Szerb and Attila Varga for comments on earlier drafts of this chapter.

A. Marx (✉)
Leuven Centre for Global Governance Studies, University of Leuven, Leuven, Belgium
e-mail: axel.marx@kuleuven.be

M. Sanders et al. (eds.), *The Entrepreneurial Society*, International Studies in Entrepreneurship 44, https://doi.org/10.1007/978-3-662-61007-7_5

competence to make policy. For other policy areas, other levels of governance might be more important. This chapter will make clear that several institutions which might be reformed in the context of creating a more entrepreneurial society fall under the 'shared' or 'supporting' competence category of EU policy-making. This implies that the centre of gravity for institutional reform remains firmly on the level of the EU Member States (EU MS) or on the level of sub-national regions (especially in federal states).

In order to illustrate the prominence of EU MS and the more limited scope for institutional reform on the EU level, this chapter will first discuss the importance of the principle of subsidiarity in EU policy-making. Next, the division of competence within the EU with regard to policy areas relevant to entrepreneurship will be discussed. The chapter will then proceed by discussing the current EU policy towards entrepreneurship and introduces the main objectives and instruments of EU entrepreneurship policy to show where the EU can make a contribution. The chapter ends with a discussion and summary which clearly shows that fostering entrepreneurship will require a multi-level approach with a strong focus on the level of EU MS.

5.2 Reforms Towards an Entrepreneurial Society in the EU

To propose reforms for an entrepreneurial society in Europe, one needs to understand that policy within the European Union requires a multi-level approach (Marks et al. 1996). Policy is made on the European, national, regional and local level. However, not all levels are equally relevant to each policy area. The importance of a governance level is determined by multiple factors and is enshrined in national and European Union law.

EU law is guided by a set of general principles by which the lawfulness of administrative and legislative measures of the EU is assessed. A number of these principles have been singled out as particularly important in relation to policies to promote entrepreneurship and competitiveness, namely the principles of subsidiarity, proportionality and better regulation (Juncker 2014a, b, p. 2).

Of the above principles, the principle of subsidiarity is of crucial importance for determining the potential reach, ambit and ambition of EU initiatives to reform the institutional basis of the EU's approach to entrepreneurship. As the previous Commission President Juncker noted, "we should leave action to the EU MS where they are more legitimate and better equipped to give effective policy responses at national, regional or local level" (Juncker 2014a, p. 2). Before going over the specific types of competences that determine the EU's powers in the different policy areas, we should therefore briefly go over the meaning and importance of the principle of subsidiarity.

The principle of subsidiarity has been defined in general EU primary law and case law, and in the existing policy documents on entrepreneurship in particular. Article 5 Treaty of the European Union (TEU) stipulates that the use of Union competences is governed by the principles of subsidiarity and proportionality (Article 5.1 TEU). These principles are the logical complements to the fact that the limits of EU are governed by the principle of conferral, where powers are voluntarily conferred to the EU by its Member States through international treaties and can hence only be exercised by the EU within these limits and in order to achieve the goals set out therein.

Competences that have not been conferred upon the EU in its constitutive treaties rest with the EU MS (Article 5.2 TEU). The principle of conferral hence places strict limitations on the policy areas in which the EU may act, but also on the types of actions that may be initiated by the EU in those areas where it is, in principle, competent to act. For example, fiscal measures may not be taken by the EU as part of the industrial policy to promote the regulatory environment in which SMEs in Europe can operate, though industrial policy is a (supporting) competence of the EU.[1]

Specifically, the principle of subsidiarity means that the EU shall, in those policy areas that do not fall within the exclusive competence (see below) of the EU, "act only if and in so far as the objectives of the proposed action cannot be sufficiently achieved by the EU MS, either at central level or at regional and local level, but can rather, by reason of the scale or effects of the proposed action, be better achieved at Union level" (Article 5.3 TEU). As the EU competences on entrepreneurship policy are almost solely either shared or supporting (see below), respect for the principle of subsidiarity is of utmost importance in all proposals aiming to reform the European entrepreneurial society.

A critical corollary to the principle of subsidiarity is the principle of proportionality, which stipulates that the content and form of EU actions shall not exceed what is necessary to achieve the objectives of the Union's treaties (Article 5.4 TEU). The legal and policy implications of both principles are explained in more detail in a separate protocol to the TEU and Treaty on the Functioning of the European Union (TFEU), setting out the conditions to ensure respect for the principles by the institutions of the EU and the procedure to be followed by the national parliaments of the EU MS when verifying compliance at Union level. EU MS as well as the Committee of the Regions (CoR) may bring actions on grounds of infringement of the principle of subsidiarity against such legislative acts as for the adoption of which the TFEU requires that the CoR be consulted (Art. 8 Protocol No 2; for a discussion, see Schmitt et al. 2014).

The principles of subsidiarity and proportionality are informed by a concern that the EU shall not act unnecessarily in policy areas where the conferral of competences by EU MS to the EU has consciously been restricted, for a number of reasons, for example because regional and local conditions vary to such an extent across Europe that central EU regulation is considered to be sub-optimal. The current Union approach to entrepreneurship is one such policy area, guided by considerations of neutrality and born of the necessity to allow the regional differences in Europe to take effect, which render it undesirable, overly time-consuming and impractical to

[1] EU tax decisions can only be taken in very limited instances.

implement centralized EU legislation using a top-down approach (De Man et al. 2015).

The importance of national and regional differences in entrepreneurship is illustrated by several chapters in this book. The great diversity in the national and local environments in which entrepreneurs operate, as well as the nature of enterprises and entrepreneurs themselves, informs the long-standing approach by the EU to policies addressing the needs of entrepreneurs as requiring fully recognition of this diversity and, hence, respect for the principle of subsidiarity (European Commission 2008a, p. 2). In order to implement the ambitious agenda for reinvigorating the European economy through entrepreneurship and SMEs, the Commission's approach (see below) is therefore based on "a genuine political partnership between the EU and EU MS that respects the principles of subsidiarity and proportionality" (European Commission 2008a, p. 4).

5.3 Division of Competence

The distribution of powers, or competences, between the EU level of governance and the Member State level is governed by the TEU and the TFEU. The EU can take a particular action—whether legislative, administrative or in the nature of soft law (e.g. recommendations)—only to the extent that EU MS granted it the relevant competence by way of a treaty provision. According to the 'principle of conferral', enshrined in Article 5(2) of the TEU, "the Union shall act only within the limits of the competences conferred upon it by the EU MS in the Treaties to attain the objective set out therein". Article 5(2) further clarifies that "competences not conferred upon the Union in the Treaties remain with the Member States" (see also Article 4(1) TEU).

The competences conferred upon the Union are classified into three principal categories: (1) exclusive competences; (2) shared competences; and (3) competences to carry out actions to support, coordinate or supplement the actions of the EU MS. First, there is the exclusive competence. Article 3 of the TFEU grants the EU exclusive competence with respect to the following matters: the customs union; competition law necessary for the functioning of the internal market; the monetary policy of the Eurozone; the conservation of marine biological resources under the common fishery policy; and the common commercial policy. It should be noted that the list of areas covered by exclusive competence is exhaustive. Where a matter falls within the EU's exclusive competence, it is only the EU that can legislate or adopt legally binding acts with respect to that matter, in principle to the exclusion of Member State action.

In the areas of shared competence, both the EU and the EU MS are entitled to regulate, however not at the same time. The EU enjoys a right of pre-emption over EU MS when it comes to the exercise of shared competences. Pursuant to Article 2(2) TFEU, a Member State may take action in an area of shared competence only to the extent that the Union has not exercised its competence in that area. In other words, if an area is regulated at the EU level, the EU MS must abstain from also regulating that area at national level. EU MS may, nonetheless, regulate aspects of the area that are not addressed by the EU legislation.[2] In addition, where EU action takes the form of minimum harmonization—that is, the EU act established minimum requirements—EU MS may enact legislation setting stricter requirements (Craig and de Búrca 2015, p. 85). Nonetheless, the EU MS will regain their right of exercising a shared competence, to the extent that the Union has ceased to exercise that competence, for instance by repealing EU legislation covering the relevant area.[3] Article 4(2) of TFEU provides that the EU shares competences with the EU MS "in the following *principal* areas" (emphasis added): internal market; social policy, for the aspects defined in the TFEU; economic, social and territorial cohesion; agriculture and fisheries, excluding the conservation of the marine biological resources; environment; consumer protection; transport; trans-European networks; energy; area of freedom, security and justice; and common safety concerns in public health matters, for the aspects defined the TFEU. Several of these policy areas are relevant in the context of institutional reform for a more entrepreneurial society.

Finally, there are competences to coordinate, support or supplement the EU MS' actions. Article 6 of the TFEU provides that "the Union shall have competence to carry out action to *support, coordinate or supplement* actions of the Member States" (emphasis added). The following areas are covered by such competences: protection and improvement of human health; industry; culture; tourism; education, vocational training, youth and sport; civil protection; and administrative cooperation. The competences belonging to this category are the weakest among the three principal categories of competences. EU MS retain their power to regulate these policy areas at the national level. As clarified by Article 2(5) of the TFEU, the Union's exercise of its competences in these areas does not supersede the EU MS' competences. The same provision also stipulates that "[l]egally binding acts of the Union adopted on the basis of the provisions of the Treaties relating to these areas *shall not entail harmonization of Member state's laws or regulations*" (emphasis added). Hence, harmonization in these areas is quite clearly excluded. Also, this list of policy areas contains several policy areas which are of crucial importance for institutional reform for a more entrepreneurial society.

Table 5.1 summarizes the type of competence for some of the key policy areas for institutional reform. The table confirms that, while most of the legal bases invoked by the EU institutions to act towards entrepreneurial reform are shared, the key competences of industrial policy, education, training and youth are supporting, and the shared competence of employment is mainly of a coordinating nature.

For the shared competences listed in Table 5.1, the regulatory room remaining for the EU MS is usually dependent on the extent to which the EU has exercised its powers in that same field. For some policy areas such as research and technological development, EU action will not preclude the EU MS from exercising their (parallel) competences (see De Man et al. 2016).

Suggestions for reforming the entrepreneurial society in Europe need to take into account the legal nature of the competences of the EU in the main policy areas for

[2]Protocol No. 25, to the TEU and TFEU, on the Exercise of Shared Competences.

[3]Declaration No. 18 in relation to the delimitation of competences, attached to the Treaty of Lisbon.

Table 5.1 Division of competences related to ecosystem of entrepreneurial society

Legal basis (TFEU)	Policy area	Competence
79	Immigration	Shared
114	Internal market (approximation of laws)	Shared
145–150 (and 9)	Employment	Shared (emphasis on coordination in Art. 5 TFEU)
151–157	Social policy	Shared (for the aspects defined in the TFEU)
162–164	European Social Fund	Shared (social policy)
165–166	Education, vocational training and youth	Supporting
172	Trans-European networks	Shared
173	Industrial policy	Supporting
174–178	Economic, social and territorial cohesion	Shared
179–188	Research and technological development	Shared (though EU action will not preclude parallel national actions)
195	Tourism	Supporting
212	Economic, financial and technical cooperation with third countries	Shared

entrepreneurship policy, as well as the requirements following the general principles of subsidiarity and proportionality in areas of shared and supporting competences. The specific implications of these types of competences and principles on the vertical division of powers between the EU and its Member States are illustrated by the addressees of the recommendations for reform in the key Commission documents outlining the current approach to entrepreneurship (see also Table 5.2). Even if the proposals by Elert et al. (2019) may wish to suggest a departure from this approach, the recommendations remain relevant for they reveal the legal limitations to an EU-centralized approach to entrepreneurial reform. Let us now delve deeper into the specific policy actions taken by the EU in the area of entrepreneurship policy.

5.4 EU Entrepreneurship Policy

The starting point for the entrepreneurship policy as being implemented by the current incarnation of the European Commission is the Small Business Act (SBA) adopted in 2008 (European Commission 2008a). It builds on the framework and concepts elaborated in the 2005 Community Lisbon Programme for a Modern SME Policy

(European Commission 2005b).[4] In 2010, the Commission labelled the SBA "the main instrument for promoting SMEs' competitiveness and entrepreneurship within the Single Market and beyond" (European Commission 2010b, p. 13). The act and the continued relevance it holds for the realization of the broader entrepreneurship policy of the EU demonstrate the pivotal importance of the SME concept as an anchoring point for most initiatives for entrepreneurial reform. Most concrete initiatives taken today for reforming the entrepreneurial society in Europe involve SMEs, even if the societal actors addressed can also include students and employees. Considering the role of the SME notion as one of the basic anchoring points for EU policy to promote entrepreneurship, it is useful to recall the Union's definition of what a small- and medium-sized enterprise entails. The category of micro-, small- and medium-sized enterprises (SMEs) includes those enterprises that employ fewer than 250 persons, with an annual turnover not exceeding €50 million and/or an annual balance sheet total not exceeding €43 million.[5] The importance of SMEs for the European economy has long been recognized by the European Commission. It was only with the adoption of the SBA that 'Entrepreneurship' became one of the main tools for promoting the competitiveness of European SMEs and an overarching notion for a number of diverging yet interrelated initiatives at EU and Member State level. The Commission page for the SBA links to a definition of the term 'entrepreneurship', which is conceived as "an individual's ability to turn ideas into action. It includes creativity, innovation, risk taking, ability to plan and manage projects in order to achieve objectives".[6]

Building on the European Charter for Small Enterprises[7] and the 2006 European Council conclusions detailing the relaunched Lisbon strategy for jobs and growth (Presidency Conclusions 2006), the 2008 SBA compiles four priority areas and 10 principles that should guide the conception and implementation of policies for SMEs, at both EU and Member State levels. The four priority areas were promoting entrepreneurship, lessen the regulatory burden, provide access to finance and provide access to markets through internationalization. The 10 principles are: (1) education and training for entrepreneurship; (2) efficient bankruptcy procedures and second chance for entrepreneurs; (3) institutional and regulatory framework for SME policy-making; (4) operational environment for business creation; (5) support services for SMEs and public procurement; (6) access to finance for SMEs; (7) supporting SMEs to benefit from Euro-Mediterranean networks and partnerships; (8) enterprise skills and innovation; (9) SMEs in a green economy; and (10) internationalization of SMEs.

---

[4]The EU entrepreneurship policy is very focused on supporting SMEs. This is a narrow interpretation of entrepreneurship policy which has been criticized by several economists.

[5]SME's are defined in Commission Recommendation of 6 May 2003 concerning the definition of micro-, small- and medium-sized enterprises, https://eur-lex.europa.eu/legal-content/EN/TXT/PDF/?uri=CELEX:32003H0361&from=EN.

[6]Definition taken from http://ec.europa.eu/growth/smes/promoting-entrepreneurship/index_en.htm.

[7]European Charter for Small Enterprises, endorsed at the Feira European Council on 19 and 20 June 2000. The Charter recognized entrepreneurship as "a valuable and productive life skill, at all levels of responsibility" (p. 8).

An important consideration for the identification of the 10 principles was the need to create an environment in which entrepreneurship is rewarded. According to the SBA, the notion of entrepreneurship is considered essential to "bring added value at EU level, create a level playing field for SMEs and improve the legal and administrative environment throughout the EU" (European Commission 2008a, p. 4). Both EU and EU MS are therefore required to foster entrepreneurial interest and talent, devoting particular attention to young people and women, and simplify the conditions for business transfers (European Commission 2008a, p. 5).

The four priority areas of the SBA were further developed in later EU policy documents as (i) encompassing the facilitation of SMEs' access to finance; (ii) facilitating their access to markets; (iii) reducing the administrative burden for SMEs; and (iv) promoting entrepreneurship (European Commission 2015). A number of intensive rounds of pubic consultation initiated after the adoption of the SBA centred on these four policy areas, as did the follow-up process of the Commission for implementing the act (European Commission 2009b). The fourth priority to promote entrepreneurship as such received rather little attention in the implementation rounds, however, as illustrated by its conspicuous absence from the SBA Action Plan adopted by the Council in 2008 (Council of the European Union 2008b). Nevertheless, this follow-up process resulted in a comprehensive review of the SBA in 2011, which took stock of the progress made by the EU and the EU MS in realizing the main principles of the 2008 Act and promoting entrepreneurship. Noting that EU MS could still do more in this respect, the 2011 Review of the SBA also identified good practices for stimulating the implementation of the ten principles (European Commission 2011b, pp. 19–24).

The SBA is governed by a dedicated performance review mechanism and a specialized organizational structure for monitoring compliance at Member State level, headed by the network of SMEs (Muller et al. 2014). Moreover, the Think Small First principle of the SBA has been implemented as a key factor for determining the score of legislative proposals of the EU in the so-called SME test. To this day, these mechanisms and actors remain central to the EU's approach to entrepreneurship.

Continuing down the road of the 2008 SBA, the Europe 2020 Strategy for smart, sustainable and inclusive growth was developed in 2010 in an attempt to address the structural weaknesses in the economic and social fabric of the EU laid bare by the 2007–2008 financial crisis (European Commission 2010a). To catalyse progress in each of the three objectives for a (1) smart, (2) sustainable and (3) inclusive growth, the 2020 Strategy formulated seven flagship initiatives focusing *inter alia* on innovation, youth employment, the digital economy and a reinvigorated industrial policy.

Taken together, these seven initiatives significantly broaden the ambit and ambitions of the Europe 2020 Strategy as compared to the 2008 SBA. Stressing the need to take action in a wide variety of policy areas, the 2010 document noted that "[a]ll EU policies, instruments and legal acts, as well as financial instruments, should be mobilised to pursue the strategy's objectives" (European Commission 2010a, pp. 5–6). Still, the approach advocated by the 2020 Strategy is largely in line with the priorities of the SBA. Moreover, one of the main goals of the strategy is to improve access to the single market for SMEs, which was one of the four priority areas of the SBA. In that respect, the Commission notes that "[e]ntrepreneurship must be developed by concrete policy initiatives, including a simplification of company law (bankruptcy procedures, private company statute, etc.), and initiatives allowing entrepreneurs to restart after failed businesses" (European Commission 2010b, p. 13).

Six of the seven flagship initiatives that make up the Europe 2020 Strategy explicitly refer to SMEs, highlighting the overall importance of the strategy for the stimulation of an entrepreneurial culture in Europe (COSME Regulation, Para. (1)). Indeed, several of the Europe 2020 flagship initiatives touch upon crucial aspects of Europe's policy for SMEs and entrepreneurial inclusion.

Building on previous initiatives, the 2010 Integrated Industrial Policy represents the most comprehensive attempt on behalf of the European Commission to draw up such a policy in support of entrepreneurship in Europe (European Commission 2010c). Reiterating the fundamental importance of SMEs for the economy of the EU, the 2010 document is clear in its statement that the promotion of the creation, growth and internationalization of SMEs should be at the core of the Union's integrated industrial policy (European Commission 2010c). In pursuit of this central objective, the industrial policy gives a detailed overview of the variety of policy areas in which action should be undertaken by the EU and its Member States in the coming years. Most of these areas had already been identified in the 2008 SBA and under the various flagship initiatives of the Europe 2020 Strategy. They concern both cross-sector and sector-specific initiatives and include, most prominently, improving framework conditions for industry, facilitating businesses' access to finance and reducing the mismatch between skills currently taught and those that are required for Europe's industry (European Commission 2014, p. 18).

The SBA, Europe 2020 and Integrated Industrial Policy Commission documents, taken together, are cited as the most important policy documents on which the current Competitiveness of Enterprises and SMEs (COSME) Regulation is built (COSME Regulation paras (1)–(4)). Adopted by the Council and the European Parliament on the basis of Articles 173 and 195 TFEU, the COSME Regulation establishes a Programme for the Competitiveness of enterprises and small- and medium-sized enterprises for the current 7-year period (2014–2020). It is the immediate successor to the Competitiveness and Innovation Programme (CIP) that ran from 2007 to 2013. Like COSME, the CIP was primarily geared towards supporting innovative SMEs and entrepreneurs by improving their access to markets, support services and finance, mainly through facilitating the access to risk capital (European Commission 2005a, b, pp. 6–7). For that purpose, the CIP established a specific Entrepreneurship and Innovation Programme that set out EU actions to support, encourage and promote: access to finance for the start-up and growth of SMEs and investment in innovation activities; the creation of an environment favourable to SME cooperation, particularly in the field of cross-border cooperation; all forms of innovation in enterprises including eco-innovation; entrepreneurship and innovation culture; enterprise and innovation-related economic and administrative reform (COSME Regulation, Arts. 2.2.a and 10.2).

COSME is a key initiative to implement several flagship initiatives of the Europe 2020 Strategy, in particular through actions for realizing the objective of smart, sustainable and inclusive growth, with a clear focus on employment (Art. 3 (4) COSME Regulation). It does so in accordance with the overarching principles and priorities identified in the SBA and industrial policy documents, and in policy areas almost indistinguishable from those listed in the CIP Decision, though with a less visible focus on innovation as a goal in and of itself. The COSME programme represents the most comprehensive legal initiative at EU level to address all relevant policy areas of the Union's approach to stimulating entrepreneurship, both as a means for competitiveness and as a direct aim of the regulation. It is the only EU initiative currently in effect that focuses specifically on SMEs (COSME Regulation, Para. (21)).

The COSME programme aims to put into place the necessary institutional and policy arrangements for creating the conditions for achieving sustainable growth of enterprises, in particular SMEs (COSME Regulation, Para. (10)). One of the means of achieving a more competitive society in a sustainable manner is to take actions that directly address the need for a more entrepreneurial culture in Europe. Hence, the regulation not only recognizes that the EU MS and the EU need to work together to create a favourable business environment, but also notes that SME competitiveness is affected by "the relatively weak entrepreneurial spirit in the Union" (COSME Regulation, Para. (22)). Particular reference is made in that regard to the requirement to address all situations that entrepreneurs may face and all stages in the life of an enterprise, "including start-up, growth, transfer and bankruptcy (second chance)". Other priority areas are the promotion of entrepreneurship education, as well as "coherence and consistency enhancing measures such as benchmarking and exchanges of good practices" (COSME Regulation, Para. (22)).

With particular attention to SMEs, the COSME programme aims to contribute to two closely intertwined objectives, both directly and indirectly aimed at promoting a more entrepreneurial culture in Europe, namely strengthening the competitiveness and sustainability of the Union's enterprises, particularly SMEs, and encouraging entrepreneurial culture which promotes the creation and growth of SMEs (COSME Regulation, Art. 3 (1)).

The overview so far demonstrated that the EU has for some time now recognized the importance of taking action in the area of entrepreneurship policy. It long lacked a concerted policy basis for elaborating a comprehensive approach to create a more entrepreneurial society in Europe. This changed in 2013 with the adoption of the Entrepreneurship 2020 Action Plan 'Reigniting the entrepreneurial spirit in Europe' (European Commission 2013). The Action Plan was announced in the 2012 Commission Communication on a 'Stronger European Industry for Growth' as a policy tool to improve the framework conditions and support measures for entrepreneurship on the EU level and level of EU MS (European Commission 2012b, p. 18). Table 5.2 presents the Action Plan and which actor should take which type of action with regard to specific policy initiatives.

The central role of the Entrepreneurship 2020 Action Plan is illustrated by the Commission's intention to conceive it as the "blueprint for decisive joint action to unleash Europe's entrepreneurial potential, to remove existing obstacles and to revolutionize the culture of entrepreneurship in Europe" (European Commission 2013, p. 5). It explicitly builds on the Europe 2020 agenda, the 2008/2011 SBA and the Integrated Industrial Policy to formulate a comprehensive response to the question of how to increase levels of enthusiasm among Europeans for going down a more entrepreneurial career path.

The 2020 Action Plan proposes three areas for immediate intervention that substantively overlap with the policy areas identified in the COSME programme and SBA agenda, though with a more outspoken focus on education and training. These areas reflect many of the preoccupations and priority concerns identified in the FIRES project related to employment, knowledge and financial institutions:

1. Entrepreneurial education and training to support growth and business creation;
2. Strengthening framework conditions for entrepreneurs by removing existing structural barriers and supporting them in crucial phases of the business lifecycle; and
3. Dynamizing the culture of entrepreneurship in Europe: nurturing the new generation of entrepreneurs.

While these areas have been singled out as subject to 'immediate intervention', they relate to policy areas and actions that have been a long time in the making, and fit in with a spate of legislative initiatives at EU level started over the course of the past decade. The connection between regulatory simplification and the promotion of entrepreneurship (areas 2 and 3 above), in particular, has been front and centre of the EU answer to the recent financial crises. This follows from the 2008 European Economic Recovery Plan, which focused on removing administrative burdens for start-ups and micro-enterprises as a means of helping more people to become entrepreneurs (European Commission 2008b). The 2009 Action Programme for Reducing Administrative Burdens in the EU also pays attention to the particularities of EU legislative impact on SMEs (European Commission 2009a). Since 2011, it has been standard Commission policy to exempt micro-enterprises from EU legislation when possible or to introduce special regimes in order to minimize regulatory burden on these businesses (European Commission 2011b).

As noted in the previous section, these different initiatives need to be implemented on several levels of governance ranging from the European to the local. At the EU level, the Commission is the central actor in developing and executing the EU's entrepreneurship policy. However, given the wide ranges of different policy areas and priority areas in the different instruments, many departments (DGs) of the Commission need to work together to realize the overarching objectives of the entrepreneurship policy. Some DGs are undoubtedly more important than others. The key DG for entrepreneurship is DG GROW, responsible for internal market, industry, entrepreneurship and SMEs. Its pivotal role is confirmed in the Entrepreneurship 2020 Action Plan, which notes that "This Action plan and its key actions will be followed up by the Commission through the competitiveness and industrial policy and the Small Business Act governance mechanisms, including in their external dimension with the candidate, potential candidate and neighborhood countries" (European

Commission 2013, p. 28). Besides DG GROW, several other DGs are involved in implementing the entrepreneurship policy (for a detailed description, see De Man et al. 2015).

5.5 Discussion

The above discussion makes clear that in the context of the European Union fostering institutional change towards a more entrepreneurial society involves different actors and institutions on different levels of governance. In this context, there is a strong emphasis on subsidiarity and most of the policy leverage to foster an entrepreneurial society is on the level of an EU MS or even a lower level of governance (see also chapter by Varga et al. 2020).

The Europe 2020 Strategy underscores the vital importance of subsidiarity and ensuring comprehensive cooperation with national, regional and local authorities in all forms and capacities in order to make progress in realizing the objective of smart, sustainable and inclusive growth. As such, according to the Europe 2020 Strategy, EU MS are invited to work together by increasing their exchange of policy information of good practices (European Commission 2010a, p. 29). Further, the strategy also stresses the role of the European Parliament, not only in its capacity as co-legislator to implement Europe 2020, but also as a 'driving force' for mobilizing EU MS, both their citizens and their national parliaments (European Commission 2010a, p. 29). Finally, the monitoring process set up by the European Commission for overseeing the implementation of the strategy relies heavily on country-specific progress reports, which also detail the progress made by the sub-national (regional) units of those countries. This emphasis on EU MS can be read in two directions. On the one hand, it can be read in the sense that the diversity of entrepreneurial environments between EU MS and their regions is invoked as a key consideration warranting a strict application of the principles of subsidiarity and proportionality in developing an entrepreneurship policy. On the other hand, it can also be read as an indicator of the urgent need for a more closely coordinated approach to entrepreneurial reform.

Also, the 2013 COSME Regulation reiterates the need to respect the fundamental principle of subsidiarity. The COSME Regulation emphasizes that the subsidiarity principle will inform the subsequent actions that can and should be included in the work programme of the Commission when implementing this regulation. The Council and Parliament are keen to emphasize the priority consideration for executing the COSME programme as being that "[t]he Union's actions should be coherent, consistent and complementary to the EU MS' financial instruments for SMEs, provide a leverage effect and avoid creating market distortion, in accordance with [relevant regulations]. The entities entrusted with the implementation of the actions should ensure additionality and avoid double financing through Union resources" (COSME Regulation, Para (15)).

The key mechanism for reaching the objective of facilitating access to capital for SMEs and entrepreneurs, the European Fund for Strategic Investment (EFSI), is also fundamentally guided by concerns for subsidiarity. Rather than underscoring what the EU cannot do, however, the reference to the principle of subsidiarity is phrased positively as a justification for a European initiative. As such, the European Parliament and the Council note that the objectives of the 2015 EFSI Regulation "cannot, as far as financial constraints to investment are concerned, be sufficiently achieved by the EU MS by reason of the disparities in their fiscal capacity to finance investment but can rather, by reason of its scale and effects, be better achieved at Union level, the Union may adopt measures, in accordance with the principle of subsidiarity as set out in Article 5 TEU"(EFSI Regulation, Para (63)).

The text of the COSME and EFSI Regulations makes it clear that, even in those policy areas and with respect to those initiatives central to the EU approach to entrepreneurship, subsidiarity considerations keep the focus squarely on actions and activities of EU MS.

The application of the principle of subsidiarity and the inherent multi-level nature of entrepreneurship policy with a strong focus on the national, regional and local level is illustrated in Table 5.2. By giving a detailed overview of the recommendations in this Action Plan by policy area and type of action, Table 5.2 is revelatory for the lengths the Commission thinks the EU and its Member States can and/or should go in order to reform the entrepreneurial society in Europe. The table provides a complete overview of the complexity of EU entrepreneurship policy identifying the different levels of policy-making involved and the different actors involved on the European level. It should be noted that the broad policy areas identified by the Action Plan correspond on a more aggregate level to the policy areas and recommendations identified in the FIRES project (Elert et al. 2019) policy areas such as taxation, capital provision, education, etc. In other words, there is quite a lot of overlap and consensus on what needs to be reformed.

Table 5.2 illustrates that institutional reform for an entrepreneurial society is pursued on multiple levels. It recognizes the need for a consolidated approach involving both the EU institutions and the EU MS to comprehensively reform the entrepreneurial education, environment and mindset of European citizens and businesses. Out of the 86 proposals for reform, 40% or 46.5% are directed to the European Commission, while the remaining 46% or 53.5% address the EU MS at national, regional or local level. If a quick quantitative analysis hence shows that, though balanced on the whole, a small majority of the actions for entrepreneurial reform should be taken by EU MS, a more qualitative approach reveals that the vertical distribution of responsibility for instigating entrepreneurial reform is skewed a lot more strongly towards the level of EU MS. It is at this level that more fundamental institutional reforms should be pursued.

For those areas such as education and industrial policy, where the EU has a supporting competence, the table confirms that proposals for Union activity remain limited to actions that support, coordinate or supplement the actions of the EU MS. Overall, out of the 40 proposals addressed by the European Commission to the EU, no less than 29% or 72.5% take the form of actions aiming to support national, regional and local initiatives, coordinate of national actors, exchange best practices across the Union, disseminate information and study possible future actions at EU or

Table 5.2 E2020 Action Plan addressees

Action pillar	Recommendation	Area	Action	Addressee
Entrepreneurial education and training to support growth and business creation				
	Develop pan-European learning initiative	Education	Coordination/best practice exchange	EU
	Reinforce cooperation with Member States to assess introduction of entrepreneurship education in each country	Education	Coordination/best practice exchange	EU
	Establish guidance framework to encourage development of entrepreneurial schools and VET institutions	Education/training	Support/promote	EU (+OECD)
	Promote recognition and validation of entrepreneurial learning in informal/non-formal learning environment	Education/training	Support/promote	EU
	Disseminate entrepreneurial university guidance framework, promote framework and facilitate exchange between universities	Education	Coordination/best practice exchange	EU

(continued)

Table 5.2 (continued)

	Endorse successful mechanisms of university-driven business creation	Education/SMEs	Support/promote	EU
	Embed key competence of entrepreneurship into curricula of primary, secondary, vocational, higher and adult education	Education/training	Legislative	Member States
	Give young people opportunity to have entrepreneurial experience before end of education	Education	Policy/legislative	Member States
	Boost entrepreneurial training for young people and adults in education by means of structural fund resources in line with national job plan	Training	Initiate EU funding	Member States
	Promote entrepreneurial learning modules for young people participating in national youth guarantee schemes	Education	Support/promote	Member States

(continued)

Table 5.2 (continued)

Create an environment where entrepreneurs can flourish and grow				
Better access to finance	Finance programmes aimed at developing market for microfinance in Europe	SMEs/finance	Funding	EU
	Facilitate direct access of SMEs to capital market through development of an EU regime for SME growth markets	SMEs/finance	Legislative/funding	EU
	Assess need of amending national financial legislation and simplifying tax legislation to facilitate alternative forms of financing for start-ups and SMEs	SMEs/finance/taxation	Legislative	Member States
	Make use of structural funds' resources to set up microfinance support schemes	SMEs/finance	Initiate EU funding	Member States
	Utilize full potential under the European Agricultural Fund for Rural Development (EAFRD)	SMEs/finance/agriculture	Initiate EU funding	Member States

(continued)

Table 5.2 (continued)

Supporting new businesses in crucial phases of their lifecycle and help them grow	Identify and promote Member States best practices to create more entrepreneur-friendly fiscal environment	SMEs/taxation	Best practice exchange	EU
	Support cooperation between clusters and business networks	SMEs	Support	EU
	Support networking and exchange of best practice between agencies running schemes on resource efficiency for SMEs	SMEs/energy	Support/best practice exchange	EU
	Reinforce enterprise Europe network partnership with hosting organizations, single points of contact and all SME support organizations by informing, encouraging and providing assistance	SMEs	Coordination/support/information	EU
	Revise rules prohibiting certain misleading marketing practices	Internal market	Legislative	EU

(continued)

Table 5.2 (continued)

	Unlock full potential of digital single market for SMEs by tackling existing barriers to cross-border online business	Internal market/ICT	Legislative	EU
	Continue development of Erasmus for young entrepreneur programme	SMEs/training	Coordination	EU
	Encourage exchanges of young entrepreneurs between EU and third countries	SMEs	Promote	EU
	Help Member States develop integrated support schemes through capacity-building seminars financed by ESF technical assistance	Education/training	Support/capacity-building	EU
	Continue to develop your Europe business portal	SMEs	Coordination	EU
	Make national tax administration environment more favourable to early stage business	SMEs/taxation	Legislative/policy	Member States

(continued)

Table 5.2 (continued)

	Promote tax coordination to ensure that inconsistencies in tax treatment do not lead to double taxation or other harmful tax practices	SMEs/taxation	Legislative/coordination	Member States
	Reassess corporate income tax regimes to consider extending the statute of limitation of losses and deductions	SMES/taxation	Legislative	Member States
	Implementing option offered for small businesses of cash accounting scheme for VAT	SMEs/taxation	Legislative	Member States
	Adopt necessary measures to support commercialization of innovation, research and development projects	SMEs/R&D	Legislative/policy	Member States
	Consider option for owners of new enterprises to request possible adjustments of payment schedules for social contributions	SMEs/employment	Legislative	Member States
	Take full advantage of EAFRD	SMEs/finance/agriculture	Initiate EU funding	Member States

(continued)

Table 5.2 (continued)

Unleashing new business opportunities in the digital age	Foster knowledge base on major market trends and innovative business models to facilitate dialogue and lead to a shared agenda for action	SMEs/ICT	Coordination/support/best practice exchange/study	EU
	Raise awareness through Europe-wide information campaign for entrepreneurs and SMEs on benefits from new digital evolutions	SMEs/ICT	Coordination/information	EU
	Facilitate networking to support new business ideas for training, advice and coaching on how to do business in the digital age	SMEs/ICT/training	Support	EU
	Launch specific actions for Web entrepreneurs such as platforms for mentoring and skill-building	SMEs/ICT/training	Coordination	EU
	Strengthen competences and skills by intensifying e-skills actions for managerial and entrepreneurial skills to address new technological and markets	SMEs/ICT/training	Coordination	EU

(continued)

Table 5.2 (continued)

	Reinforce national or regional support for digital and Web start-ups and foster alternative financing for early stage technology start-ups	SMEs/ICT/finance	Support/funding	Member States
	Promote access for entrepreneurs to open data and big data compiled in public or industry-backed programmes	SMEs/ICT	Support/promote	Member States
	Support talented entrepreneurs by encouraging bright graduates to begin a career in start-ups	SMEs	Support/promote	Member States
	Support adoption of ongoing policy initiatives such as the data protection reform and the proposal for a common European sales law	SMEs/ICT	Legislative/policy	Member States
	Ensure the best use of European funds for Web and digital entrepreneurship	SMEs/ICT	Initiate EU funding	Member States

(continued)

Table 5.2 (continued)

Easier business transfers	Develop guidelines on most effective programmes and best practices to make business transfers easier through expert working groups with Member States	SMEs	Coordination/best practice exchange	EU
	Improve legal, administrative and tax provisions for transfers of business	SMEs/taxation	Legislative	Member States
	Use existing European funds according to their applicable rules and priorities to support SME transfers	SMEs	Initiate EU funding	Member States
	Improve information and advice services for business transfers	SMEs	Information	Member States
	Effectively publicize business transfer platforms and marketplaces and launch campaigns to raise awareness	SMEs	Information	Member States
	Review tax regulation with respect to impact on liquidity of SME in case of succession of ownership	SMEs/taxation	Legislative	Member States

(continued)

Table 5.2 (continued)

Second chances for honest bankrupts	Launch public consultation to invite views from stakeholder on issues related to European approach to business failure and insolvency	SMEs	Consultation/study	EU
	Reduce discharge time and debt settlement for honest entrepreneurs after bankruptcy	SMEs	Legislative	Member States
	Offer support services to businesses for early restructuring, advice to prevent bankruptcies and support for SMEs to restructure and relaunch	SMEs	Support/information	Member States
	Provide advisory services to bankrupt entrepreneurs and develop programmes for 'second starters' for mentoring, training and business networking	SMEs/training	Support	Member States
Regulatory burden: clearer and simpler rules	Vigorously pursue reduction of regulatory burden in EU proposed legislation	SMEs	Legislative	EU

(continued)

Table 5.2 (continued)

	Review and revise EU regulation to reduce unnecessary or excessive burden in areas identified as 'top ten most burdensome'	SMEs	Legislative	EU
	Propose legislation abolishing burdensome authentication requirements for SMEs wanting to conduct cross-border business	SMEs/internal market	Legislative	EU
	Set up working group to assess needs of liberal profession entrepreneurs regarding issues of simplification, internationalization or access to finance	SMEs	Study	EU
	Monitor progress via points of single contact under services directive and encourage Member States to take more business-oriented approach	SMEs/internal market	Monitor/promote	EU

(continued)

Table 5.2 (continued)

	Assist business with a view to ensuring that they can effectively access and make use of SOLVIT platform to deal with issues of EU rights	SMEs/internal market/employment	Support	EU
	Reduce time for licensing and other authorizations necessary to start a business activity to one month	SMEs	Legislative	Member States
	Fully implement European code of best practices facilitating SMEs' access to public procurement	SMEs	Legislative/best practice exchange	Member States
	Modernize labour markets by simplifying employment legislation and developing flexible working arrangements	SMEs/employment	Legislative	Member States
	Extend the points of single contact to more economic activities and make them more user-friendly	SMEs	Support/coordination	Member States

(continued)

Table 5.2 (continued)

	Set up one-stop shops for entrepreneurs to bring together all business support services including mentoring, facilitation and advice	SMEs	Coordination/information	Member States
Role models and reaching out to specific groups				
Entrepreneurs as role models	Establish Europe-wide EU entrepreneurship day for students in their last year of secondary education	Education	Information	EU
	Step up entrepreneurship promotion activities and appoint known entrepreneurs as national entrepreneurship ambassadors	Entrepreneurship	Promote	Member States
	Take into account variety of business models and legal statuses in national or local business support schemes, and develop social entrepreneurship education and training	Entrepreneurship/education/training/social affairs	Promote/policy	Member States

(continued)

Table 5.2 (continued)

Women	Create Europe-wide online mentoring, advisory, educational and business networking platform for women entrepreneurs to promote exchange of best practices	Inclusion/education/training	Coordination/best practice exchange	EU
	Design and implement national strategies for women's entrepreneurship	Inclusion	Promote/policy	Member States
	Collect gender-disaggregated data and produce annual updates on state of women entrepreneurs nationally	Inclusion	Information	Member States
	Continue and expand existing networks of female entrepreneurship ambassadors and mentors for women entrepreneurs	Inclusion	Promote	Member States
	Implement policies enabling women to achieve adequate work-life balance, by taking full advantage of support options under EAFRD, ERDF and ESF	Inclusion	Initiate EU funding	Member States

(continued)

Table 5.2 (continued)

Seniors	Help exchange best practices helping senior executives and entrepreneurs to mentor new entrepreneurs	Inclusion/training	Best practice exchange	EU
	Foster senior entrepreneurs interested in transferring know-how to new entrepreneurs and match senior entrepreneurs with inexperienced entrepreneurs	Inclusion/training	Promote	Member States
	Ensure that participation of senior entrepreneurs and retired executives in projects is compatible with their pension prospects	Inclusion	Legislative	Member States
Migrant entrepreneurs	Propose policy initiatives to attract migrant entrepreneurs and to facilitate entrepreneurship among migrants	Migration	Policy	EU
	Propose legislation aimed at removing legal obstacles to establishment of businesses and giving qualified immigrant entrepreneurs a stable permit	Migration	Legislative	EU

(continued)

Table 5.2 (continued)

	Remove legal obstacles to establishment of businesses by legal migrant entrepreneurs by giving them stable permits	Migration	Legislative	Member States
	Facilitate access to information and networking for migrant entrepreneurs and prospective migrant entrepreneurs	Migration	Information	Member States
Unemployed, in particular young people	Launch future microfinance facility under the programme for social change and innovation to target vulnerable groups	Employment/inclusion/finance	Funding	EU
	Use ESF to provide technical assistance to set up support schemes for young business starters and social entrepreneurs	Employment/inclusion/social affairs	Funding	EU
	Organize microfinance and social entrepreneurship stakeholders' forum	Employment/inclusion/social affairs/finance	Study	EU
	Analyse situation of entrepreneurship for the unemployed	Employment/inclusion	Study	EU (with OECD)

(continued)

Table 5.2 (continued)

	Analyse results of study on contribution of public employment services to job creation, and organize dissemination event	Employment/inclusion	Study/information	EU
	Connect public employment services with business support services and (micro)finance providers to help unemployed find their way into entrepreneurship	Employment/inclusion	Support/coordination	Member States
	Design business training programmes for out-of-work youngsters on basis of clearly defined stages	Employment/inclusion/training	Policy/legislative	Member States
	Launch active labour market programmes that provide financial support to all unemployed people for starting a business	Employment/inclusion	Funding	Member States
	Establish and run entrepreneurship education schemes to enable unemployed to (re-)enter business life as entrepreneurs based on successful models from Member States	Employment/inclusion/education	Best practice exchange/policy	Member States

Member State level. This is in line with the instructions of the European Parliament and the Council in the 2013 COSME Regulation for EU initiatives in each of the four priority areas identified in the programme, which consistently ask the Commission to 'support' actions which aim to facilitate and improve access to finance for SMEs in their start-up, growth and transfer phases; to continue improving the competitiveness and access to markets of SMEs; to improve the framework conditions for the competitiveness and sustainability of SMEs; and to promote entrepreneurship and an entrepreneurial culture (COSME Regulation Arts. 8,9, 11 and 12).

The supporting nature of the activities of the EU is particularly apparent for those areas covered by Action Pillars 1 and 3 of the E2020 Plan concerning education and training, and the promotion of entrepreneurship and social inclusion of certain demographic groups. The second pillar of the Action Plan, based largely on the Union's industrial policy competence, proposes more legislative actions and the setting up of dedicated funding mechanisms. These proposals are largely confined to actions that aim to facilitate access to finance for SMEs. However, as we have seen, the most prominent of the measures adopted in this area so far also relied on legal bases for shared competences in other policy areas such as economic, social and territorial cohesion, research and technological development, and trans-European networks. Likewise, it appears that, where cross-border competitiveness is addressed as a factor that can improve the regulatory environment of entrepreneurs, the EU-shared powers regarding the functioning of internal market offer more leeway, which translates into more assertive legislative action.

5.6 Conclusion

This chapter makes clear that policies towards promoting entrepreneurship have become more prominent on the agenda of the European Union. It was also one of the key policy areas of the Juncker Commission. As a result, several regulatory and financial initiatives have been taken on the level of the EU. However, as the EU recognizes as well, promoting entrepreneurship entails reforms in many different policy areas. This was also the starting point of the FIRES project. Making changes in these different policy areas is difficult due to the complex nature of policy-making competences in the EU. Some policies can only be changed on the level of the EU (exclusive competence of the EU), while most others fall under shared competence or the competence of the EU MS. In addition, the principle of subsidiarity requires that policy reform should be approached on the appropriate level, including the local and regional level.

Given the historical evolution of (national) entrepreneurial ecosystems and the institutional frameworks that shape them, the EU MS need to be in the driver's seat in terms of institutional reform for a more entrepreneurial society. The European Commission has legally committed to helping and supporting them as well as coordinate their efforts, but reforms for an entrepreneurial society remain decidedly a responsibility of EU MS. The possibilities and limitations for institutional reform on the level of EU MS are analysed and discussed in other chapters of this volume.

References

Council of the European Union (2008a) Council conclusions on think small first—a small business act for Europe of 1/2 Dec 2008
Council of the European Union (2008b) Council action plan for a small business act for Europe, annexed to the council conclusions on think small first—a small business act for Europe of 1/2 Dec 2008
Craig P, de Búrca G (2015) EU law: text, cases and materials, 6th edn. Oxford University Press, p. 85
De Man P, Munters W, Marx A (2015) EU enterpreneurial policy. Report for FIRES Project
De Man P, Munters W, Marx A (2016) EU entrepreneurial policy. Report for FIRES Project, pp. 200
Elert N, Henrekson M, Sanders M (2019) The entrepreneurial society: a reform strategy for the European Union. Springer Verlag
European Commission (2005a) Common actions for growth and employment: the community Lisbon program, 20 July 2005, COM (2005) 330 final
European Commission (2005b) Implementing the community Lisbon program—modern SME policy for growth and employment, 10 Nov 2005, COM (2005) 551 final
European Commission (2008a) Think small first—a small business act for Europe, 25 June 2008, COM (2008) 394 final
European Commission (2008b) A European economic recovery plan, 26 Nov 2008, COM (2008) 800 final
European Commission (2009a) Action program for reducing administrative burdens in the EU sectoral reduction plans and 2009 actions, 22 Oct 2009, COM (2009) 544 final
European Commission (2009b) Report on the implementation of the SBA, s.d., COM (2009) 680
European Commission (2010a) Europe 2020—a strategy for smart, sustainable and inclusive growth, 3 March 2010, COM (2010) 2020
European Commission (2010b) Toward a single market act—for a highly competitive social market economy: 50 proposals for improving our work, business and exchanges with one another, 11 Nov 2010, COM (2010) 608 final/2
European Commission (2010c) An Integrated Industrial Policy for the globalisation era—putting competitiveness and sustainability at centre stage, s.d., COM (2010) 614
European Commission (2011b) Minimizing regulatory burden for SMEs—adapting EU regulation to the needs of micro-enterprises, 23 Nov 2011, COM (2011) 803 final
European Commission (2012b) A stronger European industry for growth and economic recovery—industrial policy communication update, 10 Oct 2012, COM (2012) 582 final
European Commission (2013) Entrepreneurship 2020 action plan—reigniting the entrepreneurial spirit in Europe, 9 Jan 2013, COM (2012) 795 final
European Commission (2014) For a European industrial renaissance, s.d., COM (2014) 14/2
European Commission (2015) Report on the public consultation on the new SME policy, 2015, at http://ec.europa.eu/growth/tools-databases/newsroom/cf/itemdetail.cfm?item_id=7744
Juncker JC (2014a) Mission letter to Jyrki Katainen, Vice-President for jobs, growth, investment and competitiveness, 1 November 2014, at https://ec.europa.eu/commission/sites/cwt/files/commissioner_mission_letters/katainen_en.pdf
Juncker JC (2014b) A new start for Europe: my agenda for jobs, growth, fairness and democratic change—political guidelines for the next European commission, 15 July 2014, at http://www.eesc.europa.eu/resources/docs/jean-claude-juncker—political-guidelines.pdf
Marks G, Hooghe L, Blank K (1996) European integration since the 1980s: state-centric versus multi-level governance. J Comm Market Stud 34:343–378
Muller P, Gagliardi D, Caliandro C, Bohn NU, Klitou D (2014) Annual report on European SMEs 2013/2014—a partial and fragile recovery, July 2014, at http://ec.europa.eu/DocsRoom/documents/16121/attachments/1/translations/en/renditions/native
Presidency Conclusions (2006) Brussels European council of 23–24 March 2006

Schmitt P, Ruys T, Marx A, in consultation with Jeffery C, Swenden W, Pamphilis N, Gaweda B (2014) Involvement of regional parliaments, regional assemblies and other relevant stakeholders in the subsidiarity early warning system of the Lisbon treaty, pp. 274. Committee of the Regions, Brussel

Varga A, Szerb L, Sebestyén T, Szabó N (2020) Economic impact assessment of entrepreneurship policies with the GMR-Europe model. In: Marx A, Sanders M, Stenkula M (eds) The entrepreneurial society. Reform strategies for Italy, Germany and the UK. Springer, Berlin

Part II
Country Studies

Chapter 6
A Reform Strategy for Italy

Mark Sanders, Mikael Stenkula, Luca Grilli, Andrea M. Herrmann, Gresa Latifi, Balázs Páger, László Szerb and Elisa Terragno Bogliaccini

Abstract In this chapter, we outline a reform strategy to promote an entrepreneurial society in Italy. From a Varieties-of-Capitalism perspective, Italy has been classified as a Mixed or Mediterranean Market Economy. It boasts a vibrant entrepreneurial economy of locally embedded, often family-owned small- and medium-sized firms

All authors acknowledge financial support from the European Union's Horizon 2020 research and innovation program under grant agreement No 649378. László Szerb and Balázs Páger also acknowledge support from the National Scientific Research Fund of Hungary (OTKA/NKFI grant no. 120289, titled as Entrepreneurship and Competitiveness investigations in Hungary based on the Global Entrepreneurship Monitor surveys 2017–2019). Mikael Stenkula also gratefully acknowledges financial support from Jan Wallanders och Tom Hedelius stiftelse and from the Marianne and Marcus Wallenberg Foundation.

M. Sanders (✉) · E. Terragno Bogliaccini
Utrecht School of Economics, Utrecht University, Utrecht, The Netherlands
e-mail: m.w.j.l.sanders@uu.nl

E. Terragno Bogliaccini
e-mail: e.m.terragnobogliaccini@uu.nl

M. Stenkula
Research Institute of Industrial Economics, Stockholm, Sweden
e-mail: mikael.stenkula@ifn.se

L. Grilli
Department of Management Economics and Industrial Engineering,
Politecnico di Milano, Milan, Italy
e-mail: luca.grilli@polimi.it

A. M. Herrmann
Copernicus Institute of Sustainable Development, Utrecht University, Utrecht, The Netherlands
e-mail: A.M.Herrmann@uu.nl

G. Latifi
TUM School of Management, Technical University of Munich, Munich, Germany
e-mail: gresa.latifi@tum.de

B. Páger · L. Szerb
Department of Management Science, University of Pécs, Pécs, Hungary
e-mail: pagerb@rkk.hu

M. Sanders et al. (eds.), *The Entrepreneurial Society*, International Studies
in Entrepreneurship 44, https://doi.org/10.1007/978-3-662-61007-7_6

that make up a major share of its economy. The main bottlenecks in the Italian entrepreneurial ecosystem are low ambition levels, the lack of skills and education flowing into entrepreneurial ventures, and a bureaucratically encumbered, non-meritocratic, business environment that feeds back into a low familiarity with ambitious entrepreneurship. Italy could strengthen its entrepreneurial ecosystem in several areas, ranging from boosting human capital investments to reducing the clientelism in the business environment and recruitment culture. This would open up more opportunities for the young and talented, eager to engage in productive and innovative venturing in Italy.

Keywords Italy · Entrepreneurship · Varieties-of-capitalism · Entrepreneurial ecosystem · Entrepreneurship policy

6.1 Step 1: Historical Roots of Institutions and Recent Policies

6.1.1 North and South—A Short History of Italy

Italy has only been a unified state since 1861 and has been a bicameral parliamentary democracy under the current constitution since 1948. But Italy has a long and rich history that influenced and permeated areas well beyond its geographical boundaries. The Italian city-states of the Renaissance saw the rise of banking and the principles of Roman Civil Law persist in continental European legal traditions. In many ways, the deep-rooted institutions in Italy are the deep-rooted institutions in large parts of Europe. Foremost among these, the Catholic Church in Rome left a deep imprint.

During the Middle Ages, the Catholic Church (The Church) was promoting corporatism to pacify the conflicts of interests between aristocracy, farmers, and trade through the various sponsored function-based groups and institutions including universities, guilds of artisans and craftspeople, and other professional associations. The establishment of a system that relies on guilds involved the allocation of power to regulate trade and prices to guilds (Wiarda 1997).

This role of the Church was also evident during industrialization. While workers asserted their rights, the Church supported them on the one hand, but also fiercely opposed communism on the other. Nowadays, the Catholic Church in Italy is characterized by widespread worship throughout Italy and is still very much alive in Italy through institutions such as schools, hospitals, nursery schools, rest homes, shelters for the chronically ill and the handicapped, special institutions for education and retraining, and publishing, to give just some examples (Garelli 2007). Italy is the nation with the highest level of baptized Catholics, at 97% (55 million) of the population (Garelli 2007). The Church has provided Italy with a long-standing

L. Szerb
e-mail: szerb.laszlo@ktk.pte.hu

tradition of charity, still actively promotes an inclusive, family-based corporatist model of economic governance, and is an important factor in cementing social cohesion in Italy.

But although Italians throughout the country share this Catholic heritage, there is also the sharp divide between North and South, known as the "Italian *Mezzogiorno*" (Ichino and Maggi 2000). This division of Italy dates to the sixth century, with the fall of Rome in 568, and persists to this day. In the middle of the eighteenth century, the country was organized into seven separate states: The Kingdom of Sardinia (with Piedmont and Liguria), the Kingdom of the Two Sicilies, the Papal State (Lazio, Umbria, the Marches, and parts of Emilia and Romagna), Lombardy-Veneto which was under Austrian rule, controlled directly from Vienna, and the Grand Duchy of Tuscany and the duchies of Parma and Modena that were dependent on the Habsburg scions (Barbagallo 2001). The Mezzogiorno extends from Abruzzo and the southern parts of Lazio down, includes Sicily, and often Sardinia is also considered part of Italy's South. Only in 1860, with the Italian *Risorgimento*, was the territory brought together into a single politically organized community (Barbagallo 2001). But even today, some would claim that Italy was never truly one country and geography, and the lack of infrastructure continues to widen the economic and social divide (Barbagallo 2001). Policies to address this have met limited success.

The *Cassa del Mezzogiorno*, or the "Fund for the South," created in the early 1950 to encourage economic growth and industrialization in the Southern part of the country (Baum et al. 1990), largely failed because of administrative ineffectiveness (D'Attorre 1987). The public work projects and the jobs it funded were either short-term or highly inadequate, and the fund was criticized for promoting "large-scale capital-intensive projects" that required administrative capacities largely absent in the South (Bohlen 1996). Instead of convergence, institutional failure ended up promoting the Mafia in the South, while the North was growing (Spooner 1984).

According to Graubard and Cavazza (1974), the ineffectiveness of public administration in Italy was mainly related to the so-called *clientelismo*—a sort of political patronage allowing certain groups of citizens to connect to politicians through special laws and a system of kickbacks offered to public officers for influencing public decisions. The signs of a diminished tolerance toward corruption in Italian society appeared especially in the 1980s (Cazzola 1988). The fight against public bribery and corruption took shape in the *Mani Pulite* ("Clean hands") judicial investigation into political corruption held in the early 1990s and led to the disappearance of many political parties and to the end of the so-called "First Republic." But while these improvements at the national level have been hopeful, corruption and organized crime organizations have not been wiped out and at times heavily encumber economic activity (e.g., D'onza et al. 2017; Spanò et al. 2016, 2017; Allini et al. 2017).

Today, the regional divide is still obvious in the quality of institutions such as schools, public administrations, hospitals, and large private corporations (Ichino and Maggi 2000; Viesti 2016). Even the judicial system, which is the backbone of a modern state, works differently in the Northern and Southern part of Italy. In the South, to get a ruling in civil cases still takes much more time than in the North, even though the legal system and the career paths for judges have essentially been the same in both parts of the country for 150 years now (Tabellini 2010).

This gap between the two regions, in fact, requires policy makers to bear in mind that any reform strategy proposed for the North should not blindly be suggested for Italy's South and vice versa. Historically, economically, and institutionally, Italy often constitutes two distinct regions rather than one country with some regional heterogeneity. Thus, Italy probably needs different policy interventions in its two regions, building on the deep-rooted institutional frameworks inherited from the past. In what follows, we, therefore, discuss how institutions for the creation and diffusion of knowledge, the allocation of finance and labor have evolved in Italy.

6.1.2 Institutions for Knowledge Creation and Diffusion

In modern economies, the institutions for knowledge creation and diffusion are largely concentrated in the academic system of education and research and the system of intellectual property rights. These institutions, notably universities and patent systems, both have their historical roots in Europe and in fact in renaissance Italy.

6.1.2.1 Universities

Italian universities rank among the oldest in the world. The University of Bologna is the oldest recognized university, established in 1088 (Università di Bologna n.d.). Other Italian universities that have obtained the official status of university institutions early in the Middle Ages include Padua, Naples, Rome, Perugia, Pisa, and Florence (Simonini 1954). Universities initially emerged as institutes where theology, law, and philosophy were taught, and their histories comprise a long struggle to keep external influences from clerical and secular authorities out and conquering and protecting scholarly and academic freedom. Today, Italian universities are typically very broad institutions of academic research, which are publicly funded, while both universities and professors enjoy high levels of autonomy and focus on academic knowledge creation and diffusion.

There are two important technical universities in Italy which first appeared at the end of the nineteenth century. The oldest technical university in Italy is based in Torino and was established in 1859 under the name *Scuola di Applicazione per gli Ingegneri* (Technical School for Engineers). In 1906, it transformed into what today is known as *Politecnico di Torino*. Its creation coincided with the new era of industrialization that put the focus on Electrotechnics and Building Science (Politecnico di Torino n.d.). Today, this university strives to enhance technological and scientific research capabilities and integrate them into a higher education framework (Statute of Politecnico di Torino 2011).

The other important technical university of the country, the *Politechnico di Milano*, was founded only 4 years later in 1863. Its original name was *Regio Instituto Tecnico Superiore* ("Royal Higher Technical Institute") and the only majors that were taught were Civil and Industrial Engineering. In 1987, the school expanded to regional campuses of Como (1987) and Lecco (1989), and regional facilities in Cremona (1991), Mantova (1994), and Piacenza (1997) (Politecnico di Milano n.d.). Importantly, both technical universities were founded in the North at the time when industrialization took off in Italy.[1]

Complementing the formal academic teaching and research institutes, Italy recently also invested in the creation of science parks. In these parks, firms and academic research are physically located close to one another to facilitate knowledge spillovers and cement the links between research and commerce. According to The Bank of Italy survey of 2012 on Science and Technology Parks, there was a boom in the number of science parks in the 1990s. Some 25 were founded at a rate of up to three per year over a period of about 25 years (Liberati et al. 2016).

There were important first-mover advantages in this area. For example, the regional government of Turin, focused on policies promoting initiatives such as incubators and science parks early on and today we see two highly regarded Science and Technology Parks, the Environment Park, and the Bio-Industry Park (Salvador 2010) in Turin. The *Politecnico di Milano* was also an early mover in this domain, and today, its incubator "Polihub" is considered excellent, and ranked as the third best university incubator in the World Top University Business Incubator Ranking 2017/2018 by the Association UBI Global.

In recent years, Italian universities and Polytechnics have also increasingly started to teach entrepreneurship and engage in technology transfer in order to generate spin-offs. Yet, the literature considers entrepreneurship education in Italy still as "immature" (Iacobucci and Micozzi 2012).

In conclusion, Italian universities and Polytechnics have a proud history and tradition to build on, but they face challenges preparing for their emerging role in the modern knowledge-based economy. The curriculum and didactic approaches would probably benefit from modernization, but deeply entrenched interests and hard-won academic freedom imply that this is hard to engineer top-down. Instead, the Italian academic system would have to accept a more engaged role in society and be convinced that it is also in their interest to make the transition to a system of more modern, entrepreneurial universities that adopt evidence-based methods and focus more on engaging academic research with societal challenges.

---

[1]Two more universities have been awarded the label *Politecnico*. *Politecnico di Bari* is in the capital city of the Apulia region, established in 1990 (Politecnico di Bari n.d.), and the University of Ancona changed its name to *Università Politecnica delle Marche* and was recognized as a technical university in 2003 (Politecnica delle Marche 2017). These institutions are based in the South and Middle of the country, respectively, and were founded to become important actors in the respective local industrial ecosystems. To date, however, they do still not play the role the older schools play in the Northern economic system.

6.1.2.2 The Patent System

The use of patents as an institution to encourage knowledge production and its diffusion is relatively old and, in fact, it was in Italy where the first real patents appeared. There is a lot of discussion among historians whether Florence or Venice was the first to grant patent rights on innovations, but Italy led the way. There was strong and systematic interest of the Venetian Republic in promoting inventions long before 1400, but it was the city of Florence which recorded Filippo Brunelleschi as the first patentee in 1421. He was granted an exclusive right of 3 years to use his invention—a barge with hoisting gear for marble—protected from potential imitators. The patent stated clearly that all those that would replicate the invented device should be burned at the stake (Frumkin 1945).

This first patent, however, was still very ad hoc. The first more general system of intellectual property rights protection was adopted by the Venetian Senate on March 19, 1474. The decree called upon every person who invented ingenious devices to first disclose their invention to *Provveditori di Comun*. Doing so would benefit inventors by protecting them for 10 years (Long 1991). The Statute is clear on several things that still characterize patents today. The decree mentions the originality of the work as a substantial ingredient in the way of getting a patent, industrial applicability, and the exclusive right to exploit the invention for 10 years. One of the early Venetian patent receivers was Galileo Galilei for his invention of a "Mechanism for Raising Irrigation Water to Fields" in 1594 (Maynard 1980). With the foundation of the Kingdom of Italy in 1861, the country implemented a national patent law, similar to that in most industrialized economies (Moradei 2009) and Italian legislation on intellectual property has since evolved considerably. Today's Italian patent law has been revised following the patent provisions of the 1995 Agreement on Trade-Related Aspects of Intellectual Property Rights (TRIPS). The patent does not substantially differ from its initial form, but the width, breadth, and extent of patent protection have changed substantially over time.

The debate on patent protection is not new to Italy. According to Sirilli (1986), the rise of technical and scientific development and the role of economists in the acknowledgement of patents as an incentive for innovation (e.g., Schmookler 1966; Scherer 1965), have both driven the debate. Textbook economics claims that without patent rights, inventors would have no incentives to produce valuable knowledge. But Sirilli (1986) shows that for Italian inventors who applied for a patent, three-quarters of the respondents admitted that the absence of patent protection would not have prevented them from pursuing the invention. Also in Italy, patents serve a useful purpose in keeping track of and building a public registry of useful inventions, but it is especially the commercially applicable ones that should be registered and protected from imitation. Thus, like in many industrialized countries, there is much debate about the usefulness of patents and the application of strict rules of protection of intellectual property as they are applied today (e.g., Panunzi 2012; Boldrin and Levine 2008).

6.1.3 Development of Financial Institutions

Italy is a well-known example of a bank-based economy, and it is of great relevance for understanding entrepreneurship in Italy to summarize its historical development and the culture that prevails in these financial institutions. Modern banking has its roots in Italy. In fact, the rise of banking system dates back to Medieval and Renaissance Italy and originated in the prosperous and rich cities of Florence, Venice, and Genoa (Hoggson 2007). The Bardi and Peruzzi families led banking in fourteenth century Florence, expanding with new branches in many other parts of Europe (Hoggson 2007).

In the fifteenth century, the de Medici bank, which was established in 1397 by Giovanni de Medici in Florence (Goldthwaite 1995), made a distinguished imprint in the development of banking and became the most important financial institution in Europe in the fifteenth century (The Economist 1999). The de Medici bank grew into the most international bank of Italy and for decades was a highly respected bank in Europe (De Roover 1999). It used its massive network to a degree that it attracted and maintained the Vatican as its largest client and until 1434, more than half of the bank's revenues flowed through the Rome "branch," which accompanied the pope on his travels. The strong ties with Rome and the Vatican brought the bank enormous influence on customers and the Church itself (The Economist 1999).

In the period between 1527 and 1572, important banking family groups such as the Grimaldi, Spinola, Pallavicino, Doria, Pinelli, and Lomellini rose as big players in banking during the sixteenth century (Duggan 2013; MacDonald and Gastmann 2000). Banking in the Renaissance, and thereafter, was very much a family business and it mainly catered to the needs of rich merchants who wanted to settle large transactions over increasing distances and needed sophisticated products, such as insurance for cargoes at sea, trade credit, and currency exchange services.

Throughout the centuries, Italy became home to many other banks. The *Banca Monte dei Paschi di Siena,* for example, has been operating continuously since 1472 (Boland 2009). The Economist (2017) noted that this bank is the oldest surviving bank in the world and saving it from bankruptcy in 2013 could thus almost be considered a matter of conservation of cultural heritage.

The first publicly held Italian bank that looked somewhat like a modern bank, taking deposits and giving loans, was established in Milan in 1894. Gradually then, small industrialists and a rising middle class created demand for and supply of what we now consider to be traditional banking services. Many of these banks are also still operating today and typically served society for centuries (Hertner 2016). The role of these banks in Italy was particularly relevant in the industrialization and modernization of agriculture in Europe after World War I. As shown by the seminal work of Gerschenkron (1962), banks were important in Europe, where financial markets were less developed than in the UK and USA but industrialization was more advanced than in others, such as Eastern Europe and Russia. This gave banks a vital role in the industrialization process as the financier of modern industry (Sylla 2002).

The banking system in Italy went through several reforms in the twentieth century. The Bank Law of 1936 is an example that reformed the whole banking sector by putting financial intermediaries into different categories depending on their credit activities. The law also limited the linkages between industry and financial institutions to alleviate possible conflicts of interest. Another reform, put in place in 1993, aimed at increasing privatization of the banking system and expanding the range of activities of banks. Until about 2004, there was some consolidation in the Italian banking sector but despite this M&A activity, concentration ran counter to the global trend. Even if there were fewer banks in 2004 (800) than in 1985 (1,100), the market share of the five largest banks dropped over this period (Goddard et al. 2007; Coccorese 2013), implying that consolidation took place among smaller banks whereas competition increased at the top.

European legislation, such as the 2004 New EU take-over Directive, implemented to integrate European financial markets have stimulated further consolidation in banking (ECB 2017). But Italy's banking system still has many small, diverse, relationship-based cooperative banks that support its SMEs also in times of crisis (Castellani 2018). If the banking sector continues to consolidate, however, as in the Netherlands or the UK, Italy risks losing its system of small, diverse and arms-length relationship banking, and credit will be allocated more to real estate (mortgages) and traded financial assets (Goddard et al. 2007; ECB 2017). This would harm the entrepreneurial ecosystem and reduce the access to finance for Italian entrepreneurs.

Despite the recent improvements, many Italian banks still struggle with significant bad debt overhang and a limited ability to finance new projects (Beccalli and Girardone 2016). Current mandatory reserve and equity ratios are insufficient. When banking made its biggest contributions to Italy's development, leverage was much lower, and banks could shoulder losses better. To justify financing experimental venturing with bank credit, banks, therefore, should be recapitalized.

6.1.4 Labor Institutions

Concerning its labor market institutions, Italy is commonly grouped with other Mediterranean countries such as Spain, Portugal, and Greece. Despite important differences, these countries are all characterized by labor markets with high employment protection and low social security. Union bargaining coverage is often extended and trade unions control large parts of the labor market without being representative of large parts of the workforce (Dilli et al. 2016; Hassel 2014). These institutions formed largely when Italy became a unified state and industrialization fueled the organization of labor in the early twentieth century. Italy's welfare state dates back to the aftermath of World War II, and both labor and social security regulations were frequently reformed even since the 2008 global financial crisis.

6.1.4.1 Employment Protection

Dismissals were first regulated in Italy in 1966. Any unfair dismissal obliges employers to either hire back workers or pay compensation based on individuals' experience and firm size (Boeri and Jimeno 2005). For workers with less than two and a half years of tenure, the compensation ranged between 5 and 8 months, and for those with between two and a half and 20 years of tenure, the compensation varied from 5 to 12 months. The above regulation applied to firms with more than 60 employees while those with less had to pay half the severance pay (Boeri and Jimeno 2005). In 1970, the *Statuto dei Lavoratori* obliged firms with more than 15 employees to hire back workers and pay their foregone earnings in case of unfair dismissals while firms with less than 15 employees were totally exempted (Leonardi and Pica 2006).

Historically, Italy was considered one of the strictest countries in terms of employment protection legislation (Lazear 1990; Bertola 1990; Nicoletti et al. 1999). As these arrangements proved to represent a barrier to entrepreneurship in general (Golpe et al. 2008) and to ambitious entrepreneurship in particular (Henrekson et al. 2010), important reforms were introduced in 2003 with the Biagi reform (Cirillo et al. 2017) and more recently with the Monti-Fornero reforms of 2012 and the "Jobs Act" of 2014 (Tiraboschi 2012; Carinci 2015). These reforms moved Italy's labor market firmly in the direction of the *flexicurity* camp.

The most significant modifications include the easing of dismissal regulation, more emphasis on active labor market policies and a new supervising national authority to enhance coordination among public and private actors (Raulli 2017). More generally, Italy has followed the Danish flexicurity recipe and decided to move from security of employees and jobs to security of income and work. In general, such reforms could support a more entrepreneurial society in Italy, but a careful evaluation of these reforms will have to show how they perform in the Italian context.

6.1.4.2 Wage Bargaining

Regarding the wage setting institutions, this is based on the tripartite agreement of July 23, 1993. Italy has an industry-wide bargaining model, applied at the national level (Eurofound 2009). As Calmfors and Driffill (1988) have shown, such a system of wage bargaining tends to increase wage pressure, which in turn may result in high long-run unemployment. Specifically, for entrepreneurs, such national coverage implies that vested interest parties can directly influence a major cost component for any (new) employer in their sector.

More importantly, these vested interest parties will also negotiate additional job-related rights and entitlements that have limited portability across industries, are easy for incumbents to administer, but put a large burden on new ventures. Trade unions, for example, negotiate the terms of pensions, sickness and maternity leave, working hours per week, month and year, leave, and education on the job. In the Italian corporatist tradition employers, state and workers will negotiate in relative harmony

(Regini 1997), but Italy also has a strong history of class struggle and communism (Kertzer 1980), making unions more militant and willing to strike for their rights than in other Continental European countries. They share this labor militancy with the Mediterranean countries, although in recent decades, strikes are declining and labor relations seem to become more harmonious (Gall 1999).

Alternatively, one can interpret this as trade unions becoming less powerful and representative as organization rates decline in new industries. As unions typically protect the position of their (long-term employed) members, their decline would level the playing field for more entrepreneurial employers, but reforms in this area should respect the tradition of paying "decent wages for decent jobs" not to clash with other important aspects of the Italian institutional framework.

6.1.4.3 Social Security

Social security is typically less developed in Italy compared to other European countries, but compared to the rest of the Mediterranean countries, it is probably one of the most developed. Social insurance was first introduced between 1898 (work injuries) and 1919 (old age, invalidity and unemployment). In the period 1945–1975, the Italian welfare state was expanded significantly (Ferrera 2005). A generous state-funded pension, universal health care, constitutionally guaranteed unemployment benefits, and social security benefits were put in place and typically funded on a pay-as-you-go basis.

These systems have all been built up after World War II and thus have a relatively short history. Still, some rights are considered inalienable and the pay-as-you-go financing implies that current generations have paid for social security and entitlements they were (implicitly) promised would also be available for them in the future. Reforming such systems can, therefore, be politically complicated. In the 1980s and 1990s and more recently after the financial crisis, we have seen significant reforms in this domain. This suggests that social security is probably not a deeply rooted institution and reforms can be proposed to promote more entrepreneurship. But such reforms should not simply lower protection and security and rather make entitlements and rights more portable across jobs and industries.

6.1.5 Recent Entrepreneurship Policies in Italy

6.1.5.1 Innovative SMEs

In the 1990s, Italy was still highly dominated by small businesses. More than 99% of active firms employed less than 50 employees and less than 3,000 firms employed more than 250 employees (Unioncamere 2005). Increasingly, more attention was paid to SMEs by industrial policy, especially that concerning innovation, which was usually thought to be of sole concern to larger firms. In addition, improvements in the bureaucratic structure of state-aid-provision entities created a more "SME-friendly" environment. It is relevant to note that, at the national level, systems of support have favored process innovation rather than product innovation (Rolfo and Calabrese 2003).

At the end of the 1990s, the Ministry for University and Scientific Research introduced the research program "Road Map for Italy." The program covered 300 SMEs and found that typically Italian entrepreneurs play a very proactive role in the management of their firms. Consequently, it is the background and competence of the entrepreneur that largely determines the ultimate success of the firm. The lack of specialization, networking, and teambuilding also has big consequences for the technological culture of SMEs in Italy (Rolfo and Calabrese 2003).

The Environmental Concessions law around 2000 established a tax relief system for SMEs that make environmental investments. As a lot of energy and resource-saving equipment and investments would fall under this legislation, the program gives Italian SMEs an incentive to develop sustainable business practices and develop new competitive advantages in doing so.

6.1.5.2 Entrepreneurship and Entrepreneurship Policy after the Recent Financial Crisis

The Italian response to the financial crisis of 2009 was focused on strengthening its innovative SME sector and initially even on increasing spending to maintain investment in innovation and R&D. In 2009, Italy was one of the first EU countries to approve the European Commission's 2008 Small Business Act (SBA) proposal and adopted it domestically. The approval of this program allowed for the immediate mandatory and continuous monitoring of SME policies and for the arrangement of "one law a year" regarding small firms (Ministero dello Sviluppo Economico n.d.). Some of the interventions under the SBA included:

- *Law 185/2008*, proposed to guarantee the integrity of credit and avoid any charges to businesses;
- *Law 29/2009-2,* adopted to facilitate access to credit by introducing, the "Tremonti Bond," through which the banks can grant loans to businesses;
- *Law 78/2009* ('*Manovra anti-crisi*'), passed to promote the reinvestment of profits in capital goods;
- *Law 99/2009* ('*Legge Sviluppo*'), providing a broad mandate to the government to reorganize regulatory obligations for companies;
- "Unique Communication" launched in 2009 giving the possibility for starting a business by sending a single communication to the Chamber of Commerce;
- *Law 82/2009* establishing an 80 million euro facility for product and/or process innovations replacing or eliminating chemical substances.

Other initiatives regarding the sustained growth of SMEs included: a fund for competition and innovation; a fund for rescue and restructuring of businesses in difficulty; a fund for districts and business networks; measures for the automobile sector, domestic appliances, furniture, and apparel; the National Innovation Fund (for patents); the Made in Italy Fund (for internationalization); and various fiscal initiatives (Ministero dello Sviluppo Economico 2009).

More specific attention to entrepreneurship followed shortly after. The Program *Restart Italia!* was launched in 2012 to reshape the Italian entrepreneurial environment in order to promote economic growth and employment. Overall the project envisioned outcomes such as the development of innovation and entrepreneurship culture, social mobility, transparency, and meritocracy as well as the attraction of foreign factors of production.

Arguably, the most significant result of the implementation of the *Restart Italia!* program was the newly recognized status of start-ups—as innovative enterprises of high technological value—when it was introduced into the Italian legal system. The resulting "Law 221/2012" (the so-called Italian Start-up Act) is an organic and coherent policy for which public support for innovative entrepreneurship represents a new way of thinking about industrial policymaking (Ministero dello Sviluppo Economico 2012).

In 2014, Italy introduced the Start-up Visa (ISV) program facilitating self-employment visas to non-EU citizens who were interested in launching an innovative start-up in Italy. The initiative was composed of a novel procedure which was characterized by being "fast-track"—never taking more than 30 days to be issued—and being centralized, digitized, bilingual, and free of charge. The committee evaluating the applications has been formed by the presidents of five key associations of the Italian innovation ecosystem, including business angel firms, university incubators, and others.

Several policy initiatives followed. Among the most important was the national Plan *Industria 4.0* which became effective in 2017. The plan was designed for firms operating in the manufacturing sector and intended as "a great deed of trust from the government to enterprise." The program is to be applied without—or as few as possible—constraints by bureaucratic processes or subjected to territorial or sectorial selection and invests in all stages of the life cycle of firms, particularly focusing on investment support in the digitalization of production, the development of employee productivity, the training of applicable skills and the development of new products and procedures (Ministero dello Sviluppo Economico 2017).

These programs have of course been evaluated, but it is difficult to ascertain their true impact. It would also take us beyond the scope of this chapter to attempt an assessment here. In short, in recent years, policy attention for SMEs and later entrepreneurial venturing has risen considerably in Italy and the financial and Euro crisis have strengthened the call to reform. However, in Italy there is also a political backlash, and reformists should take care to emphasize and ensure the inclusive character of reforms toward an entrepreneurial society, creating more and better opportunities for challengers, not lining the pockets of incumbents in business and politics.

6.1.6 Conclusions

In conclusion, we can take away a few important lessons from the above. First, Italy has a long history of supporting a vibrant entrepreneurial economy of locally embedded, often family-owned small- and medium-sized firms that make up the overwhelming majority of its economy. The Italian ecosystem was supported by banks, patents, and universities early on and industrialization, especially in the North, brought deep rooted but modern financial, labor, and knowledge institutions to Italy.

From more recent policy initiatives, we may tentatively conclude that national policy makers in Italy have recognized the importance of supporting Italy's Entrepreneurial Society. Moreover, we note that recent policy initiatives seem well-informed and well-targeted. Policy makers try to reduce the regulatory burden and remove undue barriers to new initiatives. Policies are more general and targeted at entrepreneurial venturing in general, and are not specifically directed toward sectoral, geographic or size-related barriers. Building on its unique history, Italy is well-positioned to promote more entrepreneurship in its economy in both North and South. In our next steps, we will use quantitative and qualitative information to identify what factors are holding Italian entrepreneurs back.

6.2 Step 2: Data Analysis with REDI for Italy

6.2.1 Italy's International Position

To get a first impression of Italy's relative performance as an entrepreneurial ecosystem, we turn to the Regional Entrepreneurship and Development Index (REDI). For calculating the country scores of the REDI index, we used the population-weighted REDI scores. Out of the 24 countries, Italy ranks 18th with 30.0 points (Table 3.3, in Varga et al. 2020). This score is significantly lower than other developed countries, and also the EU average, lagging well behind the United Kingdom, Germany, and even some newly assessed countries like Estonia, Slovenia, and the Czech Republic.

The REDI is composed of 14 underlying pillars that together make up 3 sub-indices: Entrepreneurial Attitudes, Abilities, and Aspirations (Acs et al. 2014; Szerb et al. 2017, 2019). Figure 6.1 gives us a first glance at how Italy is performing relative to the UK, Germany, and the EU average on these 14 pillars. From Fig. 6.1, we can see that Italy is performing below the European Union average on almost all aspects of the entrepreneurial ecosystem that the REDI methodology covers.

The scores on the 14 pillars are markedly low for "Human Capital," "Opportunity Start-up," and "High Growth," but overall, the Italian entrepreneurial ecosystem needs strengthening on almost all fronts. Italy scores above the European average (and even above Germany and the United Kingdom) on "Product Innovation" and "Process Innovation". These high scores indicate that Italy's long tradition of industrial policies to support innovative SMEs (see above) have paid off. But the Italian ecosystem

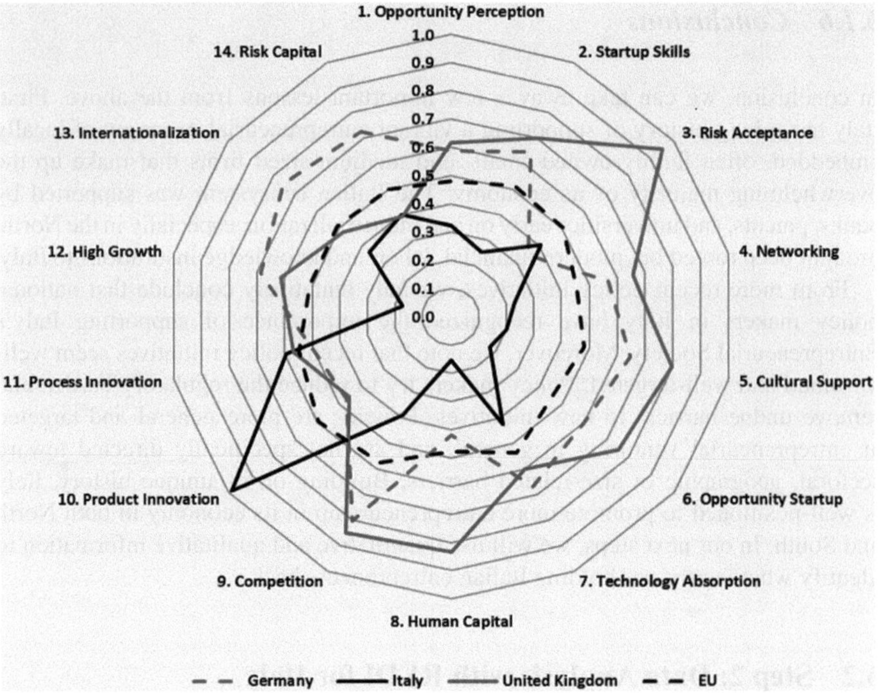

Fig. 6.1 Radar-plot REDI comparison Germany–Italy–UK and EU-average. *Source* Authors' own compilation

remains weak in the sub-index Entrepreneurial Attitudes (upper right pillars 1–5) and in Entrepreneurial Abilities (lower pillars 6–9). Even on Entrepreneurial Aspirations, it scores low because of the large imbalances between the pillars in the upper left side of the radar-plot (pillars 10–14).

The underlying algorithm in the REDI puts a penalty on bottlenecks in the ecosystem (Acs et al. 2014; Szerb et al. 2017), such that a rounder radar-plot scores higher than a more erratic one, and policy interventions should be aimed at alleviating bottlenecks with priority. As we have indicated, however, the national average potentially hides a lot of regional heterogeneity. We, therefore, focus in on Italy's main regions next.

6.2.2 A More Detailed Regional Quick Scan

If we zoom in on the regional level, in Fig. 6.2 and Table 6.1, we see that all Italian regions score between 25.7 and 33.5, with the Southern regions significantly lagging the Center and North, as expected.[2]

[2]The numbers are index numbers ranging from 0 (worst) to 100 (best) across all 125 European NUTS2/3 regions for 2012–2014.

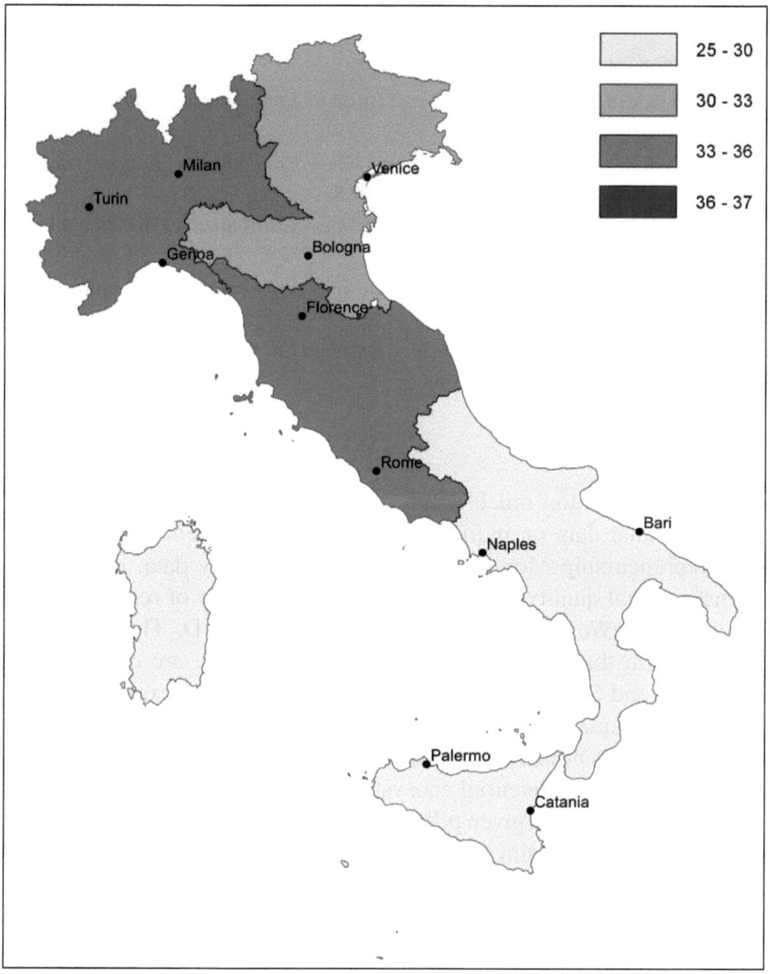

Fig. 6.2 REDI map of Italian regions. *Source* Authors' own compilation

Table 6.1 REDI-scores Italy

Region	REDI-scores 2012–2014
Nord-Ovest	33.5
Nord-Est	32.6
Centro	33.5
Sud	25.7
Isole	26.7

Source Authors' own compilation

Table 6.2 Weakest points per region

Region	Weakest pillars	Weakest variables
Nord-Ovest	5, 6, 8, 12	Open Society, Business Environment, Educational Level, Gazelle
Nord-Est	2, 4, 8, 14	Skill Perception, Know Entrepreneurs, Educational Level, Informal Investment
Centro	5, 6, 8, 12	Open Society, Business Environment, Educational Level, Gazelle
Sud	5, 6, 8, 12	Open Society, Business Environment, Educational Level, Clustering
Isole	5, 6, 8, 12	Open Society, Business Environment, Educational Level, Clustering

Source Authors' own compilation

Without going into too much detail in this chapter,[3] the intuition behind each of the pillars is that data on individual entrepreneurial agency, obtained from the Global Entrepreneurship Monitor adult population survey data, is combined with relevant institutional quality indicators from a wide variety of reputed international institutions, such as World Bank, Freedom House and OECD. The index then builds on the assumption that institutions and individual agency are complements (Acs et al. 2014; Acs and Szerb 2009). That is, high levels of, for example, Opportunity Perception in a low-quality institutional environment, will contribute little. Likewise, low Opportunity Perception in a high-quality institutional environment is also a sign of weakness in the entrepreneurial ecosystem.

To improve the score on a given pillar, policies and reforms should seek to improve the weakest link and then aim to increase both institutional quality and individual agency together. Especially because of the latter, the menu of effective interventions is not limited to improving the scores on the institutional quality indices alone. The same logic is then also imposed on the individual pillars that make up the three sub-indices: Entrepreneurial Attitudes, Abilities, and Aspirations.

The good news for Italy and its regions, based on these analyses, is that with small improvements in its weakest pillars, large improvements in the ecosystem can be expected. Moreover, from Table 6.2, we can see that, although the overall scores are lower in the Southern regions, the weaknesses in the Southern and Northern ecosystems seem largely concentrated in the same pillars and variables. This implies that national policy and reform programs addressing these weaknesses, will strengthen entrepreneurial society throughout the country and Table 6.2 gives us a clear sense of the priorities. National level policies to promote pillars 5 "Cultural Support," 6 "Opportunity Start-up," 8 "Human Capital," and 12 "High Growth" are likely to benefit Entrepreneurial Aspirations, Abilities, and Attitudes throughout the territory.

[3]We refer interested readers to Acs et al. (2014) and Szerb et al. (2017, 2019) for further details.

Improvements in these aspects would address some of the most prominent bottlenecks in the system in all regions of Italy. The recent labor market reforms as proposed under the recent Jobs Act, can, for example, prove to be beneficial in removing the penalty on growth that is present in many firm size-related social security and labor market protection provisions. It will probably take some time for such reforms and interventions to show up in the index, as the numbers will only change when people respond to the new situation by starting more ambitious and successful firms. But such fundamental reforms are what we suggest should be preferred over more direct but less fundamental policies that would boost the indicator directly, but superficially.

For Human Capital, both Educational Level and Training warrant attention, whereas for Opportunity Start-up, it is especially the poor quality of the Business Environment that keeps the pillar down. Italian entrepreneurs seem to see opportunities but are held back by deficient human capital supply and a daunting bureaucracy in starting up new ventures. To address these weaknesses, targeted interventions to improve the business environment will be needed, whereas reforms in the educational system are also advised. Not because the Italian education system does not deliver high-quality graduates, but because that quality currently does not seem to flow to the entrepreneurial ventures that need them.

In the Entrepreneurial Attitudes, the pillar on Networking is weak due to low scores on both Social Capital and Know Entrepreneur, whereas the Cultural Support pillar is weakened by the low system wide score on Open Society that negates the relatively high score for Career Status. The Start-up Skills are low in North-East mainly due to low quality of education. It is not straightforward to come up with reforms that improve these aspects, but we make some suggestions below.

6.2.3 *Overall Conclusions of the REDI Analysis*

Our reading of the data above reveals that, in all Italian regions and the country as a whole, the main bottlenecks in the entrepreneurial ecosystem are low ambition levels (High Growth), the lack of skills and education (Human Capital), and an entangled business environment (Opportunity Start-up) that feeds back into a low familiarity with ambitious entrepreneurship and a rather closed culture (Networking and Cultural Support).

Generally, it is dangerous, to rely exclusively on data and aggregate indices, even if they are composed of a broad set of sub-indicators and disaggregated as much as the data might allow. It is always important to complement a data-based quick scan with historical analysis, common sense, and more qualitative information to contextualize and complete the diagnosis. Only after triangulating the results above with the historical analysis, literature review, expert judgment, and more qualitative survey results below, we can map the diagnosis onto our menu of interventions to propose tailored reforms for Italy.

6.3 Step 3: Triangulating History, Data, and Survey Results

6.3.1 Venture Creation Processes in Italy

We assessed the ways in which the Italian institutional ecosystem influences entrepreneurial activities from two different perspectives, namely a static one, based on multiannual averages, and a process-oriented perspective (Herrmann 2020, this volume). The results obtained from both types of analyses are highly complementary. Our static analyses indicate that entrepreneurs in Italy are less likely than entrepreneurs in coordinated or liberal market economies to create radically or incrementally innovative ventures. Instead, Italy's entrepreneurs have a tendency to set up ventures based on the replication of existing technologies (Dilli et al. 2018; Herrmann 2019).

The dynamic analyses, in turn, provide insights into how the institutional environment influences different aspects of the venture creation process. With regard to human capital, we find that national labor market institutions affect the employment choices of entrepreneurs in Italy (Held 2019). In view of the benefits and security that employees enjoy in dependent employment, Italy's founders are more likely than their counterparts in the UK or the USA to start a venture in part-time rather than in full-time. Italian part-time founders, however, are more likely to transition to full-time entrepreneurship than their German equivalents (Held 2019).

Similarly, the institutional ecosystem also influences the process of finance acquisition (Held et al. 2018a). Given that stock market capitalization in Italy is low while debt finance to start-up firms is limited, venture founders in Italy very often need to finance the initial stages of venture creation with their personal funds as well as the funding provided by their family or friends. Finally, the propensity of nascent ventures to engage in R&D collaborations with external partners (universities and labs) also seems to be institutionally influenced. Given that it takes years to obtain a ruling, legal action is typically not perceived as a means of recourse in case of IP conflicts with collaboration partners. This may be the reason why nascent ventures in Italy are more reluctant to engage in R&D projects with external partners than their counterparts in Germany (Held et al. 2018b).

Taken together, these studies lend support to the argument that Italy's distinct finance-, labor-, and R&D-related institutions influence the decisions of entrepreneurs with regard to the business ideas they develop as well as the process they follow to set up their ventures. This leads to the question how entrepreneurs in Italy experience their institutional environment when setting-up a venture: Which aspects are constraining them? And what could policy makers do to facilitate venture creation in Italy?

6.3.2 Regulatory Barriers to Entrepreneurship in Italy

To examine regulatory barriers to entrepreneurship, we conducted a survey with 133 Italian founders between 2017 and 2018 (Herrmann et al. 2018). Table 6.3 provides an overview of the answers to the question: "Which regulatory requirements did you perceive as major obstacles during venture creation?".

Contrary to their German and British counterparts, venture founders in Italy frequently mentioned that they had encountered regulatory obstacles. The, by far, most frequent obstacle, encountered in almost 14.5% of cases, were bureaucratic procedures that made venture creation unnecessarily long and time consuming. Some respondents (3%) specifically mentioned the obligation to go through a notary when registering a new company and the complexity of the existing laws and specific procedures for setting-up a *Società a Responsabilità Limitata* (s.r.l.), a limited liability company. All these administrative procedures mean quite substantial implicit and explicit costs for a start-up.

Next to these bureaucratic constraints, the respondents also mentioned several financial hurdles as obstacles to venture creation, namely the taxes to be paid (5.3% of all responses), difficulties to obtain finance (5.3%), and legal initial capital requirements (2.3%). Accordingly, our survey highlights that, together with the costs arising from heavy bureaucratic requirements, nascent ventures in Italy face financing constraints. This finding did not stand out that much in the above REDI analysis. But earlier research also indicated that the absence of a vibrant angel

Table 6.3 Results survey on regulatory obstacles in Italy

Which regulatory requirements did you perceive as major obstacles during venture creation?	Times mentioned	In %
None	28	21.1
Does not answer question	15	11.3
Difficulties with bureaucratic procedures	19	14.3
Taxes	7	5.3
Difficulties with obtaining finance	7	5.3
Lacking clarity regarding regulations	5	3.8
Constantly changing regulatory environment	5	3.8
Safety regulations	5	3.8
Legal requirements to involve a notary	4	3.0
Legal initial capital requirements	3	2.3
Specific requirements related to energy sector	3	2.3

Note
1. Based on interviews with 133 founders mentioning 133 obstacles (more than one obstacle could be mentioned)
2. Only obstacles mentioned three times or more are reported in the table
Source Authors' own compilation

and VC investment community might be linked to unfavorable fiscal circumstances (Henrekson and Sanandadji 2017), tight regulation on institutional investors, and difficulties in making smooth and profitable exits in secondary markets (e.g., Bottazzi and Da Rin 2002).

A third major block of obstacles refers to unclear regulation and frequent regulatory changes. Taken together, a lack of clarity regarding regulation, as well as a constantly changing regulatory environment and specific safety regulations were mentioned in almost 12% of responses, while specific requirements related to the energy sector were mentioned as regulatory obstacles in an additional 2.3% of responses. Together, these answers indicate the detrimental effect of unclear and frequently changing rules and regulation, echoing the REDI conclusion that bureaucracy is a complicating factor in Italy.

Overall, the answers show a relevant lack of institutional support, most importantly in the form of heavy bureaucratic procedures, financial constraints, and unsteady regulation. This indicates that the aforementioned policies have thus far not (fully) succeeded in facilitating entrepreneurship in Italy.

6.3.3 Founders' Suggestions for Reforms in Italy

In the same survey, we also asked founders the following: "In your view, what can policy makers do to facilitate venture creation?". An overview of the answers to these questions is given in Table 6.4. Almost every founder had at least one suggestion of how venture creation could be facilitated by the government. The suggestions often mirror the obstacles encountered during venture creation. Accordingly, measures to alleviate bureaucracy and facilitate access to finance are listed amongst the top priorities by the founders. The respondents suggested to facilitate venture creation by reducing bureaucracy in almost 18% of all cases, to simplify bureaucratic procedures through online tools in more than 4% of responses, and to eliminate the need for a notary or to provide a notary in, together, almost 4% of cases.

Next to that, some broader suggestions were made about how to facilitate the formalities related to venture creation, namely an easier availability or accessibility of information about how to start a business (almost 5%) and better guidance of how to proceed when setting-up a new venture (slightly more than 3%). Taken together, suggestions related to facilitating administrative formalities amount to one third of all suggestions made, which illustrates the potential of this area for policy improvements.

In order to alleviate the financial constraints on nascent ventures, the respondents suggested to reduce taxes for small businesses (in more than 8% of all answers), to facilitate access to financial capital (almost 14% of responses), and to establish procedures to better detect which ventures are seeking investment (1.6% of all responses). Finance-related policy improvements make up a quarter of all policy suggestions, thus constituting another area of substantial concern.

While founders also followed-up on the third group of obstacles encountered by suggesting that constant policy changes should be avoided, this suggestion was made

Table 6.4 Results survey on suggested policies in Italy

In your view, what could policy makers do to facilitate venture creation?	Times mentioned	In %
Nothing	3	1.6
Does not answer question	13	6.8
Reduce bureaucracy	34	17.7
Facilitate financing for small businesses	26	13.5
Reduce tax rates for small businesses	16	8.3
Provide incentives for hiring people	13	6.8
Provide better training to people for starting businesses	9	4.7
Provide better information about how to start a business	9	4.7
Reduce time and difficulty of bureaucracy through online procedure	8	4.2
Provide guidance	6	3.1
Eliminate the need to have a notary for registration	4	2.1
Provide notary	3	1.6
Help market start-ups	3	1.6
Provide better networking opportunities	3	1.6
Avoid constant policy changes	3	1.6
Establish procedures to better detect whom to fund	3	1.6
Provide accountant	3	1.6

Note
1. Based on interviews with 133 founders mentioning 192 suggestions (more than one suggestion could be mentioned)
2. Only suggestions mentioned three times or more are reported in the table
Source Authors' own compilation

in 1.6% of cases. The third major block of policy recommendations, therefore, does not relate to more stable policies. Instead, it refers to facilitating access to human capital. Accordingly, founders suggested in almost 7% of their answers that policy makers should provide incentives for hiring people, in almost 5% of cases that people should be better trained in entrepreneurial skills, and in almost 2% of cases that an accountant should be provided to nascent ventures.

Finally, and unrclatcd to thc hurdlcs thcy rcportcd abovc, somc foundcrs also scc a role for the government in helping to market the products/services of start-ups (1.6%) and to provide networking opportunities (1.6%).

Overall, we, thus, find general support for the weaknesses identified in the above historical and quantitative analyses. Most importantly, Italy's founders point to the tedious bureaucratic processes as a major obstacle and, accordingly, for policy improvements. At a more general level, these suggestions can be interpreted as an invitation to move away from a non-transparent and heavy toward a leaner way of establishing new ventures. In addition, the call for easier access to human and financial capital reflects the insights gained from our analyses of the previous sections. Founders are signaling a lack of information and training and call for a more stable policy environment. We interpret this as general support for a more fundamental reform approach that creates the institutional support for those providing such services and knowledge.

6.3.4 Conclusions

In sum, the survey has confirmed most of the weaknesses identified in Sect. 6.2, but also provided some interesting additional insights. For example, the need to create a stable institutional framework that is above all transparent and clear is information that is hard to gather from quantitative data alone. The survey was, therefore, useful in nuancing some of the previous results.

Yet, when asked for the most important barriers encountered and possible policy remedies, founders—rather obviously—mention those points which they met in their personal experiences. While there certainly is valuable information in this experience, it is important to base policy recommendations on a broader basis by combining personal experiences with information of encompassing datasets. Taken together, the triangulation of our historical, quantitative and qualitative information for Italy reveals sufficient information to draw up a tentative diagnosis and turn to treatments.

6.4 Step 4: Mapping onto the FIRES-Reform Proposals

In the previous sections, we have considered the history of Italy, used an advanced diagnostic tool to scan for her most urgent problems, and asked founders how they felt and what they believed would be good treatments. Based on all this information, we can come to a diagnosis and map that diagnosis onto the menu of treatments developed in Elert et al. (2019) to propose a course of action that best fits the patient.

Italy has a long and proud history. Many of the institutions that shape an entrepreneurial society today have their roots in Italy. Italy has seen the birth of modern banking, invented intellectual property rights protection, and boasts the oldest surviving universities in the world. Consequently, Italy features a highly innovative small- and medium-sized entrepreneurial sector that competes at the global level. Innovative entrepreneurship has deep historical roots in Italy.

But time has progressed while the quality of the Italian entrepreneurial ecosystem seems to have eroded. The Italian data show quite serious weaknesses and importantly significant imbalances across the pillars that make up the REDI. Italy still performs quite well on innovation and technology absorption, but this is not complemented by a supportive culture, networks, and human capital. To face the challenges of the future, Italy will have to build on its historical strengths but should urgently address these bottlenecks. Fortunately, our regional analysis has shown that the same weaknesses hold back entrepreneurship across the country, despite significant and lasting overall level effects between regions in the North and Center, and the South. This implies that Italy can strengthen its entrepreneurial ecosystem in all regions by boosting human capital investments and, more importantly, opening up opportunities for the young and talented to engage in productive and innovative venturing across Italy. In the recent crisis, but also before, Italy has experienced an exodus of talent. It seems there are more opportunities abroad than at home and young Italians are entrepreneurial enough to go after them.

Of those that stayed and started up ventures in Italy, we heard complaints about cumbersome bureaucracy resulting in lacking growth ambitions and stunted economic dynamics. Our survey among Italian founders also revealed that complexity of the tax system, an inefficient judicial system, and cumbersome bureaucratic requirements add to the uncertainties that entrepreneurs already face and put a break on venture creation.

Taking this diagnosis to our menu of policy interventions and reform proposals in the companion volume of this book (Elert et al. 2019), we have selected what we believe to be fifteen suitable interventions for Italy. They are listed in Table 6.5. In Column 1, we find the number under which they were presented in Elert et al. (2019). Column 2 lists the policy area and 3 the proposal, where Column 4 gives our motivation for the case of Italy tying it in with the analysis presented above.

The first proposal (1) resulted from the discussions we have had with Italian founders in our surveys and was confirmed in a literature search. The need for simplicity, transparency, and predictability is high in any business venture, but certainly important in entrepreneurial ones where technical and market uncertainty is already high. Adding legal, bureaucratic, and fiscal uncertainties and complexities to this mix is not productive.

The set of fiscal and financial reform proposals (6, 8, 13 and 19) aim to eliminate that uncertainty in the tax sphere, and at the same time leave more financial resources in the hands of the people who can invest it in small amounts and in more experimental ventures at arm's length. When combined with investment in a reliable ICT infrastructure that can support the emergence of platform-based finance, this may prove a powerful push toward the decentralization of entrepreneurial finance. Still, we chose to focus first on setting the framework conditions for such a strategy to work. Proposal 19, instead, aims to strengthen Italy's traditionally diverse, decentralized, and deeply rooted system of local banking, that would also benefit from intermediating more privately held and managed wealth.

The proposals referring to Italian labor market institutions (23, 25, 27 and 31) all aim to mobilize labor across regions, sectors, and jobs, while at the same time maintaining a social security level that people are by now accustomed to in Italy. This balancing act involves making social security entitlements less conditional and more portable, while reducing job protection and barriers to job mobility.

Reducing barriers to new business formation (32) is a direct and obvious proposal in light of our aim to promote a more entrepreneurial society in Italy. New ventures typically come in the form of new businesses and organizations that need to be established also formally before they can reach their full potential. At the same time, we propose (40) to also carefully monitor these new firms and collect and disseminate the knowledge that is gained, even, or perhaps especially, when new businesses fail.

Table 6.5 FIRES-reform proposals for Italy[a]

No.	Policy area	Proposal	Italy
1	The rule of law	Strengthen monitoring and enforcement mechanisms to improve and safeguard the performance of all member states on rule of law, protection of property rights, and government effectiveness.	It takes too long to settle commercial disputes in civil cases. This creates uncertainty and works in the advantage of large, established, and incumbent firms. An entrepreneurial society needs fast, predictable, and clear legal proceedings to thrive. A lot has been done, but more is needed still.
6	Corporate income taxation	Eliminate discrepancies between statutory and effective corporate income tax rates.	This is a general advice we would give to the European Commission that also applies to Italy. Founders in Italy complain about taxes but more than their level, their complexity and unpredictability make growing a firm unattractive. Simplification and transparency are more important than lowering the levels and granting tax complex exemptions and deductions.
8	Dividend and capital taxation	Countries should aim for low dividend and capital gains tax rates with few exceptions and few (opaque) concessionary schemes.	A tax system benefits from an occasional cleaning-up. Simplicity and transparency should be the goal, not necessarily reducing rates for targeted groups. But at an overall tax pressure of 64% against 40.8% in Europe, Italy should also reduce taxes, especially on the sources of income that matter most to new ventures and their financiers.
13	Private wealth	Allow for more wealth to accumulate and remain in private hands and make it possible, easy and attractive to invest such wealth in entrepreneurial ventures.	Italy has a strong family-based tradition. This creates opportunities also for financing ventures, especially in their early stages. Italy could consider banking on extended family ties to increase the flow of financial resources into entrepreneurship. The Anglo-Saxon Angel and VC model may be less appropriate in the Italian context, given the lack of skills and incompatibility with its deep-rooted informal institutions.

(continued)

Table 6.5 (continued)

No.	Policy area	Proposal	Italy
19	Banks	Increase the mandatory equity ratio in banking gradually to 10–15% to allow them to take on more risk responsibly in their lending portfolios.	Italy still has a rather diverse and locally embedded banking system. This can be an asset in the entrepreneurial society, but these small, local banks are increasingly brought under European rules and supervision made for large, system banks. By requiring higher equity in banks, they can justifiably engage in riskier but also in the long run more productive lending, while diversity ensures stability in the system.
23	Employment protection	Relax the stringency of employment protection legislation for permanent contracts.	Italy has already implemented some fundamental reforms in the labor market in recent years. In part, this was done under pressure of the financial and Euro crisis and external creditors. The general direction of these reforms was the right one, but more can be done. Specifically, the "reinstatement" provision in employment protection is often mentioned as a burden on small and young firms. In reforming its labor markets, Italy should not forget that of the Mixed Market Economies it is actually closest to the Coordinated Market Economies and should seek to combine individual flexibility with reliable social security.
25	Employment protection	Lift the legal enforceability of confidentiality agreements between employers and their employees.	Specifically, for Italy, this proposal should be understood in light of the overall argument for investment in mobility and reducing barriers for switching jobs, industries and occupations. This will create opportunities for the young and talented to remain actively engaged in Italy and reduce the brain drain to the rest of Europe and the world.

(continued)

Table 6.5 (continued)

No.	Policy area	Proposal	Italy
27	Social security	Carefully consider the impact of flexicurity reforms on young firms and do not force them to take on excessive risks and burdens.	It is tempting for governments with tight budgets to have employers pick up the bill for their employees' training, mobility and social security. This, however, tends to reduce mobility and strengthens the insider–outsider effect. On the labor demand side, such schemes work in (relative) favor of large firms and block young firms' expansion. This keeps youth unemployment up and pushes also educated Italian youngsters to leave the country.
31	Active labor market policy	Establish or strengthen training programs to prepare workers for new occupations.	In a more flexible labor market, more flexible and mobile employees are key. Italy will not be isolated from technological and economic trends and flexibility is needed to engage opportunities and exit declining jobs, industries and trades. We propose Italy invests in the flexibility of its workforce. To the extent that people underinvest in their own flexibility due to behavioral biases and information asymmetries, public interventions and finance can be justified.
32	Entry barriers	Excessive barriers to new business formation and new entry should be lifted where possible.	Key in this proposal is the word "excessive." Founders in Italy report quite a wide variety of bureaucratic and administrative barriers to starting up a venture in Italy. Some of these barriers may serve a valid purpose, but simplicity, transparency and predictability are essential. Data shows Italian SMEs spend 52% more time dealing with bureaucracy than their European competitors and WEF ranks Italy 44th on doing business index. There is a lot of room for improvement.

(continued)

Table 6.5 (continued)

No.	Policy area	Proposal	Italy
40	Insolvency	Setup publicly funded "entrepreneurial knowledge observatories" where knowledge accumulated in the entrepreneurial process is collected, curated and freely diffused.	Creating a real hub, rich in events, infrastructure, and networking between teams could be useful for the Italian entrepreneurial ecosystems. This involves concentration. Today Milan (14.7%), Rome (8.5%) and Turin (4.7%) have less than 30% of the total number of start-ups. Our research has shown how geographical proximity is important for success. It is a tough choice, but it would be useful to invest in a start-up capital (Milan) that can perform a national function.
41	Education system	Reforms in primary and secondary education should provide pupils with a solid and coherent knowledge base and promote initiative, creativity and a willingness to experiment.	Italy's educational system can be characterised as traditional. The state sets the curriculum, provides uniform tests, and most children attend public schools. The curriculum is demanding, geared toward cognitive skills and textbook based, leaving little room for creativity and diversity. Italy considers its educational system of high quality, but making pupils work hard is not the same as teaching them useful skills. Countries ranking high on, e.g., the WEF, OECD and EU rankings, such as Finland and Norway have less homework and formal testing and more autonomy for highly trained and well-paid professional teachers. Italy should consider reforms in that direction.
42	Education system	Promote STEM education and English as a (mandatory) second language early on and then throughout educational career.	Italy ranks 20 out of 27 EU countries plus Turkey when it comes to knowledge of English as a second language. This is a handicap when Italy seeks to compete at the EU or global level. Italy scores around rank 30 out of 80 in the OECD PISA-scores on Math and Science behind countries like the Czech Republic and Luxemburg, while on STEM topics Italy has EU average levels of enrollment, but high levels of dropout. The situation can be improved by reforming curricula in primary and secondary education and ensure that sufficient vocational tertiary educational options exist in Italy.

(continued)

Table 6.5 (continued)

No.	Policy area	Proposal	Italy
44	Universities/Entrepreneurial clusters	The link between universities and external stakeholders should be strengthened by encouraging universities to stimulate entrepreneurial initiatives and university spin-offs.	Many Italian universities started offering courses focused on entrepreneurship. Courses usually taught by a researcher with no work experience outside academia, and no experience in start-ups. The average curriculum therefore deals with writing business plans and how to get financing. Italy lacks a start-up culture and those trying to provide it have no hands-on experience. This is not easy to address, but a good start would be to promote the involvement of entrepreneurs in (academic) curricula and opening up universities to external stakeholders.
45	Universities/Entrepreneurial clusters	Both the EU and its member states should create healthy, well-funded, academic institutions that allow Europe's most talented academics to pursue their research interests.	For the Italian context, it is important to open up its academic institutions. Many reforms have already been undertaken, but most in a time of aging, financial constraints, and budget cuts. With vested interests and gilded contracts hard to reform, the rate at which Italian academic institutions open up for competition and meritocracy is slow. It makes little sense to spend a lot of money on institutions before such structural issues have been addressed. Unfortunately, the (poor) students, not the aging staff is driven out.

Source Authors' own compilation
[a]Numbered as in Elert et al. (2019)

Finally, we propose Italy should consider urgent reforms to its educational system (41, 42, 44 and 45) to ensure its young and talented are better prepared for a future in a more entrepreneurial Italy. This starts in primary schools and even earlier, with a reorientation on creativity and experimentation, whereas English proficiency and STEM topics will prepare Italian youths for a future in a globalized and technologically rapidly changing economy. Meanwhile, Italy's established academic institutions should open up to the world outside of academia, preferably from a genuine position of scholarly curiosity and interest, rather than driven by financial and policy incentives.

The proposals, individually and in combination, aim to strengthen the knowledge base and talent pool from which Italian entrepreneurs can draw and aim to open opportunities for not only starting but also growing firms in all regions in Italy. All Italian regions stand to benefit from these interventions. However, the fact that density and clustering tend to promote the quality and impact of entrepreneurial venturing will imply that the same policy improvements benefit the already prosperous regions most. Still, that should not stop policymakers from pursuing these interventions as it is the Italian citizens, not its regions per se that governments should care about. Creating opportunities for Italian entrepreneurs in a few entrepreneurial hotspots is better than not creating such opportunities at all, also for people living in regions that do not have such hotspots.

Of course, these proposals will need a much more detailed discussion and form the starting point, not the final word on the policy agenda. Moreover, even if adopted, our proposals all require careful implementation and evaluation to complete the 7-step policy cycle presented in Chap. 1 of this volume. But based on our analysis of the situation, we proposed Italy consider this set of interventions to build up its strengths and restore health to its ailing entrepreneurial ecosystem. To conclude this chapter, we now turn to the discussion of these proposals in their proper policy context.

6.5 Step 5: the FIRES-Reform Proposals in Light of the Countries' Historical, Geographical and Institutional Context

To put our proposed reform program in its proper context, it is important to discuss the diagnosis and proposed treatments with experts in the field. In this case that is Italian policy makers that are active in the field every day. Moreover, given the wide diversity of policy areas involved, it is important to not only discuss this with policy makers that are active in "entrepreneurship policy" in the narrow sense. Our approach emphasizes the importance of reforming institutions that determine the allocation of financial, labor, and knowledge resources to entrepreneurial activity in the broadest and most inclusive sense of the word. Broadening the scope was motivated by the fact that entrepreneurship policy in the narrow sense has been around for some three decades or more, also in Italy, and to date has achieved only limited success.

Because of its breadth, our reform agenda inevitably cuts across many policy areas, traditionally less associated with entrepreneurship policy, including, for example, wealth taxation, financial and labor market regulation, social security, and science policy. As the institutions in these areas have evolved historically and policy makers in these areas pursue different, equally relevant, public policy priorities, the challenge is to discuss the proposed agenda in sufficient depth, but with a sufficiently diverse group of policy makers and practitioners. Policies and institutions in these different areas overlap and interact in ways that affect the quality and performance of the entrepreneurial ecosystem (Stam 2015, 2018). The challenge is to not only propose policies and reforms that will strengthen the ecosystem, but to do it in such a way that other important policy priorities are also achieved.

In order to receive a first round of feedback on the proposals for Italy presented in Table 6.5, a policy round table was held at the CDP Group (*Cassa Depositi e Prestiti*) in Rome on March 5, 2018. This step can be seen as an attempt to allow our patient, or perhaps more accurately, her team of medical specialists, intimately familiar with our patient, to give feedback about our diagnosis and proposed treatments. What proposals would this team endorse, question or maybe want to drop?

In this policy round table, the diagnosis presented above was broadly shared among the participants. The group included representatives from the Bank of Italy, the OECD, UNCTAD and the Italian Ministry of Economic Development (Sanders and Grilli 2018). Participants recognized the encumbered bureaucracy and inflexible educational system as well as the long-standing North–South divide and issues of effective and high-quality governance. There was general consensus that universities could function as catalysts by playing a more important role in supporting financial education and putting entrepreneurship at the center of the stage. Another important deficiency in the Italian entrepreneurial ecosystem is the shortage of dedicated networking events. Italy has many, small, high-quality centers of excellence, but they lack mass and local governments could act to improve this situation. Participants added that it is also important to improve attitudes toward risk taking and reduce the cultural stigma arising from failure.

Given the background and natural inclinations of the host institution, there was perhaps a slight bias in the selection of participants and emphasis on financial policies and institutions in Italy, even when these issues did not stand out as the main bottleneck in Italy in our diagnosis. This fact was recognized in the group, but as many were interested in and actively involved in financial policy making, the issue was still on the table. Concerning financing issues and venture capital, it was mentioned that the small VC industry may not only be a result of insufficient demand for this type of capital. It may also stem from the VC lack of competencies and a shortage of professional skills in this area. Crowdfunding platforms providing an alternative route to financing scale ups and exits, may fit well with the Italian tradition of family-based share holdings and finance and preserve an orientation on long-run value creation.

There were also weaknesses that were not mentioned in our analysis so far but were deemed important. Public procurement and the governance of the public administration were considered to be the most prominent problems by many participants. Too many ministries and public bodies are responsible for too many parts of a too complex puzzle. In addition, there is a problem with the quality of governance in general and of innovation and entrepreneurship policy specifically due to an aged workforce with outdated skills in the public sector—only 40% of Italian civil servants hold a university degree and the share of central government employees below the age of 35 is just 2.2%. High levels of job protection in civil service make it difficult to change these numbers, but it is evidently a problem when young and dynamic entrepreneurs have to deal with an ossified and outdated civil service.

Finally, all participants stressed the need to implement policies to promote the formation and strengthening of industrial districts. The benefits of knowledge spillovers, agglomeration, and scale can only be realized in specialized districts. The resulting geographical heterogeneity should not be politically opposed but rather be managed and accomodated. Consequently, there was a great attention from all stakeholders for the geographical dimension that is considered crucial for triggering virtuous dynamics in the Italian entrepreneurial ecosystems.

6.6 Conclusions

This chapter on Italy illustrates the FIRES-approach to formulating a tailored institutional reform strategy to promote a more entrepreneurial society in Europe. It shows how the tools, discussed and introduced in the first part of this volume, have been used to systematically analyze the situation in Italy. After carefully analyzing Italy's historically rooted institutional foundations, this chapter triangulated historical, qualitative, and quantitative information to identify Italy's strengths and weaknesses. Based on this diagnosis the most relevant proposals were then selected from the menu of policy interventions and reform proposals in the companion volume of this book (Elert et al. 2019).

We conclude that many of the institutions that shape an entrepreneurial society have their roots in Italy. Italy has seen the birth of modern banking, invented intellectual property rights protection, and has the oldest universities in the world. Even today, Italy boasts a highly innovative small- and medium-sized entrepreneurial sector that competes on quality at the global level.

Italy could strengthen its entrepreneurial ecosystem in the area of boosting human capital investments and more importantly, opening up opportunities for the young and talented to engage in productive and innovative venturing in Italy. In the recent crisis Italy has seen an exodus of talent. This diaspora perhaps had benefits in the past. It created demand for Italian products abroad and served as an alternative for high domestic unemployment. But with an aging and shrinking population, such an exodus is a bad sign that suggests there are more opportunities abroad than at home. When those that do stay and start-up ventures then complain about cumbersome bureaucracy resulting in lacking growth ambitions and stunted economic dynamics, there is a clear reason to act.

The chapter discussed proposals concerning the legal system, the mobility of talent, and the regulatory burden for new firms. It also discussed reforms of the tax and educational system and presented suggestions about how to improve the flow of financial resources into experimenting firms. The proposals, individually and in combination, aim to strengthen the knowledge base and talent pool from which Italian entrepreneurs can draw and aim to open opportunities for not only starting but also growing firms in all regions in Italy. Both North and South stand to benefit from these interventions. Of course, these proposals will need a much more detailed discussion and only form the starting point, not the final word in the policy debate. Moreover, even if eventually adopted, our proposals all require careful implementation and evaluation to complete the FIRES Seven Step cycle.

References

Acs ZJ, Autio E, Szerb L (2014) National systems of entrepreneurship: measurement issues and policy implications. Res Policy 43(3):476–494. https://doi.org/10.1016/j.respol.2013.08.016
Acs ZJ, Szerb L (2009) The global entrepreneurship index (GEINDEX). Found Trends Entrep 5(5):341–435. https://doi.org/10.1561/0300000027
Allini A, Ferri L, Maffei M, Zampella A (2017) The effect of perceived corruption on entrepreneurial intention: evidence from Italy. Int Bus Res 10(6):75–86
Barbagallo F (2001) Italy: the idea and the reality of the nation. J Mod Ital Stud 6(3):388–401
Baum CF, Munro JM, Schachter G (1990) Structural change and economic development in Southern Italy. J Dev Stud 27(1):54–71
Beccalli E, Girardone C (2016) Banking in Italy. In: Beck T, Casu B (eds) The Palgrave handbook of European banking. Palgrave Macmillan, London, pp 521–540
Bertola G (1990) Job security, employment and wages. Eur Econ Rev 34(4):851–879
Boeri T, Jimeno JF (2005) The effects of employment protection: learning from variable enforcement. Eur Econ Rev 49(8):2057–2077
Bohlen C (1996) North-South divide in Italy: a problem for Europe, too. New York Times. Retrieved from: http://www.nytimes.com/1996/11/15/world/north-south-divide-in-italy-a-problem-for-europe-too.html
Boland V (2009) Modern dilemma for world's oldest bank. Financial Times, June 12. Retrieved from: https://www.ft.com/content/a034542e-5771-11de-8c47-00144feabdc0
Boldrin M, Levine DK (2008) Against intellectual monopoly. Cambridge University Press, Cambridge
Bottazzi L, Da Rin M (2002) Venture capital in Europe and the financing of innovative companies. Economic policy 17(34):229–270
Calmfors L, Driffill J (1988) Bargaining structure, corporatism and macroeconomic performance. Economic policy 3(6):13–61
Carinci F (2015) Labour law and industrial relations in Italy: update to the jobs act (no. 183-2014). IPSOA/Wolters Kluwers, Milano
Castellani D (2018) Mortgage-backed securitization and SME lending during the financial and economic crisis: evidence from the Italian cooperative banking system. Econ Notes 47(1):187–222
Cazzola F (1988) Della corruzione. Il Mulino, Bologna
Cirillo V, Fana M, Guarascio D (2017) Labour market reforms in Italy: evaluating the effects of the jobs act. Econ Polit 34(2):211–232
Coccorese P (2013) Assessing the competitive conditions in the Italian banking system: some empirical evidence. PSL Q Rev 51(205):171–191
D'Attore PP (1987) Italian reconstruction and "depressed areas": the Marshall plan in the Mezzogiorno. Center for European studies working paper series no. 11. Harvard University
De Roover R (1999) The rise and decline of the Medici bank: 1397–1494. Beard Books, New York
Dilli S, Elert N, Herrmann AM (2018) Varieties of entrepreneurship. Exploring the institutional foundations of different entrepreneurship types through 'varieties-of-capitalism' arguments. Special issue on "financial and institutional reforms for an entrepreneurial society." Small Bus Econ, 51(2):293–320
Dilli S, Henrekson M, Westerhuis G (2016) The institutional evolution of labour market institutions in Europe and entrepreneurship. Retrieved from https://projectfires.eu/wp-content/uploads/2017/09/D2.5-The-Institutional-Evolution-of-Labour-Market.pdf

D'Onza G, Brotini F, Zarone V (2017) Disclosure on measures to prevent corruption risks: a study of Italian local governments. Int J Public Adm 40(7):612–624
Duggan C (2013) A concise history of Italy. Cambridge University Press, Cambridge
ECB (2017) Report on financial structures 2017. ECB, Frankfurt
Economist (1999) Those Medici. Retrieved from http://www.economist.com/node/347333
Economist (2017) Italy's fourth-biggest bank returns to the stock market. Retrieved from https://www.economist.com/news/finance-and-economics/21730672-shares-bailed-out-bank-start-trading-again-italys-fourth-biggest-bank
Elert N, Henrekson M, Sanders M (2019) The entrepreneurial society: a reform strategy for the European Union. Springer, Berlin
Eurofound (2009) Italy: 'wage formation'. Retrieved from https://www.eurofound.europa.eu/observatories/eurwork/comparative-information/national-contributions/italy/italy-wage-formation
Ferrera M (2005) Welfare states and social safety nets in Southern Europe: an introduction. In: Ferrera M (ed) Welfare state reform in southern Europe: fighting poverty and social exclusion in Greece, Italy, Spain and Portugal. Routledge, London, pp 1–24
Frumkin M (1945) The origin of patents. J Pat Off Soc 27(3):143–149
Gall G (1999) A review of strike activity in Western Europe at the end of the second millennium. Empl Relat 21(4):357–377
Garelli F (2007) The public relevance of the church and Catholicism in Italy. J Mod Ital Stud 12(1):8–36
Gerschenkron A (1962) Economic backwardness in historical perspective: a book of essays. Belknap Press of Harvard University Press, Cambridge, MA
Goddard J, Molyneux P, Wilson JO, Tavakoli M (2007) European banking: an overview. J Bank Finance 31(7):1911–1935
Goldthwaite RA (1995) Banks, palaces and entrepreneurs in renaissance Florence. Variorum, Aldershot
Golpe AA, Millán JM, Román C (2008) Labor market institutions and entrepreneurship. In: Congregado E (ed) Measuring entrepreneurship: building a statistical system. Springer, New York, NY, pp 279–296
Graubard SR, Cavazza FL (1974) Il caso italiano. Garzanti, Milano
Hassel A (2014) Adjustments in the Eurozone: varieties of capitalism and the crisis in Southern Europe. LSE Europe in question discussion paper series no. 76/2014
Held L (2019) Part-time entrepreneurship: the role of institutions, venture and individual characteristics in entry and transition choices. In: Held L (ed) Unravelling the patterns in venture creation processes, Ph.D. thesis. Utrecht University, Utrecht, pp 25–55
Held L, Herrmann AM, Polzin F (2018a) Follow the money: the funding acquisition process of nascent ventures. Horizon 2020 Project on "Financial and Institutional Reforms for an Entrepreneurial Society" (FIRES), Workpackage 5, Deliverable 5.1; currently under review. Also available in Held L (2019) Unravelling the patterns in venture creation processes. Ph.D. thesis. Utrecht University, Utrecht, pp 91–122
Held L, Herrmann AM, Storz C (2018b) Whom do nascent ventures search for? Variance of linkage formation activities during new product development processes. Horizon 2020 Project on "Financial and Institutional Reforms for an Entrepreneurial Society" (FIRES), Workpackage 5, Deliverable 5.1; currently under review. Also available in Held L (2019) Unravelling the patterns in venture creation processes. Ph.D. thesis. Utrecht University, Utrecht, pp 123–150
Herrmann AM (2019) A plea for varieties of entrepreneurship. Special issue on "entrepreneurship in context." Small Bus Econ 52(2):331–343
Herrman AM (2020) On the institutional foundations of the varieties of entrepreneurship in Europe. In: Sanders M, Marx A, Stenkula M (eds) The entrepreneurial society. Reform strategies for Italy, Germany and the UK. Springer, Berlin

Herrmann AM, Fischer B, Held L (2018) Internationally comparative dataset on start-up processes and their institutional foundations in Germany, Italy, the UK and the US, 1–17. Retrieved from https://projectfires.eu/wp-content/uploads/2018/10/d5.1-combined-complete.pdf
Henrekson M, Johansson D, Stenkula M (2010) Taxation, labor market policy and high-impact entrepreneurship. J Ind Compet Trade 10(3–4):275–296
Henrekson M, Sanandaji T (2017) Stock option taxation: a missing piece of European innovation policy? Retrieved from http://www.projectfires.eu/wp-content/uploads/2017/09/Complete-D5.9-submission.pdf
Hertner P (2016) Starting from scratch? The beginnings of Banca Commerciale Italiana: 1893–1894. In: Hofmann C, Müller M (eds) History of financial institutions: essays on the history of European finance, 1800–1950. Routledge, New York, NY, pp 13–38
Hoggson NF (2007) Banking through the ages: from the Romans to the Medicis, from the Dutch to the Rothschilds. Cosimo Inc., New York, NY
Iacobucci D, Micozzi A (2012) Entrepreneurship education in Italian universities: trend, situation and opportunities. Education+Training 54(8/9):673–696
Ichino A, Maggi G (2000) Work environment and individual background: explaining regional shirking differentials in a large Italian firm. Q J Econ 115(3):1057–1090
Kertzer DI (1980) Comrades and Christians: religion and political struggle in communist Italy. Cambridge University Press, Cambridge
Lazear EP (1990) Job security provisions and employment. Q J Econ 105(3):699–726
Leonardi M, Pica G (2006) Effects of employment protection legislation on wages: a regression discontinuity approach. University of Milan, Mimeo
Liberati D, Marinucci M, Tanzi GM (2016) Science and technology parks in Italy: main features and analysis of their effects on the firms hosted. J Technol Transfer 41(4):694–729
Long PO (1991) Invention, authorship, "intellectual property," and the origin of patents: notes toward a conceptual history. Technol Cult 32(4):846–884
MacDonald SB, Gastmann AL (2000) A history of credit and power in the Western world. Transaction Publishers, London
Maynard JT (1980) Understanding chemical patents. A guide for the inventor. Anal Chem 52(6):660A–660A
Ministero dello Sviluppo Economico (n.d.) Small business act. Retrieved from http://www.sviluppoeconomico.gov.it/index.php/it/impresa/piccole-e-medie-imprese/small-business-act
Ministero dello Sviluppo Economico (2009) Small business act: le iniziative in materia di sostegno alle pmi nell'europa A 27. Retrieved from http://www.sviluppoeconomico.gov.it/images/stories/recuperi/Notizie/SBA27_2009.pdf
Ministero dello Sviluppo Economico (2012) Restart Italia! Report of the task force on startups set up by the ministry of economic development
Ministero dello Sviluppo Economico (2017) Italia start-up visa hub, 4th quarter report. Summary of the main findings, 31 Dec 2017
Moradei G (2009) Patent information in Italy. World Pat Inf 31(1):19–31
Nicoletti G, Scarpetta S, Boylaud O (1999) Summary indicators of product market regulation with and extension to employment protection legislation. OECD working paper no. 226
Panunzi F (2012) Contro il monopolio sulla proprietà intelletuale. Lavoce. Retrieved from http://www.lavoce.info/archives/27450/contro-il-monopolio-sulla-proprieta-intellettuale/
Politecnico di Bari (n.d.) History. Retrieved from http://www.en.poliba.it/university/history
Politecnica delle Marche (2017) Historical highlights: the origins. Retrieved from http://www.univpm.it/Entra/Informations_about_University/Historical_Highlights
Politecnico di Milano (n.d.) Towards the present. Retrieved from https://www.polimi.it/en/university/history/towards-the-present/
Politecnico di Torino (n.d.) History. Retrieved from https://www.polito.it/ateneo/storia/index.php?lang=en
Raulli L (2017) Transformation of the Italian labor market under the Renzi government: explaining the shift to flexicurity. Master Thesis, Ludwig-Maximilians-Universität, München

Regini M (1997) Still engaging in corporatism? Recent Italian experience in comparative perspective. Eur J Ind Relat 3(3):259–278

Rolfo S, Calabrese G (2003) Traditional SMEs and innovation: the role of the industrial policy in Italy. Entrep Reg Dev 15(3):253–271

Salvador E (2010) Are science parks and incubators good "brand names" for spin-offs? The case study of Turin. J Technol Transf 36(2):203–232

Sanders M, Grilli L (2018) Policy Roundtable Report. Retrieved from https://projectfires.eu/wp-content/uploads/2018/05/d5.12-roundtable-report-italy.pdf

Scherer FM (1965) Firm size, market structure, opportunity, and the output of patented inventions. Am Econ Rev 55(5):1097–1125

Schmookler J (1966) Invention und economic growth. Harvard University Press, Cambridge, MA

Simonini R (1954) The universities of Italy. Bull Am Assoc Univ Profr (1915–1955) 40(4):563–592

Sirilli G (1986) The researcher in Italy: a profession in search of recognition. Res Policy 15(6):329–337

Spanò R, Ferri L, Fiondella C, Maffei M (2017) Accountability and reporting in the fight against corruption: preliminary evidences from the Italian setting. Int J Bus Manag 12(4):1–9

Spanò R, Paola ND, Caldarelli A, Vona R (2016) Accountants' hybridization and juridification: a critical reflection on the fight against organized crime. Public Money Manag 36(6):441–446

Spooner DJ (1984) The southern problem, the Neapolitan problem and Italian regional policy. Geogr J 150(1):11–26

Stam E (2015) Entrepreneurial ecosystems and regional policy: a sympathetic critique. Eur Plan Stud 23(9):1759–1769

Stam E (2018) Measuring entrepreneurial ecosystems. In: O'Connor A, Stam E, Sussan F, Audretsch DB (eds) Entrepreneurial ecosystems. Springer, Cham, pp 173–197

Statute of Politecnico di Torino (2011) Retrieved from https://www.swas.polito.it/services/docuff/default.asp?id_documento_padre = 10358

Sylla R (2002) The role of the banks. In: Sylla R, Toniolo G (eds) Patterns of European industrialisation: the nineteenth century. Routledge, New York, NY, pp 45–63

Szerb L, Lafuente E, Horváth K, Páger B (2019) The relevance of quantity and quality entrepreneurship for regional performance: the moderating role of the entrepreneurial ecosystem. Reg Stud 53(9):1308–1320. https://doi.org/10.1080/00343404.2018.1510481

Szerb L, Vörös Z, Komlósi É, Acs ZJ, Páger B, Rappai G (2017) The regional entrepreneurship and development index: structure, data, methodology and policy applications. Retrieved from http://www.projectfires.eu/wp-content/uploads/2018/07/d4.4-the-regional-entrepreneurship-and-development-index_-structure-data-methodology-and-policy-applications.pdf

Tabellini G (2010) Culture and institutions: economic development in the regions of Europe. J Eur Econ Assoc 8(4):677–716

Tiraboschi M (2012) Italian labour law after the so-called Monti-Fornero reform (law no. 92/2012). E-J Int Comp Labour Stud 1(3–4):47–86

Unioncamere (2005) Le nuove imprese in Italia 1998–2002—Osservatorio Unioncamere sulla demografia delle imprese. FrancoAngeli, Milan

Universita di Bologna (n.d.) The numbers of history. Retrieved from http://www.unibo.it/en/university/who-we-are/our-history/the-numbers-of-history

Varga A, Szerb L, Sebestyén T, Szabó N (2020) Economic impact assessment of entrepreneurship policies with the GMR-Europe model. In: Sanders M, Marx A, Stenkula M (eds) The entrepreneurial society. Reform strategies for Italy, Germany and the UK. Springer, Berlin

Viesti G (2016) Fondazione Res. Università in declino. Un'indagine sugli atenei da Nord a Sud. Donzelli, Rome

Wiarda HJ (1997) Corporatism and comparative politics: the other great "ism". M.E., Sharpe, Armonk, NY

Chapter 7
A Reform Strategy for Germany

Mark Sanders, Mikael Stenkula, Michael Fritsch, Andrea M. Herrmann, Gresa Latifi, Balázs Páger, László Szerb, Elisa Terragno Bogliaccini and Michael Wyrwich

Abstract In this chapter, we outline a reform strategy to promote a more entrepreneurial society in Germany. Germany has developed a successful model of capitalism in which high productivity growth is driven by on-the-job learning and firm-specific skill accumulation. The economy is rooted in a strong and regionally

All authors acknowledge financial support from the European Union's Horizon 2020 research and innovation program under grant agreement No 649378. László Szerb and Balázs Páger also acknowledge support from the National Scientific Research Fund of Hungary (OTKA/NKFI grant no. 120289 titled as Entrepreneurship and Competitiveness investigations in Hungary based on the Global Entrepreneurship Monitor surveys 2017–2019). Mikael Stenkula also gratefully acknowledges financial support from Jan Wallanders och Tom Hedelius stiftelse and from the Marianne and Marcus Wallenberg Foundation.

M. Sanders (✉) · E. Terragno Bogliaccini
Utrecht School of Economics, Utrecht University, Utrecht, The Netherlands
e-mail: m.w.j.l.sanders@uu.nl

E. Terragno Bogliaccini
e-mail: e.m.terragnobogliaccini@uu.nl

M. Stenkula
Research Institute of Industrial Economics, Stockholm, Sweden
e-mail: mikael.stenkula@ifn.se

M. Fritsch
Friedrich Schiller University of Jena, Jena, Germany
e-mail: m.fritsch@uni-jena.de

A. M. Herrmann
Copernicus Institute of Sustainable Development, Utrecht University, Utrecht, The Netherlands
e-mail: A.M.Herrmann@uu.nl

G. Latifi
TUM School of Management, Technical University of Munich, Munich, Germany
e-mail: gresa.latifi@tum.de

B. Páger · L. Szerb
Department of Management Science, University of Pécs, Pécs, Hungary
e-mail: pagerb@rkk.hu

L. Szerb
e-mail: szerb.laszlo@ktk.pte.hu

M. Sanders et al. (eds.), *The Entrepreneurial Society*, International Studies in Entrepreneurship 44, https://doi.org/10.1007/978-3-662-61007-7_7

embedded *Mittelstand,* which supports an export-oriented industry mainly based on incremental innovations, but which is less conducive to more radical innovation. We, therefore, suggest a reform agenda for Germany that encourages more entrepreneurial experimentation with the aim of facilitating radical innovation, both in incumbent and new firms. Germany's entrepreneurial talent should be encouraged to take on more risk, the education system could promote initiative, creativity and a willingness to experiment, and a more equal playing field between dependent employment and self-employment/employer could be created.

Keywords Germany · Entrepreneurship · Varieties of Capitalism · Entrepreneurial ecosystem · Entrepreneurship policy

7.1 Step 1: Historical Roots of Institutions and Recent Policies

7.1.1 United, Divided, Reunited—A Short History of Germany

In the centuries following the rule of Charlemagne (800–814), countries such as France, Spain, England, and Habsburg Austria developed into centralized states. In contrast, the so-called Holy Roman Empire of German Nation became increasingly fragmented because rulers had to "buy" the loyalty of kings, princes, and dukes within the empire. Between the emergence of Martin Luther's critique of the Church in Rome (1517) and the Thirty Years' War (1618–1648), many German states, mostly in the North and Center, adopted the new Protestant faith while others, more Southern and Western parts of Germany, remained Catholic (Cantoni 2012).[1] Religious tensions erupted in a civil war and devastated many of the German states. When the Treaty of Westphalia ended the Thirty Years' War in 1648, the area that we know as Germany today was comprised of hundreds of sovereign kingdoms, principalities, and dukedoms.

This fragmentation lasted until the (second) German Empire was established in 1871 (Falck et al. 2011; Chickering 2014) by the Prussian chancellor Otto von Bismarck. The immediate years after the formation of Germany are historically remembered as the *Gründerzeit* (start-up boom/founding era), as the country went through a process of economic expansion, quickly followed by the first wave of bankruptcies

M. Wyrwich
Faculty of Economics and Business, University of Groningen, Groningen, The Netherlands
e-mail: m.wyrwich@rug.nl

[1] This has implications for entrepreneurship today. Nunziata and Rocco (2018) show that Protestants in Germany have a stronger entrepreneurial intention than Catholics under certain conditions.

known as the *Gründerkrach* (Uebele and Ritschl 2009; Burhop 2011). Germany integrated and industrialized rapidly until World War I. But Germany inherited a distinct regional variation that left traces to this day (Tipton 1976; Gutberlet 2014).[2]

The Great War imposed an enormous burden in lives lost and resources wasted. Due to the massive reparation payments imposed in the Versailles Treaty, Germany had a hard time recovering (Broadberry and Harrison 2005).[3] Hyperinflation left a lasting imprint on the German psyche in 1923 and the economic situation worsened after a few years of economic stability in the mid-1920s. The crash of 1929 and the following Great Depression led to massive unemployment, to the breakdown of leading banks in 1931 (James 1981; Kopper 2011), and fueled the rise of the Nazi movement. The economic system of the Nazi regime that seized power in 1933 was based on autarky (self-sufficiency) and the pursuit of central planning principles (Barkai 1988). Their policy strengthened a trend toward concentration and cartelization of the economy that was already observable since the late nineteenth century (Reckendrees 2003). In a time of slumping (export) demand, the fiscal expansion caused by the Nazi rearmament and public infrastructure worked and resulted in economic recovery and much needed employment, whereas autarky kept Germany relatively isolated from further shocks from abroad.

World War II led, however, to a total destruction of the German economy in the 1940s and fueled a second hyperinflation. Upon defeat, Germany was occupied by the Allied Powers (USA, UK, France, and Soviet Union) and lost one-third of its territory in the East to Poland and Russia. In 1949, the country was split into two separate states, namely the Federal Republic of Germany (FRG or West Germany), which became a Western-style market economy, and the German Democratic Republic (GDR or East Germany), a Soviet-style centrally planned economy. The Iron Curtain divided Germany for more than 40 years and the two German states evolved in distinctly different directions.

The economy of West Germany prospered in the 1950s and early 1960s, a period referred to as economic miracle (*Wirtschaftswunder*). East Germany, meanwhile, had to cope with a massive loss of economic activity as businesses relocated assets and activities, while some 1.3 million, mostly educated and entrepreneurial, people fled to West Germany (e.g., Hefele 1998; Falck et al. 2013) from 1950 until the Berlin Wall was erected in 1961. The East German economy also had to cope with massive war reparations to the Soviet Union which amounted to about 23% of the pre-war gross national product (Lieberman 1996). The West-German economy instead benefitted from the Marshall plan and global monetary stability under the Bretton Woods system, security assurances under the NATO-treaty, and trade liberalization under GATT.

---

[2]Some German regions, for example, long retained a primogeniture inheritance system, where in other parts inheritances were shared equally among all (male) children. This led to large estates and landed nobility in some, and a rural, entrepreneurial class in other regions.

[3]The severity of the impact of these reparations is, however, somewhat disputed in the literature (see, e.g., Hantke and Spoerer 2010).

Trends in entrepreneurship also diverged strongly. In the aftermath of the oil price shock of 1973, West Germany developed from a managed to a more entrepreneurial society, with self-employment rising to 10–12% in 1989. In East Germany, in contrast, there were several waves of expropriation driving down the rate of self-employment to 1.8% at the time of reunification (Wyrwich 2012).

The biggest challenge after reunification was the integration of the economic structures of the former East Germany into the market economy system (Hall and Ludwig 1995; Burda and Hunt 2001). There was a massive surge in start-up activity in the early 1990s and the self-employment rate in the former East Germany approached the Western level around the year 2005. At the same time, almost none of the Eastern companies that existed in 1989 were still active in the market in 2000 (Fritsch et al. 2014). Despite this massive transition and rapid convergence in self-employment, striking economic differences between both parts of the country remain until today. After a period of converging productivity levels in the first years after transition, a productivity gap of 30% still persists since the late 1990s. Massive migration and brain drain to Western Germany came to a halt only recently, and the legacy of the socialist past continues to affect people's inclinations, attitudes, principles, and behavior.[4] This legacy will last but perhaps not all of it is necessarily a barrier to growth and prosperity (former East Germany has, for example, higher female participation rates and smaller gender gaps in wages and incomes).

In conclusion, both the North-East, South-West divide between Protestants and Catholics in the seventeenth and the East-West divide between socialists and capitalists in the twentieth century are important to understand the fractionalization and regional heterogeneity of Germany today. Germany's federal political structure accommodates and consolidates this heterogeneity and helps explain the decentralized character of its entrepreneurial ecosystem(s). These deep-rooted institutional features are manifest in the institutions that govern the flow of knowledge, finance, and labor to existing and new firms alike. We discuss these in the sections below.

7.1.2 *Institutions for Knowledge Creation and Diffusion*

The institutions that govern the generation and flow of knowledge to businesses in general and to entrepreneurial ventures in particular are founded in the educational system and the institutions doing basic and applied research. The system for registering and commercially exploiting knowledge then also deserves special mention.

---

[4]See for example Alesina and Fuchs-Schündeln (2007), Brosig-Koch et al. (2011), Bauernschuster and Rainer (2012), Bauernschuster et al. (2012), Corneo and Grüner (2002), Fuchs-Schündeln and Schündeln (2005, 2009), and Ockenfels and Weimann (1999).

7.1.2.1 Universities

The first medieval universities emerged in Germany after the end of the Papal Schism in 1386 with the University of Heidelberg opening in the very same year (Cantoni and Yuchtman 2014). The political fragmentation of Germany at the time implied that a lot of universities were set up in smaller cities which are not necessarily big economic or administrative agglomerations today. Examples, apart from Heidelberg, are the universities in Rostock (1419), Greifswald (1456), and Tübingen (1477), but also the University in Marburg (1527), which was the first Protestant university in the world, and the University of Jena (1558). There were several further universities founded before the onset of industrialization where, like all "medieval" universities, their curriculum consisted of Greek and Latin classics and was focused on the study of the Bible. The art of reading, writing, rhetoric, and logic were important fields while ability and utility played a minor role. Universities' traditional tasks were to collect, codify, and teach general knowledge (Carlsson et al. 2009), not to develop any new or useful knowledge.

As a response to the rapid growth of the demand for scientific research and education (Carlsson et al. 2009; Drucker 1998) in the nineteenth century, Germany also saw a wave of universities founded with a technical focus and the adjustment of curricula in already existing universities. The first higher education institutions with a technical focus in Germany were founded in Karlsruhe and Dresden in the early nineteenth century, while the first natural science faculty opened at the University of Tübingen in 1863. Furthermore, there were several technical colleges, known as *Polytechnische Hochschulen* that were upgraded into technical universities around the year 1900. The main political force behind this process was the German Association of Engineers (*Verband Deutscher Ingenieure*, VDI).[5] All technical colleges that became technical universities were located in the capital cities of the federal states (König 2006; Manegold 1989). Again, the federal tradition of Germany implied that such universities were established in smaller cities and not necessarily in places that are the largest agglomerations today. In 1900, there were technical universities in Berlin and Munich but also in Karlsruhe, Dresden, Hannover, Stuttgart, Aachen, Darmstadt, and Braunschweig.

Today, there are many more technical universities in Germany. They represent a specific type of higher education institution that has relatively strong links to (often local) industry. Recent empirical evidence suggests that the entrepreneurial capacity of technical universities is not necessarily higher than that of "classical" universities (Goethner and Wyrwich 2019). But places close to, or even hosting, a technical university that was already present in the year 1900 have a higher level of entrepreneurship in high-tech industries (Audretsch and Lehmann 2005a, b; Fritsch and Wyrwich 2018). As many universities were founded in smaller places, this partly explains why

[5]The main aim of the initiatives to upgrade technical colleges was to overcome the lower social status of engineers as compared to university graduates. Moreover, upgrading technical colleges to technical universities was regarded an important means for improving the education of engineers (König 2006).

in Germany these smaller places (e.g., rural Baden-Württemberg) prosper today, even though they lack the agglomeration advantages that are found to be supportive for entrepreneurship and innovation in countries such as the USA (Glaeser 2011).

In the twentieth century, as was the case in most developed countries, there was a massive expansion of tertiary education in Germany. Therefore, there is no region without a significant university or university of applied science with a focus on educating people for the local labor market (e.g., Jaeger and Kopper 2014).[6] Moreover, the twentieth century saw the proliferation of scientific research institutes and the emergence of networks like the Kaiser Wilhelm Society (1911), the Max Planck Society (1948), and the Fraunhofer Society (1949). Their substantial (public) resources were aimed at further developing basic research with an explicit mandate to also disseminate this knowledge to industry (Gibbons et al. 1994; Beise and Stahl 1999). These networks have now grown into important pillars of Germany's knowledge infrastructure. As for most technical universities, however, the focus in these institutions has long been on serving the needs of large, industrial, incumbent firms. Initiatives to foster entrepreneurship at universities or research institutes did not exist until the late 1990s when the EXIST program was initiated in a few pilot universities.

The EXIST program followed a dual strategy. One building block was supporting universities in developing start-up culture at their institutions, while the other was providing direct assistance for individuals and start-up projects. In support of those activities, universities received a grant from the German Federal Ministry of Economics and Technology over a three-year period (e.g., Kulicke 2014). Although there have not yet been rigorous evaluations, the pilot in Berlin was considered a success, has gone through several revisions and extensions, and is still in operation today (Becker et al. 2011; EXIST 2019).

In conclusion, the German university and educational system mirror its regional decentralization, given that the federal states are responsible for education policy. There are also joint initiatives where the lead is at the federal level. The most famous program is the so-called excellence initiative that was initiated in 2006. Recent evidence suggests that this program was successful in concentrating excellent research. It also promoted collaborations between universities and the non-university research sector. However, it has not caused massive changes to the overall German research system (e.g., Möller et al. 2016). Moreover, a strong tradition of internships and vocational education provides German firms and entrepreneurs with a well-trained and educated workforce at the local level. In contrast to the Anglo-Saxon countries, however, the German university system faces challenges developing into research-oriented universities (Baker and Lenhardt 2008). Universities are mostly teaching-oriented and made universally accessible at low costs for students. This implies, however, that universities are tightly financed out of (state level) tax revenue and have a hard time attracting and retaining (global research) talent. As a consequence, differences in the quality of education and research between German universities are

[6] A university of applied sciences (UAS), also known as a vocational university or *Fachhochschule*, is an institution of higher education that grants professional degrees and is generally more focused on vocational education and applied research.

much less pronounced than in other countries such as France, the UK, or the US. A large part of top-level research takes place outside of the universities in industry and endowed research institutes such as those of the Max Planck Society.

7.1.2.2 The Patent System

Germany has had regional patent systems since the eighteenth century (Harhoff and Hoisl 2007). The first Central German patent office was established in 1877, some six years after Germany became a state. The Imperial Patent Office (*Kaiserliches Patentamt*) provided uniform protection for discoveries in the German Empire. Patents were based on uniform principles and were effective for the entire territory of the German Empire. In the first 13 years of the patent law, there were between 4,000 and 5,000 patents granted per year. This number increased to 10,000 before 1906, and around 13,000 after that of which more than 10% were long-living patents (Burhop 2010). During the separation of the country after World War II, two patenting agencies coexisted, but after reunification, Germany merged them into a single patent institution again.

There have been several changes to patent law over the last 120 years. One of the important recent reforms was the *Arbeitnehmererfindergesetz* in 2001, which was a Bayh–Dole Act-like change in the German patenting system to increase the commercialization of scientific research. The results of this measure, however, are rather mixed (Von Proff et al. 2012; Czarnitzki et al. 2016). Without going into detail on the issue, this can be seen as an example where transferring legal institutions to another context leads to different, perhaps unexpected, outcomes. The USA universities, for which the Bayh–Dole Act was written, operated under a different institutional setting and consequently responded very differently than those in Germany. The *Arbeitnehmererfindergesetz* was perhaps less effective because of the already strong practice of technology transfer from academia to the corporate sector in Germany (Grimpe and Fier 2010). To achieve more commercial exploitation of public research, reforms will have to be better tailored to the German context. The problem with such tailored approaches, however, is that intellectual property rights protection has developed into an international issue. That is not a reason for Germany not to speak out. As a leading industrial nation with a lot of intellectual property at stake, Germany's voice in European and international negotiations governing intellectual property carries significant weight and will be heeded. It is in the interest of Germany to push for reforms that ensure a solid protection of industrial innovations but also ensures continued access to the more generic types of knowledge (e.g., gene sequencing) that industrial innovation builds upon.

7.1.3 Development of Financial Institutions

The financial system in Germany is characterized by a complex network of financial intermediaries and a, rather dominant, three-pillar banking sector. The three sets of banks comprise the private banking sector (publicly traded and held banks like Deutsche Bank and Commerzbank), the mutual or cooperative credit unions (*Genossenschaften*), and the system of public banks consisting of local savings-and-loan banks (*Sparkassen*) and the federal state banks (*Landesbanken*), respectively. The federal state banks fulfill wholesale banking services to the savings-and-loan banks, such as taking the role of regional clearing houses for liquidity and transfer liquidity from those banks with an excess liquidity to members with less. Hence, these financial institutions already have a system of joint liability like in a banking union (Hackethal 2004).[7]

Again, this situation has evolved historically. The roots of the German banking system can be traced to the Fugger family in Renaissance Augsburg (1367). The oldest, still operating bank in Germany is the Berenberg Bank founded in 1590. The fine-grained network of local banks in Germany today has its origins in the late eighteenth century (Allen and Gale 2000; Kindleberger 2015). During the nineteenth century, savings banks spread across the country. They played a decisive role in financing the industrialization of Germany. The first credit unions originated in the mid-nineteenth century. The focus of these cooperatives was on traders, shop owners, and artisans or they were set up in rural areas to serve the needs of agrarian communities. Credit cooperatives were widespread in nineteenth-century Germany and by 1914 the ca. 19,000 credit cooperatives had issued around 7% of all banking liabilities. Guinanne (2001) explains their success from their ability to make use of superior information and their capacity to impose cheap but effective sanctions on potential defaulters. These characteristics presumably permitted credit unions to lend to clients to whom commercial banks typically did not provide credits and also to develop loan terms closer to the needs of the borrowers (Flögel 2018; Flögel and Gärtner 2018).

Today, there are still 423 savings banks and 1,116 cooperative credit unions. Savings banks and credit unions typically foster close and long-term relationships with their local clients, particularly the small and medium-sized companies in which they often have seats on the corporate supervisory board (Herrmann 2020). The savings banks and cooperative banks provide about two-thirds of all lending to *Mittelstand* companies and 43% of lending to all companies and households (Audretsch and Lehmann 2016). Therefore, savings banks and credit unions are an important building block for the success of the German *Mittelstand*.[8] When it comes to innovative

[7] In addition, the federal state banks secure market funding by issuing bonds. They are also internationally operating wholesale and investment banks. Therefore, they follow a business model different from savings banks.

[8] Although there is no "official" definition of the *Mittelstand*, one can say that it comprises firms with between 50 and not much more than 500 employees where the owner is involved in the management or at least in strategic decisions (Pahnke and Welter 2018). Hence, the *Mittelstand* is part of the

new start-ups, however, banks are typically more hesitant to invest. Innovative start-ups, also in Germany, have to rely on venture capital to finance capital-intensive high-risk projects. Empirical evidence shows that the market for venture capital in Germany is functioning relatively well (Fritsch and Schilder 2008, 2012). It remains much smaller in size and scope than in the Anglo-Saxon world, but this is arguably not a supply but a demand issue (Herrmann 2020).[9]

The German financial system, with its many small and locally well-connected banks serving many SMEs across the country, has coevolved with the German economy. It serves the needs of the decentralized, export-oriented, and industrial economy of organically growing medium-sized industrial firms and *Mittelstand*. Typically, thanks to their cooperation on corporate governance boards, such firms have long-standing relationships with their banks that use the relationship and trust as collateral and security for credit.

In conclusion, despite some important challenges in flagship banks like the Deutsche Bank and the Commerzbank, the German financial system remains quite decentralized and still has a significant share of small-scale relationship banking. Thereby, it can finance incremental innovation in existing firms but is perhaps a less favorable environment for more radical innovation by new entrants as it supplies little capital in the form of equity to newcomers. The financial system thus consolidates Germany's conservatism, while underpinning its competitive strength in high-quality incremental innovation.

7.1.4 Labor Institutions

The labor force in Germany is generally well trained and very productive, justifying high wage incomes while maintaining a strong international competitive position. Strong vocational education combined with on-the-job training promotes the accumulation of firm-specific human capital in Germany's small and medium-sized high-tech industrial sector (Herrmann 2020). Consensus-oriented labor relations support moderate wage growth while firm-specific human capital investments yield high productivity growth (e.g., Soskice 1990). German export-oriented firms thus remain competitive in global markets with high quality, high value-added products and services. But this peace and high level of investment are based on generous social security and stringent labor protection. It is important to realize that these institutions have long historical roots and coevolved with the German economy into highly complementary and interconnecting institutions that support its traditional competitive strength.

SME sector. Many firms of the *Mittelstand* are family entities that have been passed on within the family for several generations.

[9]German entrepreneurs have been found to be reluctant to give up control rights and therefore prefer organic growth and private ownership over a heavy reliance on external equity finance. One could argue that this has also led to a regulatory framework that makes this type of investment less attractive (see, e.g., Fiedler and Hellman 2001; Franzke et al. 2003).

7.1.4.1 Employment Protection

The German system of employment protection obtained its modern form during the period of the German miracle (*Wirtschaftswunder*) in the 1950s and 1960s in the Federal Republic of Germany. This was the golden era of the so-called *Normalarbeitsverhältnis* (standard employment relationship) which describes a dependent, permanent full-time job with strict dismissal protection, a full integration into status-protecting social insurance and collectively set wages at a relatively high level (Eichhorst and Marx 2011).

The West German system implied high wages for insiders but also led to underutilization of the labor force, which is reflected, for example, by low labor force participation of women and a male-breadwinner family model. Such a system comes under pressure when women push into the labor market (Esping-Andersen 2002), especially after German reunification where about 90% of all women in working age were full-time employees in the former East Germany (Maier 1993).[10] This system gave industrial producers a strong incentive to invest in productivity growth, but high wages and non-wage labor costs proved less suitable for developing a modern, labor-intensive service sector (Eichhorst and Marx 2011). Moreover, demographic changes put a heavy burden on the economy to finance the generous pension system. Reforms were deemed necessary to increase the utilization of all labor resources.

The change in the labor market structure, however, did not come along with a systematic flexibilization of the rigid *Normalarbeitsverhältnis*. Rather, a second-tier labor market consisting of atypical and much less protected employment (e.g., part-time work, marginal employment) emerged. Streeck (1997) argues that this pattern is explained by the German manufacturing system that is based on "diversified quality production." This model requires labor with highly specialized skills and enables workforces—thanks to their long-standing experience within one firm—to come up with incremental innovations and improvements that translate into high-quality products and specialization in niche markets. Tight employment protection incentivizes employees to invest in the necessary firm-specific skills, which would otherwise become sunk costs in case of a job loss (Herrmann 2020).[11]

In the mid-1990s, the firm size threshold for dismissal protection was raised from 5 to 10 employees (Eichhorst and Marx 2011), and Bauernschuster (2013) found a positive effect on hiring by small firms of this reform. The duality between well-protected insiders and precariously employed outsiders in the labor market, however, persists in larger firms and the new threshold still represents a penalty on employment growth.

[10]There is still an East-West gap in terms of female labor force participation in the year 2015. However, recent analyses show that only about 40% of that difference can be attributed to the effect of the socialist system (Wyrwich 2017). The rest is due to other factors.

[11]This explanation is perfectly in line with basic human capital theory (Becker 1964). See Hall and Soskice (2001) for further explanations on the relationship between employment regulation and incremental versus radical innovation.

7.1.4.2 Wage Bargaining

The relatively high wage costs in Germany are also institutionalized in a system of collective wage bargaining. Unions played an important role in the first decades after World War II in West Germany and wages were collectively set (Soskice 1990).[12] There was some modest flexibilization in collective bargaining (e.g., single enterprise exceptions, the introduction of working time accounts) since the 1980s. With reunification, the West-German model was extended to the East and the system remained relatively stable for standard employment contracts (Eichhorst and Marx 2011; Dustmann et al. 2014). Despite low and declining union membership, in the 2000s, still, some 60–70% of all employees were covered by collective agreements and such coverage still implied significant wage premia (Kohaut and Schnabel 2007; Burda et al. 2008; Fitzenberger et al. 2013; Kluge and Weber 2018). The contrast between marginal workers in precarious employment and the well-protected and covered insiders has increased in recent decades (Brady and Biegert 2017). Entrepreneurs have more or less equal access to the latter pool of labor, but face high wage and non-wage labor costs when recruiting from the high-quality segments. A potentially important recent development is the broadly supported introduction of a minimum wage in 2015 of at that time EUR 8.50/h (Burda 2016).[13] Its effect on the flow of labor resources to entrepreneurship is unclear and not yet empirically investigated.

7.1.4.3 Social Security

Social security also has a long tradition in Germany. The introduction of social insurance dates back to an initiative by von Bismarck in the 1880s, which implied the implementation of the first social security net in the world. The Compulsory Health Insurance Act of 1883 can be regarded as the starting point of this system. This was followed by the Accident Insurance Act (1884) and the Disability/Old-age Pension System Act (1891). Arguably, the build-up of a social security system enabled von Bismarck to pacify the threat of class struggle and create loyalty to the new state (Rimlinger 1968; Pflanze 2014). The German social security system around this time became a blueprint for Germany's current health system and was a role model for many insurance systems in other countries (Abrams 2007; Weichlein 2011; Bauernschuster et al. 2019).

The social insurance system underwent several reforms and extensions since the 1880s. Unemployment insurance was introduced in 1927. Finally, care insurance was set up in 1995. The current pension system is based on a reform in 1957 and follows a pay-as-you-go defined-benefit design. There are also state-supported private pension schemes. These were introduced in the early 2000s to make up for the demographic

---

[12]The wage agreements are negotiated at the sector level between labor unions and employers' associations. The negotiations are at the regional level (so-called *Tarifbezirk*).

[13]There have been sector-based minimum wages already in the 2000s. In the West-German construction sector, a minimum wage became effective in 1997.

transition that implies fewer contributors in the pay-as-you-go scheme face a growing number of retired people.

A significant reform of the unemployment insurance was associated with the "Agenda 2010." It was a shift from policies that were rather generous toward an approach with stricter job search monitoring, harsher sanctioning of unemployment provisions, and a reduction in the duration of job training. Another element of the reform was to combine the earnings-related and means-tested unemployment assistance with the social assistance (*Sozialhilfe*) into a new support system called *Arbeitslosengeld II*. This transfer can be regarded as a step toward a more universal minimum income support scheme (Eichhorst and Marx 2011). The regulation also came with new active labor market policy tools to promote start-ups by the unemployed (*Ich AG*/"Me Inc."). The evidence on the success of these measures to date is mixed (Zöllner et al. 2018). While some do succeed in leaving the program and generate an income, most of these start-ups are not very innovative and have low growth potential.

7.1.5 Recent Entrepreneurship Policies in Germany

7.1.5.1 Entrepreneurship in Divided Germany: 1945–1989

Before reunification, the post-war "German model" can be described as a rather distinctive kind of capitalist economy that was governed by national social institutions yielding high international competitiveness despite high wages and low dispersion with respect to inequality of incomes and living standards (Streeck 1997). A defining feature of the German model is the existence of the *Mittelstand*. Audretsch and Lehmann (2016) argue that *Mittelstand* firms represent a sort of "main street entrepreneurship" of decades-old, family-owned firms with strong linkages and social ties to their local communities, including banks. These firms attract and retain specifically skilled employees, for example, by local apprentice programs. They also often have close ties with local banks providing them with financial resources. These ties are legally in the form of loans and credit, but long relations and trust enable firms to also approach banks for financing intrapreneurial ventures and innovative projects. Their products are successful in niche markets.

Public policy strongly promoted the German SMEs (including the *Mittelstand*) in the post-war period. The state-owned *Kreditanstalt für Wiederaufbau* (KfW) provided finance for the development of technological capabilities of SMEs (e.g., long-term investment loans as well as working capital loans). The KfW measures can be regarded as small business but to a much lesser extent as entrepreneurship policies. Policy programs directly targeted at start-ups played a rather minor role in the policy menu in the post-war decades.

In contrast, in socialist East Germany, *Mittelstand* and entrepreneurship were dubbed a bourgeois anachronism (Fritsch and Wyrwich 2016, p. 263). There were many outright anti-entrepreneurship policies, such as the massive expropriation of all private industrial firms in 1972. Private business ownership was very much confined to small craft enterprises and private shops in East Germany and self-employment fell from 20.4% in 1955 to 1.8% in 1989 (Pickel 1992; Wyrwich 2012). Consequently, the *Mittelstand* had largely disappeared in the East by 1989 (Fritsch et al. 2014).

7.1.5.2 Entrepreneurship and Entrepreneurship Policy after Unification

In the 1990s, the self-employment rates were steadily increasing in West Germany, partly reflecting the increased role of service but also the fundamental shift toward a more entrepreneurial society. In East Germany, the level of self-employment converged to Western levels and reached parity around the year 2005 (Welter 2007a; Fritsch et al. 2014). Interestingly, in areas that had already a high level of entrepreneurship in the pre-socialist period, the entrepreneurial catch-up was particularly pronounced (Wyrwich 2012; Fritsch and Wyrwich 2014).

Despite convergence in the numbers, however, East German businesses tend to be much smaller, even 20 years after reunification. One reason is their comparatively low levels of productivity and much lower survival rates (Fackler 2014). There are several explanations for this weakness of East German companies, ranging from unfavorable economic framework conditions to lacking managerial and entrepreneurial skills among East German entrepreneurs (Wyrwich 2013). Furthermore, East German businesses tend to have a strong focus on regional markets and their export orientation is rather low (IWH 2010; Mattes et al. 2015).

In an attempt to also support start-ups in East and West, the KfW began creating programs, such as the *Eigenkapitalhilfe-Programm* which consisted of subordinated capital for (young) entrepreneurs. In 2010, the *Bundesministerium für Wirtschaft und Energie* (BMWi) implemented *INVEST—Zuschuss für Wagniskapital* and the *Mikromezzaninfonds-Deutschland* to strengthen and develop the entrepreneurial culture of Germany. The former provides a subsidy of 20% for venture capital, whereas the latter provides specific support for unemployed persons, women, or migrants in creative industries (Audretsch et al. 2007). Bøggild et al. (2011) show that these programs yielded both an increase in competitiveness and innovativeness for subsidized start-ups as well as generated positive employment effects. Overall, BMWi-policy initiatives include the provision of information on self-employment (e.g., by participating in the *Gründerwoche Deutschland*), special measures to strengthen interest in entrepreneurship in the education system, and the improvement of the financing options available for innovative start-ups. Under the umbrella of the *Gründerland Deutschland Initiative*, the BMWi also provides an online portal to make all information available to the public and provides young ICT entrepreneurs with means for a stay in innovative regions such as Silicon Valley under the *German Accelerator* program.[14]

In addition to these federal initiatives, the German *Länder* (states) are also quite active in developing entrepreneurship promotion programs at the regional level (Welter 2007b). In East Germany, such initiatives often relied massively on European Structural Funds which were relatively generous in view of the low GDP per capita of the East German *Länder*. It is noteworthy that there is a huge heterogeneity across the *Länder* in promoting entrepreneurship. It is particularly Bavaria in West Germany and Saxony in East Germany that developed multifaceted programs to promote innovative entrepreneurship (Fritsch et al. 2010, 2015).

Finally, at the local level, some municipalities and districts focus on the development of the entrepreneurial culture within their region. Here, the main players include business associations, chambers of commerce, economic development departments, and business development agencies. An example for local funding initiatives is the *GÖBI-fonds* (*Göttinger Fonds für örtliche Beschäftigungsinitiativen*). Established in 1997, it constitutes one of the first cases of public–private collaboration at the regional level, where banking institutions were involved. Targeting unemployed and young entrepreneurs, the *Fonds* was organized in such a way that the banks would provide the funding, while the regional government would bear 50% of the default risk and (thus) would subsidize the interest rate.

Although the three levels of policy regulation aim at closely integrating their respective instruments, inconsistencies and incoherence across these levels are a real danger. For example, most state programs do not consider part-time entrepreneurship to be desirable, arguing that this type of entrepreneurship tends to contribute little to economic and employment growth, whereas at the federal level, part-time entrepreneurship is supported and recognized as a potential first step to full-time self-employment and eventual business formation.

These programs have of course been evaluated, but it is difficult to ascertain their true impact. It would also take us beyond the scope of this chapter to attempt an assessment here. At this point, we can conclude that Germany's policy makers at various levels are clearly highly interested in promoting a more adventurous and radically innovative form of entrepreneurial venturing.

7.1.6 Conclusions

Germany's turbulent history of division and unification had a big impact on the country, its institutions and inhabitants. After World War II, the entire country experienced an institutional reset: while informal institutions persisted, East and West Germany set off on diverging trajectories on formal institutions.

[14]There have been further measures within the framework of the *Gründerland Deutschland Initiative* that are not active in 2018 anymore. For example, the *Gründerwettbewerb—IKT Innovative* which consisted of a contest for young entrepreneurs in the ICT industry.

The West developed its own unique model of capitalism, with moderate wage growth, high productivity growth driven by on-the-job learning, and firm-specific skill accumulation. This supported an export-oriented industry built on the historic legacy of strongly regionally embedded *Mittelstand*, financed by a regionally branched bank-based financial system, also fueled by science and knowledge developed in technical universities as well as institutes.

In the East, meanwhile, the socialist doctrine led to the destruction of the *Mittelstand*, while massive migration to the West before the building of the Wall contributed to depriving East Germany of a significant part of its entrepreneurial talent. Importantly, the experiment with central planning failed and the East German economy collapsed, whereas the West grew into the economic powerhouse of Europe.

Now, at 30 years after reunification and in spite of enormous efforts, the socioeconomic gap between East and West Germany has still not been bridged (Canova and Ravn 2000; Lindner 2017; Mertes 2018; Verheyen 2018). Against this backdrop, it is impossible to treat Germany as a blank canvas. Hence, we suggest policies and reforms that fit its historical heritage, consider its federal character and multi-level governance, and build on Germany's strengths in order to address weaknesses within the German entrepreneurial ecosystem. To identify these weaknesses, the next section turns to the present and examines current data.

7.2 Step 2: Data Analysis with REDI for Germany

7.2.1 Germany's International Position

To get a first impression of Germany's relative performance as an entrepreneurial ecosystem, we turn to the Regional Entrepreneurship and Development Index (REDI). For calculating an overall country score, we used the population weighted regional REDI-scores. Out of the 24 EU countries for which we have this regional data, Germany ranks seventh with 51.1 points between Finland and Austria, behind Ireland, the Scandinavian countries, The Netherlands, and the UK, but ahead of France and all the Southern and Central European countries (Table 3.3, Varga et al. 2020). This implies that the German competitive position in the European Union is supported by its strong, regionally embedded *Mittelstand* and incremental innovation system (Audretsch and Lehmann 2016). To identify where reforms would help to improve its performance, however, we need to delve a little deeper into where the entrepreneurial ecosystem in Germany could be improved.

The REDI is composed of 14 underlying pillars that together make up three subindices, namely (1) Entrepreneurial Attitudes, (2) Entrepreneurial Abilities, and (3) Entrepreneurial Aspirations (Acs et al. 2014; Szerb et al. 2017, 2019). Figure 7.1 gives us a first glance at how Germany is performing relative to the UK, Italy, and the EU average on these 14 pillars. The data show that Germany overall performs better

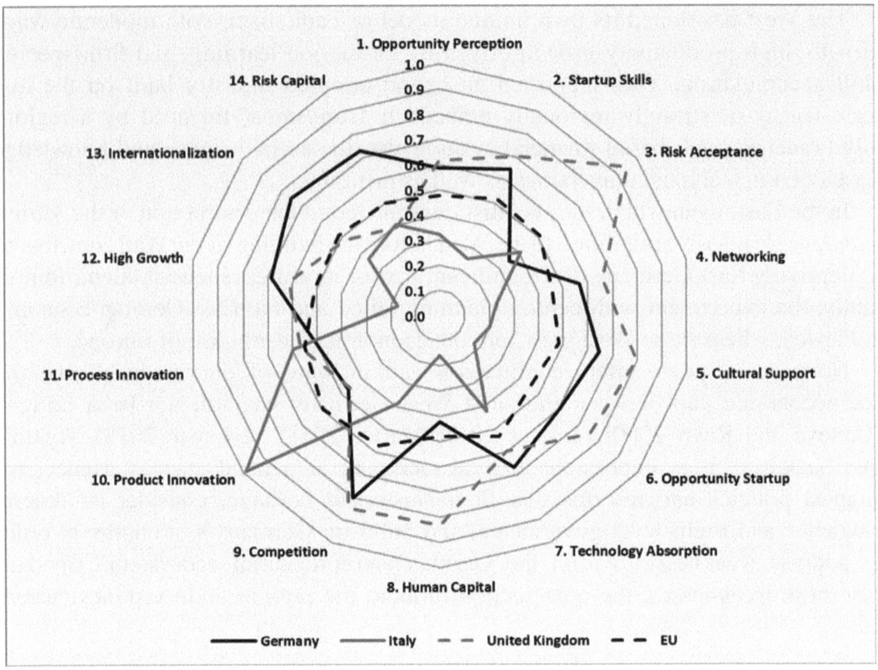

Fig. 7.1 Radar-plot REDI comparison Germany–Italy–UK and EU-average. *Source* Authors' own compilation

than the EU average and only slightly underperforms the EU average on four pillars, namely "Risk Acceptance," "Human Capital," and, perhaps surprisingly, "Product," and "Process Innovation."

The underlying algorithm in the REDI puts a penalty on bottlenecks in the ecosystem (Acs et al. 2014; Szerb et al. 2017), such that a rounder radar-plot scores higher than a more erratic one. This reflects the intuition that all pillars in the index are complementary and the ecosystem is only as effective as its weakest link. To increase the REDI-score and improve the ecosystem performance, policy interventions should therefore be aimed at alleviating bottlenecks with priority. For Germany, and based on the data, one would conclude that improving the "Risk Acceptance," "Human Capital," "Product Innovation," and "Process Innovation" pillars is most urgent.

7.2.2 A More Detailed Regional Quick Scan

A national-level analysis, however, will hide a lot of regional heterogeneity. Bottlenecks in Hamburg and Berlin may well prove to be very different from the bottlenecks in Brandenburg and Hessen. Before we draw too strong a conclusion on how to improve the German entrepreneurial ecosystem, let us therefore zoom in at the regional level.

In Fig. 7.2 and Table 7.1, we observe that there is quite some variation among German regions. The REDI-scores range between 35 (Brandenburg) and 70 (Hamburg).[15] The map and table illustrate that even at this low spatial resolution, the aggregated REDI-scores capture quite a bit of the regional heterogeneity.

Without going into technical details in this chapter, the intuition behind each of the pillars is that data on individual entrepreneurial agency (taken from the Global Entrepreneurship Monitor adult population survey data) are combined with relevant institutional quality indicators (taken from a wide variety of reputed international

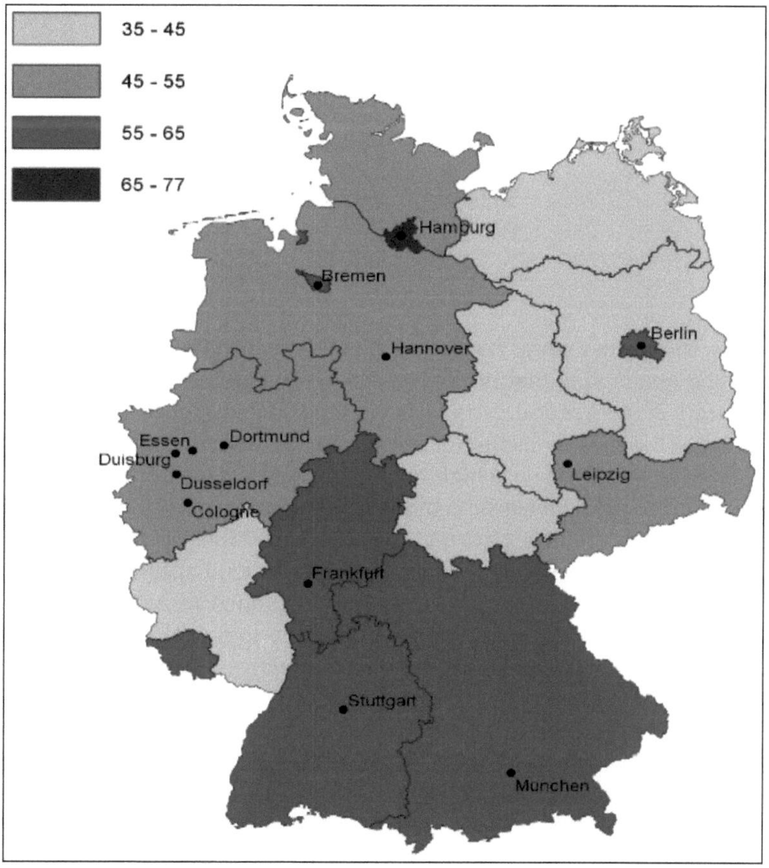

Fig. 7.2 REDI map of German NUTS2/3 regions. *Source* Authors' own compilation

[15]The numbers are index numbers ranging from 0 (worst) to 100 (best) across all 125 European NUTS2/3 regions for 2012–2014.

Table 7.1 REDI-scores Germany

Region	REDI-scores 2012–2014
Baden-Württemberg	62.0
Bayern	60.6
Berlin	62.4
Brandenburg	35.1
Bremen	57.1
Hamburg	69.5
Hessen	58.9
Mecklenburg-Vorpommern	40.2
Niedersachsen	50.3
Nordrhein-Westfalen	54.8
Rheinland-Pfalz	44.6
Saarland	56.7
Sachsen	50.5
Sachsen-Anhalt	38.2
Schleswig-Holstein	49.8
Thüringen	41.1

Source Authors' own compilation

institutions, such as the World Bank, Freedom House, and OECD).[16] The index then builds on the assumption that institutions and individual agency are complements (Acs and Szerb 2009; Acs et al. 2014). That is, for example, high levels of Opportunity Perception in a low-quality institutional environment will contribute little. Likewise, low Opportunity Perception in a high-quality institutional environment is also a sign of weakness in the entrepreneurial ecosystem. To improve the score on a given pillar, policies and reforms should seek to improve the weakest link and then aim to increase both institutional quality and individual agency together. Especially because of the latter, the menu of effective interventions is not limited to improving the scores on the institutional quality indices alone. The same logic is then also imposed on the individual pillars that make up the three subindices: Attitudes, Abilities, and Aspirations.

For all the *Länder*, we have identified those three pillars that are holding back the respective *Land* most. We then compared the *Länder* and identified the most common weak spots in regional ecosystems. The results, presented in Table 7.2, provide some clear-cut insights.

Across the best and the weakest entrepreneurial ecosystems in Germany, bottlenecks seem to arise most frequently with regard to Business Risk, which will reduce the score on Risk Acceptance and thereby Entrepreneurial Attitudes. On Entrepreneurial Abilities, the overall scores are decreased by low Human Capital

[16]We refer interested readers to Szerb et al. (2017) and the technical annex to Acs and Szerb (2016) for further details.

Table 7.2 Weakest points per region

Region	Weakest pillars	Weakest variables
Hamburg	3, 8, 11	Business Risk, Education and Training, and New Technology
Schleswig-Holstein	3, 8, 10	Business Risk, Education and Training, and New Product
Bremen	3, 8, 13	Business Risk, Education and Training, and Exports
Niedersachsen	3, 7, 10	Business Risk, Technology Level, and New Product
Nordrhein-Westphalen	3, 8, 11	Business Risk, Education and Training, and New Technology
Rheinland-Pfaltz	3, 8, 10	Business Risk, Education and Training, Educational Level, and New Product
Hessen	3, 8, 10	Business Risk, Education and Training, and New Product
Saarland	3, 8, 11	Business Risk, Risk Perception, Education and Training, and New Technology
Baden-Württemberg	3, 8, 10	Business Risk, Education and Training, and New Product
Bayern	3, 8, 10	Business Risk, Education and Training, and New Product
Thüringen	1, 8, 11	Market Agglomeration, Education and Training, Educational Level, and New Technology
Sachsen-Anhalt	1, 8, 10	Market Agglomeration, Education and Training, and New Product
Sachsen	3, 8, 10	Business Risk, Risk Perception, Education and Training, and New Product
Brandenburg	3, 7, 10	Business Risk, Technology Level, and New Product
Berlin	3, 8, 10	Business Risk, Education and Training, and New Product
Mecklenburg-Vorpommern	1, 8, 14	Market Agglomeration, Education and Training, and Informal Investment

Source Authors' own compilation

scores due to a lack of Education and Training, whereas a lack of New Product or New Technology in Product or Process Innovation generally holds back the overall performance on Entrepreneurial Aspirations. Despite significant heterogeneity across the German *Länder*, there certainly seems to be room for national-level interventions and reforms in these areas.

At the regional level, the *Länder* may well add specific interventions to strengthen specific regional weaknesses and bottlenecks, given in particular that it does not seem necessary to equally develop all pillars in all regions.

7.2.3 Overall Conclusions of the REDI Analysis

Our interpretation of the data above reveals that in all German *Länder*, and the country as a whole, the main bottlenecks in the entrepreneurial ecosystem are a limited willingness to take risk (Business Risk), an education system that can be improved (Education and Training), and a lack of radical innovation (New Products and Technology) that feeds back into a low familiarity with ambitious entrepreneurship.

As the simulation exercises in Varga et al. (2020) have shown, improving the scores on REDI in Germany would have positive effects on productivity and well-being in all regions, even if some would benefit more than others. At this point, however, it is not quite clear exactly how one could go about engineering such an improvement in the German entrepreneurial ecosystems. We know it is the bottlenecks that hold down scores, and consequently, improving on those is probably the most cost-effective way of improving the system as a whole. But a lot of research remains to be done on how exactly policy interventions and reforms would affect the various variables and pillars underlying REDI.

Moreover, it is not advised to draw conclusions exclusively on the basis of data and aggregate indices, even if they are composed of a broad set of sub-indicators. It is not yet clear from the data exactly what could be done to improve the situation or how interventions could be made to fit local specificities. Only after triangulating the results above with the historical analysis, literature review, expert judgment, and qualitative survey results below, we can map propose tailored reforms for Germany.

7.3 Step 3: Triangulating History, Data, and Survey Results

7.3.1 Venture Creation Processes in Germany

As illustrated in Herrmann (2020), we assessed the impact of Germany's institutional ecosystem upon entrepreneurial activities from both a static perspective (based on multiannual averages) and from a process-oriented perspective. Both sets of analyses provide similar and complementary results. The static analyses confirmed that entrepreneurs in Germany have a tendency to set up incrementally innovative ventures rather than to develop ventures based on radically innovative technologies or the imitation of existing business ideas (Dilli et al. 2018; Herrmann 2019).

The dynamic analyses, in turn, revealed how Germany's institutional environment influences different aspects of the venture creation process. With regard to human capital, we find that entrepreneurs in Germany, who begin to set up their ventures in part-time, are less likely to transition to full-time entrepreneurship than their counterparts in the UK or the USA. The reason seems related to Germany's regulated labor market which, in case of venture failure, makes it rather difficult for entrepreneurs to obtain a position in dependent employment. Entrepreneurs are reluctant to give up dependent employment and set up their ventures in part-time (Held 2019). In addition, entrepreneurs in Germany are unwilling or unable to hire employees and rather engage external service providers in order to access qualified labor (Held et al. 2018c).

With regard to the process of finance acquisition, Held et al. (2018a) find that various venture characteristics influence the type of funding which nascent venture acquire first and, respectively, most. These characteristics include the type of good that a venture develops, its product's novelty, size, industry, but also its institutional environment. With regard to the latter, Germany's entrepreneurs are particularly likely to make up for a low stock market capitalization by seeking debt finance, making use of the well-developed banking system instead (Held et al. 2018a).

Finally, we also find that nascent ventures in Germany are more likely to engage in R&D collaborations with external partners, such as universities and labs, than nascent ventures in the UK or the USA. The reason for this seems to be that nascent ventures are reluctant to engage in joint R&D projects whenever the institutions governing inter-firm collaborations make the outcome of lawsuits in case of IP conflicts rather unpredictable (Held et al. 2018b).

Taken together, these studies suggest that Germany's distinct finance, labor, and R&D-related institutions lead entrepreneurs to focus on incrementally innovative business ideas.

7.3.2 Regulatory Barriers to Entrepreneurship in Germany

To examine regulatory barriers to entrepreneurship, we conducted interviews with 313 founders in Germany, between 2015 and 2018. Table 7.3 provides an overview of the answers given to the question: "Which regulatory requirements did you perceive as major obstacles during venture creation?" coded to also compare the answers across countries. The table suggests that an important number of German founders did not feel constrained by regulatory barriers. Among those regulatory obstacles that were mentioned most, founders often pointed to difficulties with various aspects of administrative processes. With regard to the acquisition of labor, capital, or knowledge, only very few founders pointed to the problem of "high taxes" which, in turn, might indicate that founders considered financial constraints less important.

These findings are overall in line with the REDI analysis which indeed indicated that regulatory barriers were not the most pressing problem. In contrast, other sources and rankings, such as the World Bank's Doing Business Index (World Bank 2018a), mention regulatory barriers to starting up as a matter of concern in Germany. Part of the answer to this paradox could be that regulatory barriers are significant in Germany

Table 7.3 Results survey on regulatory obstacles in Germany

Which regulatory requirements did you perceive as major obstacles during venture creation?	Times mentioned	In %
None	130	41.0
Does not answer question	32	10.1
Stringent environmental regulations	18	5.7
Regulatory requirements for buildings	12	3.8
Bureaucracy in general	11	3.5
Specific requirements related to energy sector	10	3.2
Legal requirements for approval	10	3.2
Onerous requirements for documentation	10	3.2
Tax laws in general	8	2.5
Legal requirement to be member of IHK	7	2.2
Lengthy approval process	5	1.6
Registration procedure	5	1.6
Difficulties with obtaining finance	5	1.6
Employment regulations which hamper ability to hire employees	5	1.6
High taxes in early phases of venture creation	4	1.3
Legal initial capital requirements	4	1.3
Constantly changing regulatory environment	4	1.3
Difficulties with transition of legal form	3	0.9
Insecurity about details of law	3	0.9

Note
1. Based on interviews with 313 founders mentioning 317 obstacles (more than one obstacle could be mentioned)
2. Only obstacles mentioned three times or more are reported in the table
Source Authors' own compilation

but perceived to be justified and unproblematic by the founders that actually overcame them. Moreover, strict regulation, provided it is clear and fair, can also prevent the entry of less viable and low-quality entrepreneurs (Stenholm et al. 2013).

When looking at the top-10 obstacles more closely, we see that founders confirm the problem of a cumbersome bureaucracy. But only some (<5%) mention bureaucracy and complicated legal and regulatory requirements as a real obstacle to start a firm. From our survey, we thus get the impression that barriers to entry in Germany could be alleviated by reducing the administrative requirements for venture creation. That is confirmed by the fact that Germany ranks 113 out of 190 in the World Bank (2018a) Doing Business Index on "ease of starting a firm."

7.3.3 Founders' Suggestions for Reforms in Germany

In the same survey, founders were also asked: "What can policy makers do to facilitate venture creation?". An overview of the answers to this question is listed in Table 7.4. While an important share of the founders interviewed still thinks that policy makers cannot facilitate venture creation, the most common suggestions point to measures of financial support. This is remarkable in light of the fact that financial barriers were rarely mentioned as a regulatory obstacle. Similarly, financial constraints do not come out very strongly in the data analyses of Sect. 7.2 nor in the historical analysis of Sect. 7.1.

Two other suggestions stand out. In slightly different wordings, the founders suggest a simplification of procedures, which in itself need not make regulations less tight, only more transparent and easier to follow. And, again, in different ways, they argue that the government could promote venture creation by allowing founders to benefit more from the venture they create. Although, not strongly and perfectly, Germany's founders clearly identified some of the same weaknesses in the entrepreneurial ecosystem that our above data analysis revealed. Recall that the weaknesses of the REDI analysis revealed a low score on the pillars "Risk Acceptance," "Education and Training," and "Product Innovation." The founders' suggestions about better networking opportunities, the stimulation of a more entrepreneurial culture, and general need for more support resonate with those weaknesses, but the founders did not mention a lack of knowledge, absorptive capacity, or a lack of new product and process technology. The latter might be explained by survival bias in sampling, such that the surveyed founders may find themselves in a vibrant entrepreneurial scene and perceive a strong ecosystem where only external constraints hold venturing back. Interestingly, the survey reveals founders' frustration with the regulatory framework and bureaucracy that the REDI-analysis is ill equipped to reveal.

Rather unsurprisingly, the policies suggested are all action-oriented, whereby financial instruments are typically top-of-mind, also for founders. This may explain the high share of recommendations that suggest to supporting start-ups and new ventures financially—even though capital did not seem to be a major barrier to venturing in Germany in the REDI analysis. Those founders signaling a lack of information and training and calling for a more stable policy environment can be interpreted in support of a more fundamental reform approach that creates institutional support for those providing such services and knowledge.

When calling for lower taxation and higher financial support for founders, we should of course be very cautious. Nobody likes to pay taxes, and founders are no exception. Still, perhaps founders' complaints are not unjustified in this case. Even if Germany's founders strongly benefit from a public-funded infrastructure—including, for example, a well-developed transportation system, public incubators, and entrepreneurial support programs like the EXIST initiative—the level of taxation and social security contributions out of total profits is estimated to be about 50% (World Bank 2018a) in Germany, and on "paying taxes" Germany ranks 41 out of

Table 7.4 Results survey on suggested policies in Germany

In your view, what could policy makers do to facilitate venture creation?	Times mentioned	In %
Nothing	37	9.5
Does not answer question	30	7.7
Facilitate financing for small businesses	89	22.9
Reduce bureaucracy	39	10.1
Avoid constant policy changes	28	7.2
Provide competent advice to people starting businesses	24	6.2
Improve situation specific to energy sector	23	5.9
Reduce tax rates for small businesses	20	5.2
Provide better information about how to start a business	18	4.6
Provide better training to people for starting businesses	13	3.4
Simplify tax laws	12	3.1
Clear regulations	10	2.6
More flexible tax law adjustable to liquidity of start-up	10	2.6
Provide guidance	9	2.3
Provide incentives for hiring people	9	2.3
Reduce costs	9	2.3
Financial benefits for founder	9	2.3
Facilitate procedures for approval	8	2.1
Create feeling of support for entrepreneurs	5	1.3
Abolish compulsory membership in IHK	5	1.3
Reduce initial capital requirement	4	1.0
Offset risk of starting business	4	1.0
Simplify regulatory requirements for buildings	4	1.0
Simplify venture creation process	3	0.8
Provide better networking opportunities	3	0.8
Create entrepreneurial culture	3	0.8
Adjust tax system to encompass start-ups	3	0.8
Help market start-ups	3	0.8
Ease environmental regulations	3	0.8

Note
1. Based on interviews with 313 founders mentioning 455 suggestions (more than one suggestion could be mentioned)
2. Only suggestions mentioned three times or more are reported in the table
Source Authors' own compilation

190. Concerning financial support for founders, there are already quite a lot of public programs for entrepreneurship and it is doubtful whether even more support would be helpful.

7.3.4 Conclusions

The analysis in this section confirms some, but not all of the weaknesses identified in the REDI analysis completed in Step 2. Moreover, it provides some revealing additional insights, for example, the need to create a stable regulatory framework, and the suggestion that overall taxation on new ventures is perhaps too high. Such information is hard to gather from quantitative data or historical analyses. The more qualitative analysis presented in this step was therefore useful to complement the results obtained in Sects. 7.1 and 7.2. But given the limited perspective that most founders have, the proposed interventions typically fall in the "inform, deregulate, subsidize-more and tax-less" approach that has characterized entrepreneurship policies around the world already for decades. When asked for the most important barriers and additional policy measures, it is only logical that founders would mention those barriers and proposals that they perceived as most important in their personal experiences and direct environment. There certainly is valuable information in that experience. But as a guide to policy, this is not sufficient, as is an approach based on history or aggregate data only. The true value of this information is revealed when combined with information from other sources. Together, the insights gained from triangulating our historical, quantitative, and qualitative information on Germany now reveal enough information to formulate a "diagnosis" for Germany and propose our "treatments."

7.4 Step 4: Mapping onto the FIRES-Reform Proposals

Formulating a reform strategy to strengthen the entrepreneurial ecosystem is similar to treating a patient. In the previous sections, we have considered the medical history of the patient, used advanced diagnostic tools to scan for her health problems, and asked the patient how they feel and what they believe would be a good treatment. Based on this information, we can now come up with a diagnosis and map this diagnosis onto the menu of available treatments in order to propose a treatment that fits the patient.

In general, Germany boasts a strong entrepreneurial ecosystem. Like in most other countries, there are hotbeds of entrepreneurship in major cities alongside more rural regions. The geographic resolution of our data reveals that Germany's entrepreneurial talent and resources arguably tend to cluster in its major cities. But given that these cities are themselves spread across the country, this is also the case for entrepreneurship in Germany. Our quantitative data analyses suggested a large regional heterogeneity in entrepreneurial ecosystem performance, whereas for the country as a whole or the regions affected, this does not necessarily constitute a problem.

The results from the surveys do not suffer from this problem and confirm that the challenges and bottlenecks in the German ecosystem are indeed not formidable. Founders suggested that regulation makes the founding of new ventures difficult, especially in green tech and renewable energy sectors. This is confirmed in Germany's rankings on traditional indicators like self-employment and firm formation, especially in high-tech sectors. These show that Germany is lagging in an international comparison. But these concerns do not seem to be overly problematic. Importantly, founders did not complain about a lack of funding, skilled personnel, or knowledge. The data analysis does however reveal that German entrepreneurship is less risk seeking than in the Anglo-Saxon world. New ventures in Germany score comparatively low in radically new products and technology as well as in risk acceptance. Moreover, the rates of self-employment and start-up activity in Germany have been declining and this might be worrisome to a country that is already scoring low on these indicators. Incremental innovation is routine in German industry, but the pillars related to more radical innovation seem the weakest links in an otherwise well developed and functional entrepreneurial ecosystem. This diagnosis roughly holds for the country as a whole and the individual *Länder* separately.

Admittedly, though, it is not easy to change all these aspects together. German preferences for well-designed and (over)engineered solutions, an emphasis on quality over price and a dislike for disruptive technologies that might challenge incumbent firms and unsettle long-grown business relations, are deeply entrenched in the German culture. Furthermore, these even constitute the core of a carefully built and cherished "made in Germany" brand and reputation. It is thus important not to advise our "German patient" to become a person they are not and do not want to become. Still, a little more adventurous spirit would not hurt and more likely improve Germany's position *vis-a-vis* the competition from East-Asian tiger economies that rival its industrial and engineering dominance. Hence, making it easier to start (and end) a venture and supporting radically innovative entrepreneurship financially could go a long way in improving the entrepreneurial ecosystem in the country and its *Länder*.

Taking these general prescriptions to the menu of policy interventions and reform proposals in the companion volume of this book (Elert et al. 2019), we have selected fifteen suitable interventions for Germany. They are listed in Table 7.5. In Column 1, we find the number under which they were presented in Elert et al. (2019). Column 2 lists the title and Column 3 the proposal, whereas Column 4 gives a brief motivation for the case of Germany tying in with the analysis presented above.

The first proposal (2) refers to intellectual property. We think it is in the interest of the German entrepreneurial society that access to knowledge remains open. Germany is traditionally strong in developing generic knowledge into specific products and services, and IP protection should protect the latter, not the former. But as IP is beyond the competencies of even national authorities, our proposal here is to be

Table 7.5 The FIRES-reform proposals for Germany[a]

No.	Policy area	Proposal	Germany
2	Intellectual property	Limit the breadth, width, and span of patent protection to cover working prototypes and market-ready innovations only for a short period of time and permit economic actors to infringe upon patents that have not been commercialized.	This is an international issue, but it would certainly help if Germany were to advocate this at the appropriate levels, because Germany is an important player in this field. It may, at first sight, go against the interests of a country that patents a lot. But this will stimulate commercialization also in Germany.
9	Wealth taxation	Harmonize and reduce taxes on private wealth, private wealth transfers and inheritance if productively invested.	The transfer of wealth across generations, especially in the form of business assets, is a major issue in the family-firm dominated *Mittelstand* in Germany (Ellul et al. 2010; Getz and Peterszen 2004). By reducing taxation on private wealth transfers, the transition of ownership across generations is easier and this also frees up more so-called triple-F finance in Germany.
17	VC	Reduce barriers to the sale, acquisition, and IPO of VC-funded start-ups to facilitate profitable exits.	Germany does not seem to suffer from a direct lack of VC funds, but the market remains small because of low demand. We propose to stimulate this market by strengthening the pull-factors as direct subsidies in these circumstances will only cause too much cheap money chasing too few projects.
19	Banks	Increase the mandatory equity ratio in banking gradually to 10–15% to allow them to take on more risk responsibly in their lending portfolios.	European and international minimum standards are applied in Germany, but allow for rather low reserves and high leverage. Deutsche Bank was branded the worlds' riskiest bank by the USA FDIC in 2016 (Hofbauer et al. 2017; Moshinsky 2016). Financing entrepreneurship simply requires more loss-absorbing capacity in banking
21	FinTech	Implement a light-touch regulatory regime for equity crowdfunding and peer-to-business lending.	German crowdfunding regulation introduced in 2015 is relatively conservative. The arguments are all about stability. We would encourage experimentation with this new form of finance under tight supervision, but loose regulation.

(continued)

Table 7.5 (continued)

No.	Policy area	Proposal	Germany
23	Employment protection	Relax the stringency of employment protection legislation for permanent contracts.	Germany ranks fourth for permanent and forty-fourth for temporary contracts protection in the OECD ranking. The gap is huge. Some labor protection is needed to maintain the high levels of firm-specific human capital (e.g., Hall and Soskice 2001), but that cannot justify the gap with temporary workers. The way forward would be to close the gap by bringing protection for permanent contracts down where responsible, and award temporary work more protection where needed to level the playing field.
27	Social security	Carefully consider the impact of flexicurity reforms on young firms and do not force them to take on excessive risks and burdens.	Many of the flexicurity reforms tend to put administrative or financial burdens and risks on firms that work as a deterrent to hire and/or as a penalty on growth. In reforming the labor market, policy makers should take a dynamic view of entrepreneurship and realize that successful firms need to grow.
29	Social security	Ensure full portability of social security entitlements by making them independent of tenure at a specific employer.	Labor market mobility in Germany is relatively low. It seems that in Germany this is also due to the "orderly" educational system that sets people on a very predictable career path. Linking social security entitlements to jobs is perhaps a consequence as much as a cause but it is a good place to start.
31	Active labor market policy	Establish or strengthen training programs to prepare workers for new occupations.	Labor market mobility in Germany is relatively low. On-the-job training for mobility has to be publicly funded or funded by employees as we cannot expect employers (let alone start-ups) to invest in mobility.
32	Entry barriers	Excessive barriers to new business formation and new entry should be lifted where possible.	The survey above clearly indicates founders think bureaucracy and regulation are a barrier to business formation and the Doing Business Index of the World Bank (World Bank 2018b) ranks Germany 113 out of 190 in ease of starting a business. Compared to Georgia, at 20% below the global frontier and not improving as fast (World Bank 2018c).

(continued)

Table 7.5 (continued)

No.	Policy area	Proposal	Germany
37	ICT	Invest in excellent, open-access digital infrastructure for European citizens and businesses.	Providing such an infrastructure would promote scaling of new digital ventures and high-tech services (Baller et al. 2016). Germany ranks 15 out of 139 in the Networked Readiness Index, down from 13 and below the Nordics and UK. As this is a fertile ground for new firm formation, Germany could invest here to promote a more adventurous entrepreneurial ecosystem without jeopardizing upsetting its existing routine innovation paradigm in manufacturing. Strong improvements could also be made to the digitalization of public administration.
39	Insolvency	Insolvency regulation should protect ventures that are inherently healthy and promising and allow for a quick and ex-ante transparent liquidation of those that are not.	This proposal ties in with the Business Risk Acceptance and Fear of Failure, but this necessarily is a long run intervention. Only by signaling strongly to society that failure in business is acceptable, can cultural attitudes gradually become more supportive. German bankruptcy law seems overly stringent.
41	Education system	Reforms in primary and secondary education should provide pupils with a solid and coherent knowledge base and promote initiative, creativity and a willingness to experiment.	If we combine German performance on PISA scores and low scores on education and training plus need for more risk acceptance in the REDI-data analysis, it is clear that also in the educational system reforms are desirable. The government has put quite a few programs in place in the 2000s already and reform fatigue may be an issue, but a focus on creativity and out-of-the-box thinking remains urgent (Rothman 2017). This proposal is of course complicated by the fact that educational policy in Germany is largely a competence of the federal states.

(continued)

Table 7.5 (continued)

No.	Policy area	Proposal	Germany
45	Universities	Both the EU and its member states should create healthy, well-funded, academic institutions that allow Europe's most talented academics to pursue their research interests.	For Germany, this should be interpreted as a call for increasing the public funding for universities in particular. These institutions have a strong educational focus in Germany as it is and spending per student has declined (Füller 2017) to €9,000 per students which is less than the OECD average of €10,400. Underinvesting in academic teaching and basic research jeopardizes the knowledge base in the long run. Again, federal state and national politicians need to closely collaborate to address this issue in Germany.
48	Innovation policy	Develop highly competitive programs encouraging small businesses to engage research and development with the potential for commercialization.	Germany's unique legacy of a decentralized, innovative, and well-funded *Mittelstand* gives it a unique strength to build on. If its *Mittelstand* firms can be engaged in somewhat more risky innovation, Germany can strengthen and maintain its competitive position in the world in a way that will be hard to copy in other places.

[a]Numbered as in Elert et al. (2019)
Source Authors' own compilation

interpreted as a suggestion to raise the issue at the appropriate governing bodies and treaty negotiations.

The proposals in taxation and financial regulation (9, 17, 19, and 21) lie clearly within national competencies. They serve the dual purpose of mobilizing more capital for riskier, perhaps more radically innovative ventures and increasing the financial rewards for such venturing and investing in it. Here, we propose a different approach than the founders, whom in our survey called for more public funding and financial support. Instead, we believe that mobilizing the so-called triple-F finance by family, friends and fools, can be promoted by allowing for more wealth to accumulate and be transferred among private individuals.

Proposals on social security and labor market regulation (23, 27, 29, and 31) all aim to mobilize Germany's most knowledgeable and valuable employees. Portability of social security entitlements across jobs, sectors, and labor market statuses will reduce the lock-in of skilled labor in gilded jobs and reduce the barriers for employers. Also, this portability creates a level playing field for start-ups on the demand side and for marginalized groups on the supply side of the labor market. This will make growth in Germany more inclusive and equitable as well as more innovative.

A third group of proposals (32, 37, and 39) intends to improve the regulatory situation for start-ups and founders both at the start and possibly the end of their venture, as well as strengthen the digital infrastructure of Germany. The latter is an essential and vital infrastructure for platform-based services that account for most spectacular new firm formation in the world today.

Finally, a group of proposals (41, 45, and 48) suggests reforms to make Germany's strong knowledge generation sector more open to entrepreneurs penetrating the knowledge filter (Acs and Plummer 2005), and particularly for more radical ideas. The promotion of creativity and experimental mindsets in primary and secondary education will support this shift in the long run. Policies to support innovation in SMEs will have to be designed in close cooperation with knowledge-intensive firms in Germany, whereas greater investment in higher education and basic research is a proven recipe for improving the quality of life in the long run.

The proposals individually and in combination aim not only at making German entrepreneurs more adventurous and change their environment in ways that such adventures are rewarded more if successful and punished less if a failure. In addition, the proposals focus more directly on allowing these more adventurous entrepreneurs to start a venture with less administrative hurdles and to grow them with capital, labor, and knowledge for which they can compete on a more level playing field. These reforms would have to be implemented while keeping sensible and important regulations in place to screen out business models that add no social value.

It is likely that, even though all German *Länder* stand to benefit from these interventions, the fact that density and clustering tend to promote the quality and impact of entrepreneurial venturing will imply that the same policy improvements will benefit already prosperous cities and regions most. Still, that should not stop policy makers from pursuing these interventions as it is the well-being of German citizens, not the GRP of its administrative units per se, that the national government should primarily care about. In addition, Germany has effective automatic transfer schemes that will help maintain a high quality of life throughout the country, even if the available entrepreneurial resources are attracted to, and deployed in, only parts of the territory.

7.5 Step 5: The FIRES-Reform Proposals in Light of the Countries' Historical, Geographical, and Institutional Context

To put our proposed reform program in context, it is important to discuss the diagnosis and proposed treatments with experts in the field. Moreover, given the wide diversity of policy areas involved, it is important to not only discuss this with policy makers that are active in "entrepreneurship policy" in the narrow sense. Our approach emphasizes the importance of reforming institutions that determine the allocation of financial, labor, and knowledge resources to entrepreneurial activity in the broadest and most inclusive sense of the word. Entrepreneurship policy, in the narrow sense, has been in place for more than three decades and, to date, seems to have achieved only limited success.

Because of its breadth, our reform agenda inevitably cuts across many policy areas traditionally less associated with entrepreneurship policy, including wealth taxation, financial and labor market regulation, social security, and science policy. Policies and institutions in these different areas overlap and interact in ways that affect the quality and performance of the entrepreneurial ecosystem (Stam 2015, 2018). As the institutions in these areas have evolved historically and policy makers in these areas pursue different, equally relevant public policy priorities, the challenge is to discuss the proposed agenda in sufficient depth and with a sufficiently diverse group of policy makers and practitioners. The challenge is to not only propose policies and reforms that will strengthen the ecosystem, but to do it in such a way that other important policy priorities are also achieved.

In order to receive the first round of feedback on the proposals for Germany presented in Table 7.5, a policy round table was held at the *Bundesministerium für Wirtschaft und Energie* in Berlin on April 24, 2018. This step can be seen as an attempt to allow our patient, or perhaps more accurately, their team of medical specialists, intimately familiar with our patient, to give feedback about our diagnosis and proposed treatments. What proposals does this team endorse, question, or propose to drop?

Several participants stressed that cultural aspects and attitudes are important factors affecting the entrepreneurial activity in Germany. Discussing monetary issues, such as the size and distribution of certain items of EU's, Germany's, or the *Bundesländer's* budget, will only be of limited use if one does not see how this fits into the institutional and cultural patterns of Germany.

The participants also agreed that institutions like high employment protection and entrepreneurship-inhibiting insolvency laws increase the risks involved with entrepreneurial failure and the stakeholders also meant that institutional reforms that decrease the personal risks of failure might have an effect on individuals' risk attitude. The relatively high-risk aversion in Germany is not innate and can be altered, even if it might take some time.

Supporting business angels might work to reduce market failure in the seed stage. The idea to subsidize the investors and not the firms was regarded as a fruitful strategy. However, some participants questioned the idea that capital access was an important bottleneck and others claimed that angel investment has no detectable effect on firm productivity and development. Supporting the VC industry might have an effect on the entrepreneurial culture and the risk attitude among potential entrepreneurs in society. It was also critically discussed whether tight regulation truly is a bottleneck for start-ups.

Some proponents argued that the size threshold of the SME definition that EU uses should be increased to include more *Mittelstand* firms as well. Even if these firms are not SMEs by the today's definition, they operate under similar organizational routines, managerial practices, and firm behavior. Even if this issue was not a specific proposal, participants pointed out that this would imply that a given budget has to be distributed among more firms or that the budget must increase substantially to avoid that resources are diluted.

7.6 Conclusions

This chapter on Germany presents the FIRES-approach to formulating a tailored institutional reform strategy to promote a more entrepreneurial society in Europe. It illustrates how one could systematically analyze the situation before selecting and proposing reforms within this area. After carefully analyzing Germany's historically rooted institutional foundations, this chapter triangulated the historical, qualitative, and quantitative information to identify Germany's strengths and weaknesses. Based on this diagnosis, the most relevant proposals are selected from the menu of policy interventions and reform proposals developed in more detail in the companion volume of this book (Elert et al. 2019).

Due to its unique history, the German entrepreneurial landscape is probably the most decentralized and regionally diffused in all of Europe. This is reflected to this day in a spatial structure with a comparatively low level of concentration of economic power in the capital region and with economically strong clusters in the *Länder* capitals and other large cities around the country. Germany is home to centuries-old universities and also developed a strong system of non-university research institutes. Germany's financial system is unique with its locally embedded public bank system which supports Germany's *Mittelstand* of decentralized export-oriented medium-sized industrial firms across the country. The labor market is characterized by a model of consensual and coordinated decision making between employers and employees that facilitates and promotes high investments in firm-specific human capital.

Germany has developed its own unique model of capitalism and represents the core of the continental European model with a coordinated market economy. The reunification between West and East Germany in 1990 started an economic process that is arguably still ongoing. The socialist doctrine had drained East Germany of its entrepreneurial talent and the structure of *Mittelstand* vanished.

Germany today has, however, a rather unbalanced entrepreneurial ecosystem. It excels in competition and technology absorption, but these strengths are negated by lacking performance on human capital. Germany lags only slightly relative to the EU average on human capital and risk acceptance and scores low in Entrepreneurial Attitudes. The main bottlenecks in the entrepreneurial ecosystem are a limited willingness to take risk, an educational system that could aim for more creativity and experimentation and a lack of radical innovation that feeds back into a low familiarity with ambitious entrepreneurship and a rather closed and conservative business culture.

This chapter discusses proposals concerning taxation and financial regulations as well as ideas about how to improve the regulatory situation for start-ups and founders. Germany also needs to strengthen the digital infrastructure and the knowledge generation sector in addition to supporting innovation in SMEs.

The main message for Germany is that the German institutions could allow for more experimentation and somewhat more radical innovation by strengthening the educational system in that direction and considering creating a more equal playing field between dependent employment and self-employment/employer when it comes to labor protection and social security. While this should not go at the cost of carefully built-up competitive strengths, Germany could afford to become more adventurous. The proposals individually and in combination aim to reward German entrepreneurs more if successful and punish them less if they fail.

Of course, these proposals will need a much more detailed discussion and form the starting point, and not the final word on the policy debate. Moreover, even if adopted, our proposals all require careful implementation and evaluation to complete the seven-step policy cycle presented in Chap. 1 of this volume.

References

Abrams L (2007) Bismarck and the German Empire: 1871–1918. Routledge, London

Acs ZJ, Autio E, Szerb L (2014) National systems of entrepreneurship: measurement issues and policy implications. Res Policy 43(3):476–494. https://doi.org/10.1016/j.respol.2013.08.016

Acs ZJ, Plummer LA (2005) Penetrating the "knowledge filter" in regional economies. Ann Reg Sci 39(3):439–456

Acs ZJ, Szerb L (2009) The global entrepreneurship index (GEINDEX). Found Trends Entrepreneurship 5(5):341–435

Acs Z, Szerb L (2016) Extension of GEDI indicators. FIRES Report D4.1. Retrieved from https://www.projectfires.eu/wp-content/uploads/2016/03/D4.1-Report-on-Extention-of-the-GEDI-indicator.pdf

Alesina A, Fuchs-Schündeln N (2007) Good-bye Lenin (or not?): the effect of communism on people's preferences. Am Econ Rev 97(4):1507–1528

Allen F, Gale D (2000) Comparing financial systems. MIT press, Cambridge, MA

Audretsch DB, Grilo I, Thurik R (2007) Entrepreneurship policies in Germany: from small business to entrepreneurship policy. Handbook of research on entrepreneurship policy. Edward Elgar Publishing Inc, Cheltenham, UK, pp 47–50

Audretsch DB, Lehmann EE (2005a) Does the knowledge spillover theory of entrepreneurship hold for regions? Res Policy 34(8):1191–1202

Audretsch DB, Lehmann EE (2005b) Do university policies make a difference? Res Policy 34(3):343–347

Audretsch DB, Lehmann EE (2016) The seven secrets of Germany: economic resilience in an era of global turbulence. Oxford University Press, Oxford

Baker D, Lenhardt G (2008) The institutional crisis of the German research university. High Educ Policy 21(1):49–64

Baller S, Dutta S, Lanvin B (eds) (2016) The global information technology report 2016 innovating in the digital economy. World Economic Forum, Geneva. Retrieved from: http://reports.weforum.org/global-information-technology-report-2016

Barkai A (1988) Das Wirtschaftssystem des Nationalsozialismus: Ideologie, Theorie, Politik. 1933–1945. Fischer-Taschenbuch-Verlag, Frankfurt am Main

Bauernschuster S (2013) Dismissal protection and small firms' hirings: evidence from a policy reform. Small Bus Econ 40(2):293–307

Bauernschuster S, Driva A, Hornung E (2019) Bismarck's health insurance and the mortality decline. J Eur Econ Assoc (Forthcoming)

Bauernschuster S, Falck O, Gold R, Heblich S (2012) The shadows of the socialist past: Lack of self-reliance hinders entrepreneurship. Eur J Polit Econ 28(4):485–497

Bauernschuster S, Rainer H (2012) Political regimes and the family: how sex-role attitudes continue to differ in reunified Germany. J Popul Econ 25(1):5–27

Becker C, Grebe T, Lübbers T (2011) Evaluation der Fördermaßnahmen „EXIST-Gründerstipendium“ und „EXIST-Forschungstransfer“. Studie im Auftrag des Bundesministeriums für Wirtschaft und Technologie. Gesellschaft für Innovationsforschung und Beratung mbH, Berlin

Becker G (1964) Human capital: a theoretical and empirical analysis, with special reference to education. University of Chicago Press, Chicago

Beise M, Stahl H (1999) Public research and industrial innovations in Germany. Res Policy 28(4):397–422

Bøggild N, Heyn L, Käser-Erdtracht J, Richter TJ, Wallau F, Werner A, Zinke G (2011) Evaluierung der ERP-Programme—Endbericht. Rambøll Management Consulting, Hamburg

Brady D, Biegert T (2017) The rise of precarious employment in Germany. In: Kalleberg A, Vallas S (eds) Precarious work. Emerald Publishing Limited, Bingley, pp 245–271

Broadberry S, Harrison M (2005) The economics of World War I. Cambridge University Press, Cambridge

Brosig-Koch J, Helbach C, Ockenfels A, Weimann J (2011) Still different after all these years: solidarity behavior in East and West Germany. J Public Econ 95(11–12):1373–1376

Burda M (2016) The German labour market "miracle", an assessment. SFB 649 Discussion Paper 2016-005

Burda M, Fitzenberger B, Lembke A, Vogel T (2008) Unionization, stochastic dominance, and compression of the wage distribution: evidence from Germany. SFB 649 Discussion Paper 2008-041

Burda M, Hunt J (2001) From reunification to economic integration: Productivity and the labor market in Eastern Germany. Brookings Pap Econ Act 32(2):1–92

Burhop C (2010) The transfer of patents in imperial Germany. J Econ Hist 70(4):921–939

Burhop C (2011) Wirtschaftsgeschichte des Kaiserreichs, 1871–1918. Vandenhoeck and Ruprecht, Göttingen

Canova F, Ravn MO (2000) The macroeconomic effects of German unification: real adjustments and the welfare state. Rev Econ Dyn 3(3):423–460

Cantoni D (2012) Adopting a new religion: the case of Protestantism in 16th century Germany. Econ J 122:502–531

Cantoni D, Yuchtman N (2014) Medieval universities, legal institutions, and the commercial revolution. Q J Econ 129(2):823–887

Carlsson B, Acs ZJ, Audretsch DB, Braunerhjelm P (2009) Knowledge creation, entrepreneurship, and economic growth: a historical review. Ind Corp Change 18(6):1193–1229

Chickering R (2014) Imperial Germany and the Great War, 1914–1918. Cambridge University Press, Cambridge, UK

Corneo G, Grüner HP (2002) Individual preferences for political redistribution. J Pub Econ 83(1):83–107

Czarnitzki D, Doherr T, Hussinger K, Schliessler P, Toole A (2016) Knowledge creates markets: the influence of entrepreneurial support and patent rights on academic entrepreneurship. Eur Econ Rev 86:131–146

Dilli S, Elert N, Herrmann AM (2018) Varieties of entrepreneurship. Exploring the institutional foundations of different entrepreneurship types through 'Varieties-of-Capitalism' arguments. Special Issue on "financial and institutional reforms for an entrepreneurial society." Small Bus Econ 51(2):293–320

Drucker PF (1998) From capitalism to knowledge society. In: Dale N (ed) The knowledge economy. Butterworth-Heinemann, Boston, pp 15–34

Dustmann C, Fitzenberger B, Schönberg U, Spitz-Oener A (2014) From sick man of Europe to economic superstar: Germany's resurgent economy. J Econ Perspect 28(1):167–188

Eichhorst W, Marx P (2011) Reforming German labour market institutions: a dual path to flexibility. J Eur Soc Policy 21(1):73–87

Elert N, Henrekson M, Sanders M (2019) The entrepreneurial society: a reform strategy for the European Union. Springer, Berlin

Ellul A, Pagano M, Panunzi F (2010) Inheritance law and investment in family firms. Am Econ Rev 100(5):2414–2450
Esping-Andersen G (2002) A new gender contract. In: Esping-Andersen G (ed) Why we need a new welfare state. Oxford University Press, Oxford, pp 68–95
Exist (2019) EXIST Start-up Germany. Retrieved from: https://www.exist.de/EN/Network/EXIST-Start-up-Germany/content.html
Fackler D (2014) Establishment survival in East and West Germany: a comparative analysis. Schmollers Jahrb 134:183–208
Falck O, Fritsch M, Heblich S (2011) The phantom of the opera: cultural amenities, human capital, and regional economic growth. Labour Econ 18(6):755–766
Falck O, Günther C, Heblich S, Kerr WR (2013) From Russia with love: the impact of relocated firms on incumbent survival. J Econ Geogr 13(3):419–449
Fiedler MO, Hellmann T (2001) Against all odds: the late but rapid development of the German venture capital industry. J Private Equity 4(4):31–45
Fitzenberger B, Kohn K, Lembcke AC (2013) Union density and varieties of coverage: the anatomy of union wage effects in Germany. ILR Rev 66(1):169–197
Flögel F (2018) Distance and modern banks' lending to SMEs: ethnographic insights from a comparison of regional and large banks in Germany. J Econ Geogr 18(1):35–57
Flögel F, Gärtner S (2018) The banking systems of Germany, the United Kingdom and Spain from a spatial perspective: The German case. Gelsenkirchen: Institute for Work and Technology (IAT) (IAT Discussion Paper, No. 18/04)
Franzke SA, Grohs S, Laux C (2003) Initial public offerings and venture capital in Germany. CFS Working Paper No. 2003/26
Fritsch M, Bublitz E, Sorgner A, Wyrwich M (2014) How much of a socialist legacy? The re-emergence of entrepreneurship in the East German transformation to a market economy. Small Bus Econ 43(2):427–446
Fritsch M, Noseleit F, Slavtchev V, Wyrwich M (2010) Innovative Gründungen und ihre Bedeutung für den Standort Thüringen. Studie im Auftrag des Thüringer Ministeriums für Bildung, Wissenschaft und Kultur sowie der Stiftung für Technologie, Innovation und Forschung Thüringen (STIFT). Friedrich-Schiller-Universität, Jena
Fritsch M, Schilder D (2008) Does venture capital Investment really require spatial proximity? An empirical investigation. Environ Planning A 40(9):2114–2131
Fritsch M, Schilder D (2012) The regional supply of venture capital—can syndication overcome bottlenecks? Econ Geogr 88(1):59–76
Fritsch M, Sorgner A, Wyrwich M, Zöllner M (2015) Entwicklung und Perspektiven der Förderung innovativer Gründungen im Freistaat Thüringen. Studie im Auftrag der Stiftung für Technologie, Innovation und Forschung Thüringen (STIFT) sowie des Thüringer Ministeriums für Wirtschaft, Wissenschaft und digitale Gesellschaft. Friedrich-Schiller-Universität, Jena
Fritsch M, Wyrwich M (2014) The long persistence of regional levels of entrepreneurship: Germany, 1925–2005. Reg Stud 48(6):955–973
Fritsch M, Wyrwich M (2016) Entrepreneurship in the East German transition process: lessons for the Korean Peninsula. Hist Soc Res 41(3):256–280
Fritsch M, Wyrwich M (2018) Regional knowledge, entrepreneurial culture and innovative start-ups over time and space—an empirical investigation. Small Bus Econ 51(2):337–353
Fuchs-Schündeln N, Schündeln M (2005) Precautionary savings and self-selection: evidence from the german reunification "experiment". Q J Econ 120(3):1085–1120
Fuchs-Schündeln N, Schündeln M (2009) Who stays, who goes, who returns? Econ Transit 17(4):703–738
Füller C (2017) Educational expenditure: More money for schools and universities. Munich: Goethe Institute. Retrieved from https://www.goethe.de/en/kul/wis/20925479.html on 16-04-2018
Getz D, Petersen T (2004) Identifying industry-specific barriers to inheritance in small family businesses. Family Bus Rev 17(3):259–276

Gibbons M, Limoges C, Nowotny H, Schwartzman S, Scott P, Trow M (1994) The new production of knowledge: the dynamics of science and research in contemporary societies. Sage, Thousand Oaks, CA
Glaeser E (2011) Triumph of the city: how our greatest invention makes us richer, smarter, greener, healthier, and happier. Penguin Social Science, New York
Goethner M, Wyrwich M (2019) Cross-faculty proximity and academic entrepreneurship: the role of business schools. J Technol Transf (Forthcoming)
Grimpe C, Fier H (2010) Informal university technology transfer: a comparison between the United States and Germany. J Technol Transf 35(6):637–650
Guinanne T (2001) Cooperatives as information machines: German rural credit cooperatives, 1883–1914. J Econ Hist 61(2):366–389
Gutberlet T (2014) Mechanization and the spatial distribution of industries in the German empire, 1875 to 1907. Econ Hist Rev 67(2):463–491
Hackethal A (2004) German banks and banking structure. In: Krahnen JP, Schmidt RH (eds) The German financial system. Oxford University Press, Oxford, pp 71–105
Hall JB, Ludwig U (1995) German unification and the "market adoption" hypothesis. Camb J Econ 19(4):491–507
Hall PA, Soskice D (2001) Varieties of capitalism: the institutional foundations of comparative advantage. Oxford University Press, Oxford
Hantke M, Spoerer M (2010) The imposed gift of Versailles: the fiscal effects of restricting the size of Germany's armed forces, 1924–9. Econ Hist Rev 63(4):849–864
Harhoff D, Hoisl K (2007) Institutionalized incentives for ingenuity—Patent value and the German Employees' Inventions Act. Res Policy 36(8):1143–1162
Hefele P (1998) Die Verlagerung von Industrie- und Dienstleistungsunternehmen aus der SBZ/DDR nach Westdeutschland: unter besonderer Berücksichtigung Bayerns (1945–1961). Volume 4 of Beiträge zur Unternehmensgeschichte. Franz Steiner Verlag, Stuttgart
Held L (2019) Part-time entrepreneurship: the role of institutions, venture and individual characteristics in entry and transition choices. In: Held L (ed) Unravelling the patterns in venture creation processes, Ph.D. thesis. Utrecht University, Utrecht, pp 25–55
Held L, Herrmann AM, Polzin F (2018a) Follow the money: the funding acquisition process of nascent ventures. Horizon 2020 Project on "Financial and Institutional Reforms for an Entrepreneurial Society" (FIRES), Workpackage 5, Deliverable 5.1; currently under review. Also available in Held L (2019) Unravelling the patterns in venture creation processes. Ph.D. thesis. Utrecht University, Utrecht, pp 91–122
Held L, Herrmann AM, Storz C (2018b) Whom do nascent ventures search for? Variance of linkage formation activities during new product development processes. Horizon 2020 Project on "Financial and Institutional Reforms for an Entrepreneurial Society" (FIRES), Workpackage 5, Deliverable 5.1; currently under review. Also available in Held L (2019) Unravelling the patterns in venture creation processes. Ph.D. thesis. Utrecht University, Utrecht, pp 123–150
Held L, Herrmann AM, van Mossel A (2018c) Team formation processes in new ventures. Special Issue on "Financial and Institutional Reforms for an Entrepreneurial Society." Small Bus Econ 51(2):441–464
Herrmann AM (2019) A plea for varieties of entrepreneurship. Special Issue on "Entrepreneurship in Context." Small Bus Econ 52(2):331–343
Herrman AM (2020) On the institutional foundations of the varieties of entrepreneurship in Europe. In: Sanders M, Marx A, Stenkula M (eds) The entrepreneurial society. Reform strategies for Italy, Germany and the UK. Springer, Berlin
Hofbauer G, Klimontowicz M, Nocoń A (2017) The changes in capital structure of selected banking markets as a result of new regulations. In: Proceedings of the 14th international scientific conference European financial systems 2017. Masaryk University, Brno, pp. 222–229
IWH (2010) Ostdeutschlands Transformation seit 1990. Im Spiegel wirtschaftlicher und sozialer Indikatoren, 2nd edn. Institut für Wirtschaftsforschung (IWH), Halle

Jaeger A, Kopper J (2014) Third mission potential in higher education: measuring the regional focus of different types of HEIs. Rev Reg Res 34(2):95–108

James A (1981) State, industry and depression in Weimar Germany. Hist J 24(1):231–241

Kindleberger CP (2015) A financial history of Western Europe. Routledge, London

Kluge J, Weber M (2018) Decomposing the German East-West wage gap. Econ Transit 26(1):91–125

Kohaut S, Schnabel C (2007) Tarifliche Öffnungsklauseln: Verbreitung, Inanspruchnahme und Bedeutung. Sozialer Fortschritt 56(2):33–40

König W (2006) Vom Staatsdiener zum Industrieangestellten: Die Ingenieure in Frankreich und Deutschland 1750–1945. In: Kaiser W, König W (eds) Geschichte des Ingenieurs. Carl Hanser, Munich, pp 179–231

Kopper C (2011) New perspectives on the 1931 banking crisis in Germany and Central Europe. Bus Hist 53(2):216–229

Kulicke M (2014) 15 Years of EXIST "University-based start-up programmes". Development of the EXIST funding programme between 1998 and 2013. Fraunhofer-Institut für Systemund Innovationsforschung, Karlsruhe

Liberman P (1996) Does conquest pay? The exploitation of occupied industrial societies. Princeton University Press, Princeton, NJ

Lindner A (2017) German unification: macroeconomic consequences for the country. In: Heinemann F, Klüh U, Watzka S (eds) Monetary policy, financial crises, and the macroeconomy. Springer, Cham, pp 239–263

Maier F (1993) The labour market for women and employment perspectives in the aftermath of German unification. Camb J Econ 17(3):267–280

Manegold KH (1989) Geschichte der Technischen Hochschulen. In: Boehm L, Schönbeck C (eds) Technik und Bildung. VDI Verlag, Düsseldorf, pp 204–234

Mattes A, Arnold M, Eickelpasch A, Fritsch M, Schiersch A (2015) Kleinteiligkeit der ostdeutschen Wirtschaft – Gibt es spezifische Wachstumshemmnisse für die Bildung größerer Unternehmenseinheiten? Final project report submitted to the German Ministry of the Interior. DIW econ, Berlin

Mertes M (ed) (2018) In search of Germany. Routledge, London

Möller T, Schmidt M, Hornbostel S (2016) Assessing the effects of the German excellence initiative with bibliometric methods. Scientometrics 109(3):2217–2239

Moshinksy B (2016) Meet the riskiest bank in the world. Business Insider Netherlands. Retrieved from https://www.businessinsider.nl/fdic-report-on-leverage-ratio-names-deutschebank-as-riskiest-2016-9/?international=true&r=UK on 16-04-2018

Nunziata L, Rocco L (2018) The Protestant ethic and entrepreneurship: evidence from religious minorities in the former Holy Roman Empire. Eur J Polit Econ 51:27–43

Ockenfels A, Weimann J (1999) Types and patterns: an experimental East-West-German comparison of cooperation and solidarity. J Pub Econ 71(2):275–287

Pahnke A, Welter F (2018) The German Mittelstand: antithesis to Silicon Valley entrepreneurship? Small Bus Econ 52(2):345–358

Pflanze O (2014) Bismarck and the development of Germany. The period of consolidation, 1871–1880, vol II. Princeton University Press, Princeton, NJ

Pickel A (1992) Radical transitions: the survival and revival of entrepreneurship. Westview Press, Boulder

Reckendrees A (2003) From cartel regulation to monopolistic control? The founding of the German 'steel trust' in 1926 and its effect on market regulation. Bus Hist 45(3):22–51

Rimlinger GV (1968) Social change and social security in Germany. J Hum Resour 3(4):409–421

Rothman B (2017) After the shock: the German education system in 2017. National Center on Education and The Economy. Retrieved from http://ncee.org/2017/09/after-the-shockt-he-german-education-system-in-2017/ on 16-04-2018

Soskice D (1990) Wage determination: the hanging role of institutions in advanced industrialized countries. Oxford Rev Econ Policy 6(4):36–61

Stam E (2015) Entrepreneurial ecosystems and regional policy: a sympathetic critique. Eur Plan Stud 23(9):1759–1769

Stam E (2018) Measuring entrepreneurial ecosystems. In: O'Connor A, Stam E, Sussan F, Audretsch DB (eds) Entrepreneurial ecosystems. Springer, Cham, pp 173–197

Stenholm P, Acs ZJ, Wuebker R (2013) Exploring country-level institutional arrangements on the rate and type of entrepreneurial activity. J Bus Ventur 28(1):176–193

Streeck W (1997) German capitalism: does it exist? Can it survive? New Polit Econ 2(2):237–256

Szerb L, Lafuente E, Horváth K, Páger B (2019) The relevance of quantity and quality entrepreneurship for regional performance: the moderating role of the entrepreneurial ecosystem. Reg Stud 53(9):1308–1320. https://doi.org/10.1080/00343404.2018.1510481

Szerb L, Vörös Z, Komlósi É, Acs ZJ, Páger B, Rappai G (2017) The regional entrepreneurship and development index: structure, data, methodology and policy applications. Retrieved from http://www.projectfires.eu/wp-content/uploads/2018/07/d4.4-the-regional-entrepreneurship-and-development-index_-structure-data-methodology-and-policy-applications.pdf

Tipton F (1976) Regional variations in the economic development of Germany during the nineteenth century. Wesleyan University Press, Middletown, CT

Uebele M, Ritschl A (2009) Stock markets and business cycle co movement in Germany before World War I: evidence from spectral analysis. J Macroecon 31(1):35–57

Varga A, Szerb L, Sebestyén T, Szabó N (2020) Economic impact assessment of entrepreneurship policies with the GMR-Europe model. In: Sanders M, Marx A, Stenkula M (eds) The entrepreneurial society. Reform strategies for Italy, Germany and the UK, Springer, Berlin

Verheyen D (2018) The German question. Routledge, London

Von Proff S, Buenstorf G, Hummel M (2012) University patenting in Germany before and after 2002: what role did the professors' privilege play? Ind Innov 19(1):23–44

Weichlein S (2011) Nation state, conflict resolution and culture war, 1850–1878. In: Smith HW (ed) The Oxford handbook of modern German history. Oxford University Press, Oxford, pp 281–306

Welter F (2007a) Entrepreneurship in West and East Germany. Int J Entrepreneurship Small Bus 4(2):97–109

Welter F (2007b) Book review of Deutsche Gründungsregionen, edited by Rolf Sternberg, Berlin/Münster: Lit Verlag. Raumforschung und Raumordnung 65(2):163–164

World Bank (2018a) Doing Business 2018: reforming to create jobs. International Bank for Reconstruction and Development and World Bank, Washington, DC

World Bank (2018b) Economy rankings. Doing Business: Measuring Business Regulations. World Bank, Washington, DC

World Bank (2018c) Distance to frontier. Doing Business: Measuring Business Regulations. World Bank, Washington, DC

Wyrwich M (2012) Regional entrepreneurial heritage in a socialist and a post-socialist economy. Econ Geogr 88(4):423–445

Wyrwich M (2013) Can socioeconomic heritage produce a lost generation with regard to entrepreneurship? J Bus Ventur 28(5):667–682

Wyrwich M (2017) Women and the labour market in East and West Germany: socialist legacy and pre-socialist tradition. Jena Economic Research Paper 2017–015. Friedrich Schiller University, Jena

Zöllner M, Fritsch M, Wyrwich M (2018) An evaluation of German active labour market policies: a review of the empirical evidence. J Entrepreneurship Pub Policy 7(4): 377–410

Chapter 8
A Reform Strategy for the UK

Mark Sanders, Mikael Stenkula, James Dunstan, Saul Estrin, Andrea M. Herrmann, Balázs Páger, László Szerb and Elisa Terragno Bogliaccini

Abstract In this chapter we outline a reform strategy to promote an entrepreneurial society in the UK. To put it in the words of the Varieties of Capitalism framework, the UK today represents a distinct liberal market economy with a deregulated environment, flexible labor markets, well-funded elite universities, and strong protection of intellectual property rights. Overall, the entrepreneurial ecosystem is supportive, but bottlenecks remain regarding radical innovation, export orientation, and informal investment. To address these shortcomings, the UK should aim at strengthening the

All authors acknowledge financial support from the European Union's Horizon 2020 research and innovation program under grant agreement No 649378. László Szerb and Balázs Páger also acknowledge support from the National Scientific Research Fund of Hungary (OTKA/NKFI grant no. 120289, titled as Entrepreneurship and Competitiveness investigations in Hungary based on the Global Entrepreneurship Monitor surveys 2017–2019). Mikael Stenkula also gratefully acknowledges financial support from Jan Wallanders och Tom Hedelius stiftelse and from the Marianne and Marcus Wallenberg Foundation.

M. Sanders (✉) · J. Dunstan · E. Terragno Bogliaccini
Utrecht School of Economics, Utrecht University, Utrecht, The Netherlands
e-mail: m.w.j.l.sanders@uu.nl

E. Terragno Bogliaccini
e-mail: e.m.terragnobogliaccini@uu.nl

M. Stenkula
Research Institute of Industrial Economics, Stockholm, Sweden
e-mail: mikael.stenkula@ifn.se

S. Estrin
Department of Management, London School of Economics, London, England, UK
e-mail: s.estrin@lse.ac.uk

A. M. Herrmann
Copernicus Institute of Sustainable Development, Utrecht University, Utrecht, The Netherlands
e-mail: A.M.Herrmann@uu.nl

B. Páger · L. Szerb
Department of Management Science, University of Pécs, Pécs, Hungary
e-mail: pagerb@rkk.hu

L. Szerb
e-mail: szerb.laszlo@ktk.pte.hu

M. Sanders et al. (eds.), *The Entrepreneurial Society*, International Studies in Entrepreneurship 44, https://doi.org/10.1007/978-3-662-61007-7_8

workforce's knowledge base and talent pool as well as the capital base from which UK entrepreneurs can draw. It furthermore is advisable to open opportunities for not only starting but also growing innovative firms in all regions in the UK.

Keywords UK · Entrepreneurship · Varieties of Capitalism · Entrepreneurial ecosystem · Entrepreneurship policy

8.1 Step 1: Historical Roots of Institutions and Recent Policies

8.1.1 Global Empire and Splendid Isolation—A Short History of the UK

In its current form, the UK of Great Britain and Northern Ireland has existed since the partition of Ireland as an independent country in 1922. But, of course, British history has much deeper roots. The British Isles were raided, invaded, occupied, and settled from the mainland frequently in the early middle ages. But since the invasion of William the Conqueror in 1066, the British Isles have not experienced further foreign occupation. Still, it took a long time for the country to unify. The seventeenth century saw the English Civil War (1642–1651) and the Glorious Revolution (1688). With the Acts of Union of 1707 England, Wales and Scotland formed the UK of Great Britain and with the Acts of Union of 1800 the Kingdom of Ireland joined.

In the seventeenth century, the UK started to rise as a naval superpower and built up a colonial empire that spanned the globe. The first British Empire (1583–1783) established Britain as a global power but ended with the loss of the Thirteen Colonies in the American Revolution. The Second Empire (1783–1815) saw the exploration of the Pacific and the rise and fall of Napoleon. The defeat of the latter at Waterloo left Britain without serious challengers and ushered in the *Pax Britannica* during which the UK was the unrivaled global superpower until the Great War of 1914–1918. In this imperial century, the British Empire expanded into Africa, India, and Asia. And through its dominance in global trade, finance and diplomacy the UK effectively ruled the world, while at home the Industrial Revolution turned Northern England into the workshop and London into the financial capital of the world.

With the unification of Germany, the opening up of Japan and the end of the civil war in the USA, however, new rivals to the UK's dominance rose toward the end of the nineteenth century. With the defeat of Germany and its allies in the Great War, the British Empire saw its last territorial expansion, which reached its peak in 1921. The Great War, however, had weakened the UK and boosted the confidence of colonial elites. Independence movements in India and Ireland and later the rest of the empire ushered in a gradual decline, while Britain's rivals rapidly industrialized and caught up militarily and economically.

In World War II, the UK and its allies defeated Nazi Germany and Imperial Japan, but its days of unrivaled global dominance were over. The UK had to reposition itself in the new world order, while the age of empire left a strong economic and geographical imprint on the country. The London area had developed into an economic, administrative, and cultural powerhouse, far bigger than the UK alone could have supported (Parkinson et al. 2006), whereas the Industrial Revolution had brought prosperity to the northern regions, but also left them struggling with the loss of the empire and its markets.

Therefore, by the 1980s, an economic policy focused on specific areas or *zones* was implemented by the Thatcher government. The focus of the program was to incentivize inward investment to areas experiencing severe economic problems (Potter and Moore 2000). The Regional Development Agencies Act of 1998 then divided England into nine regions, each with its own Regional Development Agency funded by six different government departments, as well as EU funds (Richardson 2011). But different regions in the UK started from very uneven starting points. Former industrial centers such as Swansea and Middlesbrough had to divest from traditional industries in the wake of globalization, whereas the British cities such as Cambridge, Oxford, and Reading all lacked such industrial heritage (NESTA 2008).

In terms of entrepreneurship, the levels in the UK have historically varied substantially across regions and localities and with different effects. With London as the administrative, financial, and political center of the Empire, a lot of the entrepreneurial talent and resources from all over the country migrated to that area. This pattern was further reinforced when globalization and international competition devastated the economy in the Northern industrial districts. A long history of political unity implies that the formal institutions have largely been built at the national level and are uniform across the country. But the economic geography of the British Isles and its diverse informal institutional make-up imply that entrepreneurship functions vary in different parts of the country. Mueller et al. (2008), for example, found that, for Great Britain as a whole, new firm formation had a positive effect on employment growth. Yet this effect was much smaller in Scotland and Wales and even negative for the lower quartile regions. This all suggests that we should not take the London area to be representative of the UK and carefully consider the heterogeneity that is hidden in aggregated data. The needs and opportunities of London are not those of Scotland and the other way around. Therefore, a one-size-fit-all reform approach to the UK is not advised and a regionally diversified approach is needed.

Against the backdrop of this rich history, Britain developed the institutions that currently define its entrepreneurial ecosystems. To establish and maintain its global Empire, the UK set up institutions that mobilized financial, human, and knowledge resources at an unprecedented scale, whereas the loss of the empire enforced an institutional adjustment process that arguably is still ongoing. Still, the most relevant institutions supporting entrepreneurship in the UK have deep roots. In what follows, we focus on its institutions for knowledge creation and diffusion, its financial institutions, and its labor markets. We then proceed to an overview of recent policy programs and initiatives to support entrepreneurship.

8.1.2 Institutions for Knowledge Creation and Diffusion

Institutions for knowledge generation and diffusion are largely concentrated in a country's academic system of education and research and its system of intellectual property rights. In this section, we will discuss the nature and historical roots of each in the UK.

8.1.2.1 Universities

The UK has a long history of higher education, beginning in the city of Oxford from the year 1096 (University of Oxford n.d.) and followed a century later by Cambridge in 1209 (University of Cambridge n.d.). In the fifteenth century, St Andrews, Glasgow, and Aberdeen—the first three Scottish universities—were founded by Papal Bull, and a century later the University of Edinburgh was established in 1583 by Royal Charter (University of Edinburgh n.d.). These six universities are classified as the "ancient universities" (established before 1800), with the classification sometimes stretched to include Durham University (Bathmaker et al. 2016).

In the nineteenth century, a major expansion of higher education occurred in the UK. St. David's College, Lampeter (Wales), and King's and University College of the University of London were awarded university status by Royal Charter (British Council n.d.), and the University of London was established as a secular alternative to Oxford and Cambridge (University of London n.d.). The need for a more localized higher education system (Barnes 1996) and a desire to increase education of the applied sciences (Heyck 2012) resulted in the founding of the civic universities (or, "redbricks") in Manchester, Leeds, Liverpool, Sheffield, Birmingham, and other industrial Victorian cities. Simultaneously, the ancient universities of Oxford and Cambridge introduced new curricula and relaxed admission requirements (Scott 2014a).

Socio-economic trends fueled by technological innovation, cheaper transportation, and the emergence of the knowledge economy put education high on the policy agenda (Clarke 2001; Ashton and Green 1996). But while the Scottish universities had historically lower tuition fees and living expenses, English universities before the twentieth century remained accessible only to the wealthy as a result of the *laissez-faire* principles of Victorian Britain (Anderson 2016). This paradigm radically changed following the infamous Robbins Report of 1963, which specified 178 recommendations for the higher education system focusing on greatly expanding the number of students in tertiary education (Moser 1988). One year prior to the report, the 1962 Education Act had already introduced state funding for full-time higher education (domestic) students in order to equalize educational opportunity and bring higher education to the masses (Wilson 1997).

The 1960s also saw the establishment of The Polytechnics (Henkel and Kogan 1993). Following Anthony Crosland's 1965 speech advocating the establishment of two parallel systems of higher education (Taylor 2003), these polytechnic institutions arose through the merger of colleges of technology, commerce, and art (later, including colleges of education) and were committed to the application of knowledge. They offered an alternative form of education to that of traditional universities by overcoming the traditional dichotomy between theory and practice (Brosan 1972). This created what is now referred to as the "binary divide" in UK higher education that lasted for over a quarter of a century (Pratt 1997). The essential difference between the two educational systems being that polytechnics continued to be controlled by local education authorities, as opposed to the greater autonomy which the older colleges enjoyed (Scott 2014b). In 1992, the binary divide ended, and the "new" polytechnics became universities (Cranfield and Taylor 2008).

In 1985, universities were finally given the rights to exploit their own innovations, which led to the spreading of science parks around universities in the UK. By 1993, almost every university in the UK had its own science park, providing a business environment for almost 1,200 firms and 20,000 employees (Storey and Tether 1998). The presence of entrepreneurship "in the classroom" is a more recent phenomenon, and as recently as the 1990s, only a handful of higher education institutes provided a serious opportunity for enterprise/entrepreneurial education (Hannon 2005). Responding to the Lambert Review of Business-University Collaboration, the government announced the Science and Innovation Investment Framework in 2004, cementing business-university collaboration within the portfolio of UK universities (Wilson 2012).

In conclusion, British universities and higher education deliver high-quality research and degrees and compete for the best and brightest at the global level. Relatively high tuition fees notwithstanding, UK universities attract students, PhDs, and staff from around the world, and these contribute to an excellent and world-class scientific research infrastructure. The relative weaknesses in the UK educational system, however, are the missing middle. Compared to countries like Italy or Germany (Sanders et al. 2020a, b) or Japan and China in Asia, the quality of vocational education is lacking due to a weak apprenticeship system and low engagement with employers (OECD 2015). Moreover, there is hardly a culture of lifelong learning or applied vocational education. This leads to over-education at the high general skills levels, and a mismatch and under-education at the low vocational skills (e.g., Green et al. 2016; Machin and Vignoles 2018). This affects the level of human capital in the UK labor supply that is needed to grow the knowledge-intensive ventures that emerge out of the knowledge created in its excellent research institutions.

8.1.2.2 The Patent System

In the British context, patents originated in the form of "letters patent" during Elizabethan England. These were essentially royal privileges granting monopoly power to the introducers of new techniques (WIPO n.d.a). However, this system came to be abused by the monarchy whose royal favors were perceived as privileges granting selective monopolies. Consequently, judicial pressure and public outcry forced intellectual property to be regulated under common law. The Statute of Monopolies enacted in 1623 made all monopolies illegal except for those "... made of the sole working or making of any manner of new manufactures within this Realm to the true and first inventor" (Statute of Monopolies 1623). While this was by no means the first form of patent protection for inventors, it is historically important for instilling the principle that only "the true and first inventor" owns the rights to a monopoly patent (Machlup and Penrose 1950).

The patent system established in 1623 remained in place for another two centuries and evolved through the work of lawyers and judges in courts without government regulation (IPO 2014a). This initial *laissez-faire* approach to patent law meant no examination was required to acquire an English patent, only its registration. The establishment of intellectual property rights was a fitting precursor to the Industrial Revolution in the eighteenth and nineteenth centuries. It is important to note that the British patent system, while present, actually provided weak and erratic protection to inventors (MacLeod 1988).

By the mid-eighteenth century, growing criticisms with the patent system included being too costly, as well as it being almost impossible to specify an invention in any such way that would satisfy the courts (Robinson 1972). Consequently, the significance of the British patent system prior to the Patent Law Amendment Act of 1852 remains debated (MacLeod and Nuvolari 2006). Mokyr (2005) concludes that in this period, innovation and industrialization were not held back by limited intellectual property protection.

In essence, the reform of 1852 made two main changes to the prior patent system. Firstly, legal fees were greatly reduced, and secondly, it implemented a single patent for the UK (Dutton 1984). However, costs were still relatively high, but the 1883 Patents Act reduced patent filing fees by another 84% (Nicholas 2014).

Patent law in recent times can be mainly derived from the Patent Act of 1902, which required patent examiners to construct an extensive archive of prior specifications. By 1907, all recorded patent specifications had been classified, with the first documented patent dating back to the year 1617 (IPO 2014b).[1] The 1977 Patents Act applied more stringent novelty tests to patents, while also implementing the European Patent Convention of 1973 and the Patent Co-operation Treaty of 1970 (WIPO n.d.b). The UK is still signatory to these treaties and will remain so after Brexit, making intellectual property rights in the UK a matter of international negotiations.

The skepticism toward monopolies—such as expressed in the Act from 1623 mentioned above—may be one reason for the fact that British firms, unlike their German counterparts, are less inclined to engage in large-scale collaborations within the framework of over-arching industry associations (Herrmann 2020). Given that large-scale collaboration is discouraged, British firms lack an important tool, via industry-wide coordinated associations, to access a broad knowledge base (Tate 2001; Teubner 2001).

[1]Patent No. 1 of 1617 granted to Rathburn and Burges for "Engraving and Printing Maps, Plans &co."

8.1.3 Development of Financial Institutions

Banking in the UK began during the seventeenth century. The Bank of England was founded by Royal Charter in 1694 and was primarily used to fund the war effort against France (Bank of England n.d.). The Bank of Scotland was established one year later in 1695 following an act made by the Parliament of Scotland providing a legal monopoly on banking (Lloyds Banking Group n.d.). It initially fulfilled a different role to its English counterpart, acting mainly to develop Scotland's business and trade with England and the Low Countries. In 1696, the Bank of Scotland became the first European commercial bank to successfully issue a paper currency (BBC 2008). When its legal monopoly ended in 1716, the Royal Bank of Scotland was chartered in 1727, creating a historic rivalry between the two Scottish banks (White 1992). The Bank of Scotland's monopoly ended much earlier than the Bank of England's. Scotland then enjoyed a significant expansion in banking services and by the end of the century had one of the most developed banking sectors in Europe (Collins 2012). The Royal Bank of Scotland even invented the overdraft (BBC 2009).[2]

From 1709 onwards, the Bank of England was the only bank allowed to operate on a joint-stock basis (Ferguson 2009). The next big leap in the history of UK banking was the Bank Charter Act of 1844 (Bank of England n.d.), which restricted the issuance of banknotes solely to the Bank of England. With restrictions on joint-stock banking lifted by 1858, corporate branch deposit banking developed in the UK (Newton and Cottrell 1998) and large commercial banks such as Lloyds (1884) and Barclays (1896) began to emerge. On the eve of the World War I, residents' deposits in British banks totaled almost £1.2 billion, with a total bank-note circulation of only £45.5 million (Ferguson 2009). UK SME finance was left predominantly to the big four modern banks—Barclays PLC , HSBC Holdings PLC, Lloyds Banking Group PLC, and Royal Bank of Scotland Group PLC—who still hold 78% of the SME market and 95 percent in the case of Scotland (Han et al. 2012).

In 1945, the Industrial and Commercial Finance Corporation was created (3i Group n.d.) via a political decision to increase funding availability for SMEs. By then, larger banks and the London Stock exchange mainly focused on overseas commerce (Merlin-Jones 2010) so no "readily accessible channel, corresponding to the new issue market for larger firms, through which the small industrialist can raise long-term funds" existed (Radcliffe Committee on the Working of the Monetary System cited in Merlin-Jones 2010, p. 5). In addition, the National Research Development Corporation, founded in 1948, and the National Enterprise Board, conceived by the Labour government in 1973, acted to provide loans to small firms to improve R&D and boost innovation (Rothwell 1985). The inauguration of the Thatcher government in the 1980s brought the reduction of corporate and personal taxes to encourage greater entrepreneurship, alongside the new Business Expansion Scheme which offered up to £40,000 in tax relief to individuals investing in non-public UK

[2]The bank allowed William Hog, a merchant, to take £1,000—the equivalent of £63,664 today—more out of his account than he had in it.

companies (Mason and Harrison 1989). Over the 1990s and early 2000s, liberalization and globalization implied that the UK financial system grew in number and became more concentrated in terms of market participants and geographically. The financial sector in the UK today is extremely concentrated in (the City of) London, where all superlatives still apply. The UK boasts the biggest currency, commodities, stock and asset markets in Europe and serves as a global financial center rivaling New York and Tokyo. But the skyscrapers of the city are not primarily in the business of financing SMEs and/or innovative young ventures. The UK has a significant venture capital market and new initiatives in platform-based FinTech innovation benefit from a sensible and benign regulatory regime, but the financial crisis of 2007 hit London perhaps hardest of all and revealed vulnerabilities in the strong reliance on global financial asset trading.

In conclusion, the financing of small-scale experimental ventures may not be the biggest activity in the London City, but the sheer size of UK financial markets still implies that entrepreneurs face little financial constraints in the UK. Moreover, financial regulation in the UK is arguably more flexible than in the Euro-Area, as UK financial regulators take a tougher stance on incumbent banks' interests while leaving more space for new, platform-based alternative intermediation services.

8.1.4 Labor Institutions

The labor force in the UK is typically not very loyal to the employer because that loyalty is often not reciprocated (Herrmann 2020). At the lower end of the spectrum, wages are low and jobs are insecure, making investment in firm-specific human capital a risky strategy for UK workers (OECD 2019). This implies it is easy to start a venture, but much harder to grow one into a global competitor as the latter implies accumulating also tacit and firm-specific knowledge on product, market, and process (e.g., Thirkell and Dau 1998). As in other countries, the existing equilibrium in labor relations in the UK has deep historical roots that can be traced in the history of employment protection, wage bargaining, and social security.

8.1.4.1 Employment Protection

Labor relations in the UK (and in fact the Anglo-Saxon world) have always been rather conflicting. Due to laws such as the Masters and Servants Acts of 1823 and 1867, disobedient workers could be punished for a criminal offense (Woods 1982; Choi 2010). British labor law only gradually turned in favor of the workers in the early twentieth century (e.g., the Old Age Pension Act of 1908 and the National Insurance Act of 1911).

In 1963, the Contracts of Employment Act introduced statutory protection from termination of employment and protection of wages (Brown et al. 2000), with subsequent acts addressing race (Race Relations Act 1965) and gender (Equal Pay Act

1970) related inequalities. High unemployment and large losses in nationalized industries wreaked havoc in the public sector budget, and the Thatcher years in the 1980s saw a decade of legislation to break union power and liberalize labor markets. The 2002 Employment Act was implemented and essentially shifted the responsibility of enforcement of employment rights from public tribunals to private management-controlled procedures, giving more weight to the competitiveness of the employer than the welfare of the individual (Hepple and Morris 2002; Hepple 2002). The reforms in labor protection of recent decades have brought the UK back to a position in which low wages and low employment protection create high uncertainty for and, consequently, low loyalty of employees for their employer. The flexibility of the labor market implies it is easy to hire employees, but the lack of investment in firm-specific human capital and employability makes it hard to accumulate firm-specific knowledge and retain brains. For this reason, it is easy to start a venture in the UK, but very hard to grow that venture into a globally competitive firm of significant size.

8.1.4.2 Wage Bargaining

In the UK, wage-bargaining institutions go back far in history and were formed out of conflict between the aristocratic landowners and skilled peasants and artisans of England. One of the earliest pieces of legislation, which came about after the breakout of the black death, was the "Ordinance of Laborers" legislation of 1349 that implemented a series of labor regulations and price controls to mitigate the problems of labor shortages after the plague (Craig 2007). Building on this legislation, the Elizabethan Statute of Artificers of 1563 prohibited conspiracies to raise wages and the first worker's associations formed in response to the legislation (Woodward 1980).

Unions in Britain had effectively been repressed by the aristocracy and large employers (Curthoys 2004). By 1824, unions became partly legalized due to the repeal of the combination laws (Shawl 1954).[3] But it was not until the repeal of the Masters and Servants Act (1867) and the Trade Union Act (1871) that there was a positive step toward establishing more harmonious relations between the unions and the courts (Kahn-Freund 1944).

The relationship between employers and the employed during the nineteenth century remained one of conflict, where the interests of both parties were at odds. The proposals set forth by the Whitley Committee led to the establishment of the country's first Joint Industrial Council in 1918 (Clegg et al. 1985). But this was short-lived and, following the deterioration of laborers' power due to postwar unemployment, the state abandoned its support for co-management and consultation (Lewchuk 1984).

The mid-1970s saw the turmoil of UK recession as a result of the oil crisis in 1973 and the decline of traditional British industries. This culminated in the "winter of discontent" 1978–79, where 1.5 million public sector workers took part in Britain's largest single day of industrial action since the general strike of 1926 (Hay 2010). In

[3]The combination acts of 1799 and 1800 were the embodiment of Parliament's conversion to a *laissez-faire* policy, removing protection of labor conditions up until their repeal in 1824.

1980, Thatcher's government abolished the statutory procedure that allowed independent trade unions to seek official recognition and British employers were no longer legally required to bargain with the unions (Towers 1989). Thus, the 1980s and 1990s saw a dramatic decline in trade union power and a decentralization of collective bargaining (Wooden and Sloan 1998).

In 1999, the New Labour government under Tony Blair passed the National Minimum Wage Regulations which set a minimum wage of £3.00 per hour for 18–21-year-olds and £3.60 per hour for anyone older. The wage floor improved the conditions for "outsiders," such as those employed in small businesses (Morris et al. 2005), but also increased the operating costs of smaller firms (Rusly et al. 2017).

Liberalized *laissez-faire* wage formation in the UK has arguably depressed wages by lowering union bargaining power, and the UK saw significant wage diversion between strong (insider educated white managerial jobs) and weak (outsider uneducated minority female manual) jobs in the 1990s and polarization in the 2000s (Goos et al. 2009, 2014). Labor market polarization has led to widening income inequality and reduced incentives for medium-level human capital investment at school and on the job.

8.1.4.3 Social Security

The earliest underpinnings of a modern welfare state in the UK can be traced back to the sixteenth and seventeenth centuries with the Act for the Relief of the Poor in 1597 and the Poor Relief Act of 1601 (Birtles 1999). The modern welfare state in the UK arose after the landslide victory of the Liberal government in 1906. It introduced the concept of national health and unemployment insurance in the 1911 National Insurance Act (Feld 2011). The Beveridge Report of 1941 influenced one of the most radical changes in British history by establishing three main principles for postwar policy development: the introduction of family allowances, a National Health Service, and state maintenance of full employment in order to maintain funding for such social provisions (Whiteside 2014). The centuries' old poor laws were replaced by the National Assistance Act of 1948 (Spicker 2014), and in that same year, the Attlee Labour government launched the National Health Service that is still operating today (NHS n.d.).

By the 1980s, the Thatcher government introduced various measures to shift social security into an enterprise incentivizing framework. The government for example implemented an Enterprise Allowance Scheme, which gave individuals direct transfers of between £40 and £100 per week for their first year of self-employment (Cowling and Mitchell 1997).

In conclusion, the UK labor institutions have always been, but certainly since the Thatcher Era, tilted in favor of employers. This creates great labor mobility and flexibility on the one hand, but arguably low mutual loyalty, and rather militant labor relations on the other. This results in a labor market in which it is easy to hire and fire workers, but hard to find committed employees that will invest in firms' specific human capital and are willing to go the extra mile and make sacrifices for their colleagues or employers. Moreover, in such a constellation the incentives and rewards for accumulating capital are high, whereas the incentives and rewards for accumulating skills are not. In the end, this entrenches wage and wealth inequality, creating strong incentives to start but few opportunities to grow successful new businesses.

8.1.5 Recent Entrepreneurship Policies in the UK

In our analysis of recent entrepreneurship policy initiatives in the UK, we consider the four priorities of public policy—deregulation, access to finance, innovation, and enterprise culture (based on a framework by Huggins and Williams 2009)—that have guided policy initiatives since the early 1980s.

8.1.5.1 (De)regulation

Since the 1980s, UK governments of all signatures were actively working to make regulation better for businesses (Ashmore 1988). This started with the 1985 and 1986 White Papers "Lifting the Burden" and "Building Businesses ... Not Barriers." In 1997, the government established the Better Regulation Task Force to advise the government how to reduce unnecessary burdens of regulation. Government also focused on lifting regulation for small firms specifically with the "Think Small First" campaign.

In 2011, the government introduced the *Micro-Business Moratorium*—a freeze on new regulation for start-ups and companies with fewer than 10 employees. It then applied a "one-in, one-out" rule for UK business regulation in 2012, and following a political logic, the rule was changed into "one-in, two-out" in 2013 and "one-in, three-out" in 2016. Regulation of business is, however, not a matter of quantity, but rather of quality, including transparency. More interesting initiatives in recent years develop sensible regulation in a more interactive way. Entrepreneurs need regulatory stability rather than ongoing changes. Frequent changes of regulation may be detrimental for the development of the firms, a view supported by the survey of British founders presented in Sect. 8.3.[4]

The deregulation doctrine is still very much alive today. In 2015, the Parliament passed the Small Business, Enterprise and Employment Act, requiring the government of the day to publish a "Business Impact Target". Social security burdens for especially small employers were reduced in 2014, when the government introduced the Employment Allowance for all businesses and charities and since 2016 allows start-ups and SMEs to employ four workers without paying any social security contributions. The policy has not yet been evaluated on its effects and can be expected

[4]This is particularly true for the renewable energy sector in UK (Leendertse 2017).

to promote the creation of new but hamper the growth of successful businesses in the UK.

8.1.5.2 Access to Finance

In the early 1990s, the government started supporting the development of informal venture capital. The Business Expansion Scheme, which was implemented in 1983, was replaced in 1993 by the Enterprise Investment Scheme. This scheme provided both front-end and capital gains' tax relief on investments made directly in qualifying unquoted companies, strengthening incentives for business angels (Mason et al. 2010, p. 47). Furthermore, the Financial Services and Markets Act (UK Government 2000) created the opportunity for unquoted firms to raise equity and allowing investors to obtain certification without going through an authorized institution (Mason 2009). The government then set up the Business Finance Partnership, increasing lending to small- and medium-sized businesses and the Enterprise Capital Funds, providing venture capital investment for early stage, innovative small- and medium-sized businesses with high growth potential (UK Government 2015).

With these incentives in place, a vibrant angel and venture capital sector developed (Wiltbank 2009; Mason et al. 2010), and the creation of co-investment funds to match private investments with public funds enabled business angels to increase the availability of finance for new ventures (Mason 2009, p. 548). In November 2011, the Business Angel Co-Investment Fund was launched, investing with syndicates of business angels in SMEs.

Hence, the successive governments in the UK first allowed a private business angel and venture capital market to emerge and then also channeled public funds to SMEs and start-ups through these channels, thereby avoiding the problem of having to pick winners or write extensive protocols to administer subsidies and grants.

Considerable efforts were also made to get banks to lend to SMEs (UK Government 2015). For example, in 2009, the Enterprise Finance Guarantee was initiated, allowing banks to offer small businesses a normal, secured commercial loan. In early 2011, the Bank Appeal Process, which allowed SMEs to appeal against a bank's decision to decline a loan, was also launched. More than 9,000 businesses used the process, resulting in £42 millions of further lending. But although this can be considered a success of the appeals process, it also signals that banks in the UK have not been very keen on financing SMEs.

Nevertheless, in July 2012, with support from the government, the Bank of England (BoE) launched Funding for Lending, allowing banks and building societies to borrow from the BoE at cheaper than market rates for 4 years. In 2014, the Department for Business, Innovation and Skills established the British Business Bank, managing all government programs that help smaller businesses to access finance. In the first quarter of 2018, the Funding for Lending program was discontinued as it was predestined to (Pike 2017). But it was also discontinued after it was shown to have a great detrimental effect on the savings in high-street banks, as interest rates fell by two-thirds in January 2017 (Jones 2018).

In conclusion, tax and other policy initiatives have given formal UK financial markets a great boost in recent decades. The UK now has the largest VC and angel investment market in Europe, and London, arguably, remains the financial capital of the world. But the flow of finance to SMEs and start-ups, especially in their earliest stages of growth remains limited, especially outside London.

8.1.5.3 Innovation

For decades, the UK governments tried to improve the translation of knowledge into products and services. In 2001, the government launched the Small Business Research Initiative with the aim to increase the demand for R&D from high-technology SMEs. In addition, the Knowledge-Transfer Partnerships helped entrepreneurs access expertise and skills for growth by connecting them with academic institutions. Following the recommendations of the Lambert Review (HM Treasury 2003), the UK government began to promote knowledge transfer between universities and businesses by rewarding universities for activities that enhanced collaboration. In 2004, the government established the Technology Strategy Board and launched the Science City Program in several cities to also attract investors to strong, science-based assets. In 2007, the UK Innovation Agency launched Innovate UK that was complemented with several capital funds which supported innovative businesses and university innovation (HM Treasury 2010). The Business-University Collaboration and the Business-Research Council Collaboration initiatives of 2009 and the Gateway to Research launched in 2013 all aimed to improve the flow of information between ventures and research. Finally, University Enterprise Zones were launched in 2014, where Bradford, Bristol, Liverpool, and Nottingham won the bids and started pilots that ran till 2017 and a new round of funding for 2019 has been announced (UK Government n.d.).

To improve adult literacy and numeracy, the Skills for Life strategy was initiated in 2001 (HM Treasury 2009). The National Skills Academy Programme was then launched in 2005 to train specialists and the Train to Gain program and designed to improve skill deficiencies (HM Treasury 2006). The program was discontinued in 2010, however, after it was recognized that "...it [was] simply paying for training that would have happened anyway" (Brennan 2010).

In short, the British government over the past decades has implemented many initiatives to try and strengthen the collaboration between its world-class scientific institutions and its business sector, but with mixed success. These programs have been evaluated elsewhere, but it is difficult to ascertain their impact. It would take us beyond the scope of this chapter to attempt an assessment here.

8.1.5.4 Enterprise Culture

The UK government seems to have encouraged an entrepreneurial culture through awards starting decades ago. For example, The Queen's Awards for Enterprise is prestigious awards for businesses and individuals in the UK since 1965. The Enterprise Act of 2002 made bankruptcy law more forgiving, recognizing that not all of the bankruptcies are the result of misconduct and irresponsibility (Walters 2005). The Davies Review (Davies 2002) argued that the best way to make the culture more entrepreneurial was through the educational system. In 2004, the government established the National Council for Graduate Entrepreneurship to promote a culture of entrepreneurship in higher education and launched the initiative Enterprising Britain, which since 2005 is an annual competition.

Teaching pupils to be entrepreneurial, however, is not the same as teaching them about entrepreneurship. The government therefore shifted focus with the aim to foster a more entrepreneurial youth. They launched Inspiring the future, where young entrepreneurs are volunteering to go into schools to talk about running their own business, Enterprise Village which supports teachers to set up and develop a school-based business, and the Premier League Enterprise Academy model which enabled football clubs to develop enterprise in young people, concentrating in deprived areas. The government also funded the development of Student-led Enterprise Societies. Their main activity was working together with local firms to get loans for student support and launching start-ups. The Global Entrepreneurship Week is, further, an annual event to help young people learn about the range of support programs available to entrepreneurs in the UK.

Besides awards, support, and events, the UK government encouraged entrepreneurship through Enterprise Zones, established since 2012. These Enterprise Zones are designated areas across England that provide tax breaks and government support. Initiatives to improve access to information and counseling are all part of a big umbrella campaign called Great Business, under which the government launched the Business in You Campaign with the aim to help people understand how they can start and run their own business.

In conclusion, subsequent UK governments have always had an interest in and developed (national) initiatives to promote an entrepreneurial mindset and culture throughout the UK.

8.1.6 Brexit and the LSE Growth Commission Report (2017)

In discussing the current situation in the UK, it would be incomplete not to discuss the issue of Brexit. Although the exact relationship of the UK with the European Union after Brexit remains unclear at the time of writing this book (January 2020), the LSE Growth Commission (2017) has published a noteworthy report on the growth prospects of the post-Brexit UK. The Commission reports some progress on the recommendations made in its 2013 prequel (mainly on increasing competition and investment in long-term assets and SMEs) but, interestingly, now calls for a tax and minimum wage system that is neutral with regard to forms of employment to promote lifelong learning and adaptable skills in light of rapid technological changes. Coupled with a new system of tax breaks for skills investment and better endowed technical education, this should make British workers more resilient in future labor markets while supplying British entrepreneurs with the much-needed skilled labor force.

For the financial sector, the Commission suggests maintaining the links to EU markets by developing a substitute for the financial services "passport" while also diversifying its portfolio. The latter should be done by building new links to emerging markets and tapping into domestic markets by widening SME access to bond markets and boosting equity tax relief schemes for investors in SMEs. If at the same time smart regulation would make the banking market more competitive while supporting the emerging FinTech sector, the private financial markets can be an asset, not a liability for the British economy. To complement the private sector, the Commission advised the government to strengthen the British Business Bank, to establish a new infrastructure bank, and to fill the funding gaps the private market will not fill.

Finally, the Commission challenges the UK's industrial strategy, stating that two-thirds of the workforce are now employed in sectors where productivity is below average. The Commission therefore recommends the government to establish a new framework in order to pursue six key priorities, namely:

1. Skill shortages;
2. Low productivity sectors;
3. Small firms (less obstacles in terms of taxes and regulations);
4. Universities and private sector collaboration;
5. City-growth policies (support locally);
6. Growth, environment, and well-being.

The analysis of the Commission also largely supports the proposals we present below. Still, our focus on entrepreneurship and the entrepreneurial ecosystem has led us to identify slightly different bottlenecks. Furthermore, a more historical and regionally differentiated approach leads us to focus our proposals on making the UK ecosystem more diversified and inclusive, while de-emphasizing the more traditional UK strategies of further SME deregulation, putting a strong focus on (global) finance and linking academic research to the private sector.

8.1.7 Conclusions

In conclusion, the UK has an eventful history that shaped its institutions in a unique way. The British Isles were not invaded from outside since 1066, but saw centuries of internal conflict before the country unified in the seventeenth and rose to unrivaled global supremacy in the nineteenth century. In the twentieth century, however, this unrivaled position was challenged and the UK, like any other nation going forward, will have to compete in an increasingly global marketplace with innovative and efficient competitors for the favor of consumers across the globe.

During the Thatcher years of the 1980s, the UK developed into a distinct liberal market economy (Hall and Soskice 2001) with a deregulated business environment, flexible labor markets, well-funded elite universities, and strong protection of intellectual property rights. In such a system, however, low labor protection arguably reduces incentives to invest and accumulate (firm-specific) human capital. Policies based on further deregulation and stronger market competition will not be able to address this weakness. In line with the LSE Commission on Growth (2017), we thus argue, below, that the UK needs to start paying more attention to its collective physical, digital, and financial infrastructures—factors that entrepreneurs need to succeed in global markets. A well-educated, loyal labor force, and excellent infrastructure are essential for ventures to grow into sustainable and globally competitive businesses. If, as a corollary, the UK entrepreneurial ecosystem can also become more inclusive—regionally, and across income groups and wealth levels—this may turn out to be vital for the long-run sociopolitical sustainability of the UK model.

8.2 Step 2: Data Analysis with REDI for the UK

8.2.1 UK's International Position

For calculating country scores of the Regional Entrepreneurship and Development Index (REDI), we used the population-weighted REDI-scores. Out of 24 European countries, the UK then ranks 4th with 56.0 points behind Ireland, Denmark, and Sweden (Table 3.3, Varga et al. 2020). The REDI ranking for the UK is quite consistent with other more commonly used indicators. The UK continues to be in top 10 in terms of "Ease of Doing Business" on the World Bank Doing Business report, ranking 7th out of 190 economies in the 2017–18 report.

The LSE Growth Commission (2017) identified human capital, especially among low wage employees, as a key weakness. Their report suggested leveling the playing field, now tilted in favor of self-employed, to promote long-term employment and on-the-job training in the UK. Again, this contrasts specifically with Germany, where permanent contracts enjoy very strong labor protection and on-the-job training is very strong. Clearly, the UK and Germany have developed different models, as the Varieties of Capitalism literature already suggested. In the same way as in Germany, the strengths of the UK model typically imply its weaknesses.

To address the UK's weaknesses, the LSE Growth Commission (2017) advocates, among other things, the implementation of a more directive industrial policy to shape future markets and negotiating new trade deals with the EU and USA to ensure London's bank and service-oriented dominance after Brexit. We believe the success of both these policy approaches depends to a large extent on factors beyond UK control and therefore represent high-risk strategies. The only certainty the UK has is that a lot of things will change, and the country must brace for a major shock. We would therefore argue that diversification and flexibility are the best defense and propose that a more vibrant, agile, and flexible entrepreneurial society will be able to cope with such uncertainty and change.

The UK's entrepreneurial ecosystem, though performing well in international comparison, also has its bottlenecks. The UK is known to suffer from the so-called European paradox (EC 1995). That is, on innovation scoreboards, the UK consistently ranks high (Schwanen and Wyonch 2018), but it seems the UK has problems commercializing that knowledge and bringing new technology to global markets. As the latter is the role that Schumpeter (1911) and, more recently, the knowledge spillover theory of entrepreneurship (Acs et al. 2009, 2013) foresee for entrepreneurs, this suggests there must be weaknesses in the entrepreneurial ecosystem that more traditional indicators and indices fail to identify. Figure 8.1 gives us a first glance at how the UK is performing relative to Germany, Italy, and the EU average on the 14 pillars identified in the REDI (Acs et al. 2014; Szerb et al. 2017, 2019).

It is clear from the graph that the UK entrepreneurial ecosystem is strong on almost all pillars and outperforms the Italian ecosystem on all but two pillars, "Product Innovation" and "Risk Capital." In the former pillar, the Italian ecosystem benefits from its strong emphasis and specialization in small-scale manufacturing industries, whereas the UK economy is much more characterized by services, where product innovation is simply harder to observe. The UK also outperforms the EU and Germany on several pillars, especially when it comes to Entrepreneurial Attitudes (pillars 1–5 in the figure) and Entrepreneurial Ability (6–9).

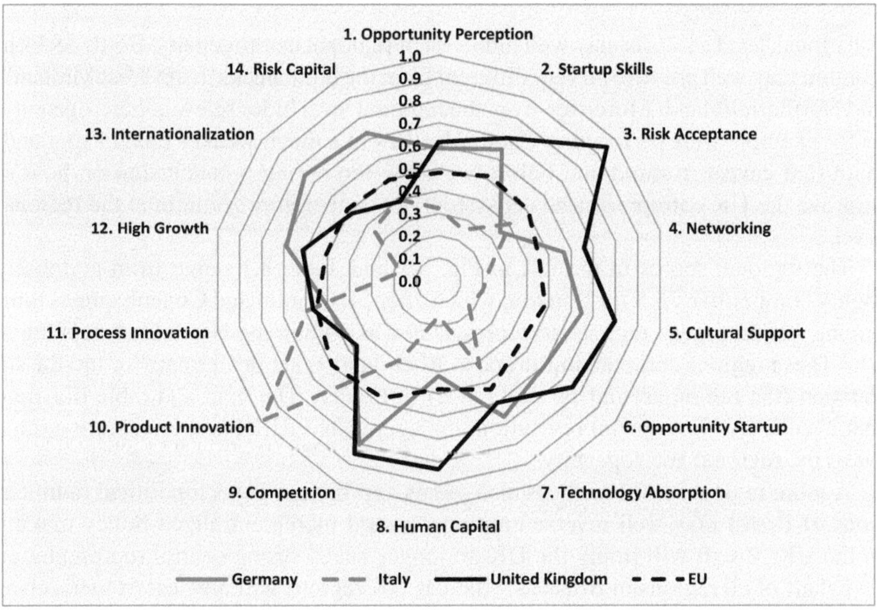

Fig. 8.1 Radar-plot REDI comparison Germany–Italy–UK and EU-average. *Source* Authors' own compilation

Concerning Entrepreneurial Aspirations (10–14), Germany and even occasionally the EU as a whole outperform the UK. These include the outcomes and availability of financial and knowledge resources, where it seems that the British ecosystem could benefit from reforms. This confirms the above-mentioned Growth Commission's analysis that it is the final step from invention to innovation and economic growth where the UK ecosystem has (relative) weaknesses. The data show that the UK performs at or above the EU average on almost all pillars and only underperforms in comparison with the EU average on three pillars: "Product Innovation," "Internationalization" and, perhaps surprisingly at first glance, "Risk Capital."

The underperformance on the pillar "Risk Capital" is mainly driven by large regional variations (see also Sect. 8.2.2), where many remote regions (e.g., in northern England) have very low values. In the central parts of UK, the financial system works better. Still, in this low score, we see a long-term challenge for the British governments since the early 1970s (HMSO 1971, 1979) is confirmed. These sources argue that paradoxically, as a result of strong formal financial markets for equity and VC capital, the funding gap for ventures that cannot gain access to these channels (and typically rely on less abundant informal finance) is more pronounced.

8.2.2 A More Detailed Regional Quick Scan

A national-level analysis may well hide a lot of regional heterogeneity. Bottlenecks in London may well prove to be very different from the bottlenecks in the West Midlands and Northern Ireland. Moreover, even the regional level hides relevant heterogeneity, as for example well-performing Cambridge lies in a much weaker East of England. With that caveat in mind and before we draw too strong a conclusion on how to improve the UK entrepreneurial ecosystem, let us therefore zoom in at the regional level.

The regional scores in the UK in Fig. 8.2 and Table 8.1 range from a globally highly competitive 75.5 for London, which after Stockholm and Copenhagen is third among 125 European regions, to scores as low as 44.3 in the North East, ranking at 61.[5] These regions compare in Europe to Rheinland-Pfalz in Germany or the Bassin Parisien (the region around Île de France) in France. The map and table illustrate that even at this low spatial resolution, the aggregated REDI scores capture quite a bit of the regional heterogeneity.

A more regional-level analysis also seems appropriate as sociopolitical ramifications of Brexit may well reverse the trend toward more centralized policy making in the UK. Brexit will imply the UK no longer needs strong central representation on behalf of all regions in Brussels, whereas UK regions will now assert themselves more in London. The Brexit vote uncovered important differences across regions that reflect economic realities as well. Investing in a more resilient entrepreneurial

[5]The numbers are index numbers ranging from 0 (worst) to 100 (best) across all 125 European NUTS2/3 regions for 2012–2014.

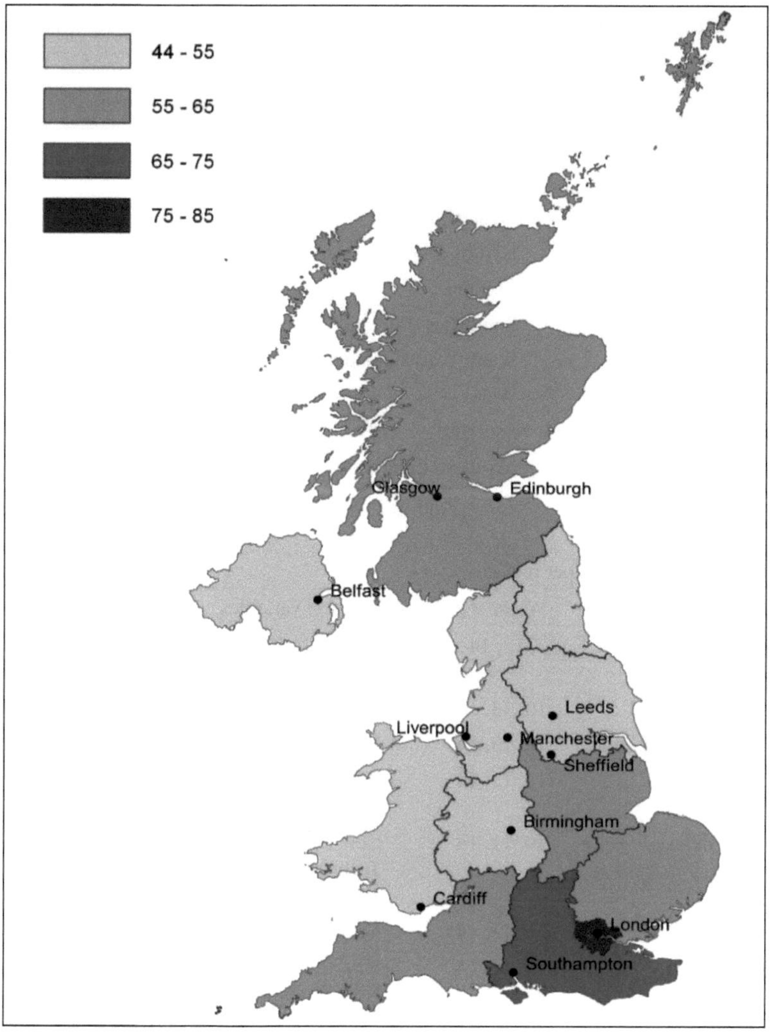

Fig. 8.2 REDI map of UK's regions. *Source* Authors' own compilation

ecosystem that generates inclusive and innovative growth across the Kingdom may well prove an important strategy to prevent further tensions.

Table 8.2 shows the weakest pillars in the REDI index across all UK regions. The analysis shows that the pillars are all concentrated in the 10–14 range, with only a few exceptions. Despite the large range between the best and worst performing entrepreneurial ecosystems in the UK, therefore, it is possible to implement policies and propose reforms that will strengthen all ecosystems alike. The frequent appearance of pillars 7, 10, and 11 suggests a bottleneck in the transfer of knowledge from basic and applied research to commercial activity, as in the aforementioned so-called

Table 8.1 REDI-score UK

Region	REDI-scores 2012–2014
North East England	44.3
North West England	50.4
Yorkshire and The Humber	51.8
East Midlands	57.9
West Midlands	54.0
East of England	58.7
London	75.5
South East England	69.6
South West England	62.3
Wales	50.4
Scotland	60.5
Northern Ireland	55.0

Source Authors' own compilation

Table 8.2 Weakest points per region

Region	Weakest pillars	Weakest variables
North East England	7, 12, 14	Absorptive Capacity and Technology Level, Clustering and Gazelles, Informal Investment
North West England	10, 13, 14	New Product, Exports, Informal Investment
Yorkshire and the Humber	10, 13, 14	New Product, Exports, Informal Investment
East Midlands	12, 13, 14	Clustering and Gazelles, Exports, Informal Investment
West Midlands	10, 11, 14	New Product and Technology Transfer, Technology Development, and New Technology, Informal Investment
East of England	10, 13, 14	New Product, Exports, Informal Investment
London	10, 11, 14	New Product, Technology Development and New Technology, Informal Investment
South East England	10, 12, 13	New Product, Gazelles, Exports
South West England	10, 11, 14	New Product, New Technology, Exports
Wales	7, 10, 11	Absorptive Capacity and Technology Level, New Product, Technology Development, and New Technology
Scotland	10, 13, 14	New Product, Connectivity and Exports, Informal Investment
Northern Ireland	1, 13, 14	Opportunity Recognition, Connectivity and Exports, Informal Investment

Source Authors' own compilation

European Paradox. It reflects the low actual uptake of new product and process technology in new ventures in the UK. This weakness is pronounced throughout the country and even the world-class London ecosystem is (relatively) weak in that respect. This calls for a targeted national approach, where interventions aim to strengthen exactly that weak link.

The frequent appearance of pillar 13, underpinned with low scores on Exports and sometimes also Connectivity, suggests UK manufacturing still has difficulty finding foreign markets and competing in the global marketplace. The strong services' orientation of, in particular, the London ecosystem can explain why this aspect of the entrepreneurial ecosystem remains underdeveloped. But although for London this does not seem to be a big problem, for the more peripheral regions in the UK it may well be. Moreover, Brexit may adversely affect the competitive position of London as the financial and business services capital of Europe. Diversification and the development of new, more industrially oriented competitive strengths could be a sensible strategy to try and strengthen these pillars in the UK entrepreneurial ecosystem.

The other pillar that stands out as remarkably and consistently weak across the UK is pillar 14 "Risk Capital." Low scores on "Risk Capital" are typically due to very low levels of informal investment being available and/or accessed. This is compensated by strong formal markets for equity in early-stage venturing, but business angel and VC markets have come under criticism for lack of regional, gender, and ethnic inclusiveness (Bates and Bradford 1992; Mollick and Robb 2016). Well-developed VC and private equity markets are of course good for the unicorns and gazelles that make the headlines, but financing the SMEs and start-ups at the base requires smaller magnitudes that promise only lower returns, making them much less interesting for VC funds and angel investors.

In Estrin et al. (2018), the authors investigated the potential for equity crowdfunding to play a complementary role in filling the funding gap. But reforms can also be proposed to strengthen the more traditional informal investment channels. This may be particularly important to boost access to informal investment, especially in the periphery.

We believe the UK is doing well in developing crowdfunding as a channel to complement formal financial markets. From Table 8.2, we may conclude that most UK regions would benefit from reforms and interventions that increase the technological sophistication and innovativeness of production and increase the flow of funds to perhaps dull, but essential small industrial firms that turn new knowledge into business. In manufacturing, this can give a boost to export performance and global competitiveness, whereas in services this will stimulate the regional and national economy.

We agree with the LSE Growth Commission (2017) that policies to level the playing field between self-employed and employees and to increase incentives for on the job training are helpful in this respect. The UK's strength in labor flexibility may well come at a cost of low loyalty and security for employees that makes investment in firm-specific human capital, especially at the lower end of the wage distribution, a less appealing proposition.

8.2.3 *Overall Conclusions of the REDI Analysis*

Our reading of the data above reveals that in all UK regions and in the country as a whole, the entrepreneurial ecosystem is strong. But even in the best ecosystem, there are always pillars that perform relatively weak and bottlenecks remain in a lack of innovation (New Products and Technology), export orientation (Exports), and informal investment. It is dangerous, however, to rely exclusively on data and aggregate indices, even if they are composed of a broad set of sub-indicators. It is always important to complement a data-based quick scan with common sense and more qualitative information to contextualize and complete the diagnosis. Only after triangulating the results above with the historical analysis, literature review, expert judgement and more qualitative survey results below, we can map the diagnosis onto our menu of interventions to propose tailored reforms for the UK.

8.3 Step 3: Triangulating History, Data, and Survey Results

8.3.1 *Venture Creation Processes in the UK*

As illustrated in Herrmann (2020), we studied in two ways how the British institutional ecosystem influences entrepreneurial activities, namely from a static perspective (based on multiannual averages) as well as from a process-oriented perspective. Both kinds of analyses provide similar insights. Our static analyses reveal that entrepreneurs in the UK are less likely to set up incrementally innovative ventures or imitate existing business ideas; they rather tend to set up radically innovative ventures (Dilli et al. 2018; Herrmann 2019).

The dynamic analyses, in turn, illustrate how the British institutional environment influences different aspects of the venture creation process. With regard to human capital, we find that national labor market institutions influence the work choices of entrepreneurs (Held 2019). Whenever labor market flexibility guarantees neither employment security nor benefits, the risk related to giving-up dependent employment in order to work full-time on venture creation is limited. Accordingly, part-time entrepreneurs in liberal market economies, such as the UK, are significantly more likely to transition to full-time entrepreneurship than their counterparts in coordinated market economies, such as Germany (Held 2019).

With regard to the process of finance acquisition, we (Held et al. 2018a) find that various venture characteristics influence the type of funding which nascent venture acquire first and, respectively, most. These characteristics also include a venture's institutional environment. Ventures in countries with a higher stock market capitalization (such as the UK) are less likely to seek debt finance. At the same time, a more limited availability of loans to the private sector also leads nascent ventures to finance their endeavors through grants.

Finally, we find that nascent ventures in the UK and the USA are less likely to engage in R&D collaborations with external partners, such as universities and laboratories, than nascent ventures in Germany (Held et al. 2018b). It seems that nascent ventures are reluctant to engage in joint R&D projects whenever the institutions governing inter-firm collaborations make the outcome of lawsuits in case of IP conflicts rather unpredictable.

Taken together, these studies lend support to the argument that the UK's distinct finance, labor, and R&D-related institutions influence the decisions of entrepreneurs with regard to the business ideas they develop as well as the modus operandi they choose to set up their ventures. This leads to the question how British entrepreneurs experienced their institutional environment when setting up a venture: Which aspects are constraining? And what could policy makers do to facilitate venture creation in the UK?

8.3.2 Regulatory Barriers to Entrepreneurship in UK

To examine regulatory barriers to entrepreneurship, we conducted interviews with 158 founders in the UK between 2016 and 2018. Table 8.3 provides an overview of the answers given to the question: "Which regulatory requirements did you perceive as major obstacles during venture creation?" that were coded to compare the answers also across countries.

The first remarkable result of Table 8.3 is that about every second founder said that they did not experience any regulatory obstacles. This lends support to our aforementioned result that it is overall rather easy to start a business in the UK. It is also in line with the UK rankings in the World Bank's (2018) Doing Business reports. A sustained pro-business attitude since the Thatcher years has successfully reduced costs and regulatory barriers to founding and managing businesses.

Still, some challenges remain. According to a recent poll among business owners (thus, not only founders), 51% of businesses think that the level of regulation in the UK is an obstacle to success, whereas 46% of small businesses identified tax administration as a burdensome area of compliance (NAO 2014). These findings are confirmed by our survey. Tax legislation, together with stringent data protection laws and onerous information requirements, was mentioned (each about 5% of all times) among the most important obstacles to venture creation. This suggests that in the UK, founders occasionally have difficulties to find the right information and navigate the complexities of government bureaucracy. It is furthermore noteworthy that unreliable or very specific regulation was perceived as an obstacle. Accordingly, legal insecurity as well as legal requirements for approval were perceived as obstacles in, together, about 8% of all times. Similarly, specific requirements related to the energy sector (almost 3% of times), stringent environmental regulation (almost 2% of times), and a constantly changing regulatory environment (almost 2% of times) were mentioned as important regulatory constraints.

Table 8.3 Results' survey regulatory obstacles in the UK

Which regulatory requirements did you perceive as major obstacles during venture creation?	Times mentioned	In %
None	81	43.8
Does not answer question	5	2.7
Data protection laws	10	5.4
Tax legislation	9	4.9
Onerous requirements for documentation	9	4.9
Legal Insecurity	8	4.3
Legal requirements for approval	7	3.8
Specific requirements related to energy sector	5	2.7
Pension scheme	5	2.7
High taxes	4	2.2
Employment regulations in general	4	2.2
Difficulties with obtaining government funding	4	2.2
Stringent environmental regulations	3	1.6
Insurance requirements	3	1.6
Constantly changing regulatory environment	3	1.6

Note
1. Based on interviews with 158 founders mentioning 185 obstacles (more than one obstacle could be mentioned)
2. Only obstacles mentioned three times or more are reported in the table

Source Authors' own compilation

Based on these insights, we conclude that it is important for governments to carefully consider not only the contents of regulations but to also pay attention that rules and regulation have a long-term perspective. If regulation is changed frequently, this leads to insecurity among founders as well as business owners.

8.3.3 Founders' Suggestions for Reforms in the UK

In the same survey, founders were also asked: "What can policy makers do to facilitate venture creation?". The answers to this question are listed in Table 8.4.

Interestingly, only a small share of founders (7.2%) opined that policy makers could *not* facilitate venture creation. This is a remarkable contrast to the above finding that about every second founder did not feel constrained by regulatory obstacles. On the contrary, British founders had numerous suggestions on how policy makers could facilitate venture creation.

By far, the most common suggestion called for facilitating access to finance for small businesses (almost 13% of all times mentioned). This is perhaps remarkable,

Table 8.4 Policy recommendations by founders in the UK

In your view, what could policy makers do to facilitate venture creation?	Times mentioned	In %
Nothing	19	7.2
Does not answer question	6	2.3
Facilitate financing for small businesses	34	12.8
Provide better training to people for starting businesses	23	8.7
Reduce bureaucracy	18	6.8
Reduce tax rates for small businesses	17	6.4
Provide better information about how to start a business	16	6.0
Provide incentives for hiring people	13	4.9
Avoid constant policy changes	13	4.9
Provide competent advice to people starting businesses	9	3.4
Centralize information for starting business	8	3.0
Improve situation specific to energy sector	7	2.6
Help market start-ups	7	2.6
Remain in EU	6	2.3
Provide better networking opportunities	6	2.3
Provide guidance	6	2.3
Be less inclined toward incumbents	5	1.9
Offset risk of starting business	4	1.5
Improve situation specific to IT sector	4	1.5
Financial benefits for founder	4	1.5
Create feeling of support for entrepreneurs	3	1.1

Note
1. Based on interviews with 158 founders mentioning 265 suggestions (more than one suggestion could be mentioned)
2. Only suggestions mentioned three times or more are reported in the table
Source Authors' own compilation

because the UK has a well-developed financial system. The reason for this discrepancy, also discussed in our REDI analysis, is related to the different types of finance that nascent ventures use. While venture or angel capital is comparatively abundant in the UK, only radically innovative ventures have access to such high-risk finance. As pointed out by Herrmann (2020), even in the UK only a small minority (of less than 10%) of all ventures founded per year are radically innovative. This would imply that the majority of ventures, pursuing incrementally innovative or imitative business ideas, need to turn to other financial sources. For these ventures, which also are the largest part of respondents to our survey, bank- or government-based finance constitutes the most important finance source—next to the founders' own and informal funding. We therefore interpret the suggestion of better access to finance as a call for improving access to bank-based, public, and informal finance.

The second most important suggestion concerns the human resources needed for venture creation. Almost 9% of responses highlighted that policy makers should provide better training to people for starting businesses, while almost 5% suggested to provide incentives for hiring people. Overall, this is in line with our above findings that, in the UK, workers with (firm-) specific skills are comparatively scarce and difficult to retain. The suggestions of UK founders indicate that the British workforce would benefit from acquiring not only more specific skills but also more entrepreneurial knowledge. In addition, policies that facilitate the hiring of skilled workers may constitute a further measure to provide nascent ventures with the necessary human capital.

While founders also asked for lower tax rates for small businesses (in almost 6.5% of cases), they asked in various ways for better and more transparent information about venture creation. Accordingly, they did not only suggest to reduce bureaucracy (in almost 7% of cases) but also to provide better information about how to start a business (in 6%), to provide competent advice to people starting businesses (in almost 3.5%), to centralize information for starting businesses (in 3%), and to provide guidance (in almost 2.5%). Taken together, this indicates that founders have experienced systematic problems in obtaining the necessary information at the right time.

Finally, and in line with the regulatory obstacles mentioned above, the founders interviewed suggested that venture creation would be facilitated by a more reliable and long-term oriented regulation. Accordingly, they suggested to avoid frequent policy changes in almost 5% of all times and to remain within the EU in almost 2.5% of times.

8.3.4 Conclusions

While our founder survey does not confirm all the weaknesses identified in REDI analyses based on composite indices, it adds several important nuances. It thus adds complementary information to the results obtained in Sect. 8.2. For example, the surveys clearly confirm the need for better opportunities for small ventures to obtain finance. But in addition, founders also highlight the lack of (access to) an appropriately skilled workforce. The REDI analysis, in contrast, did not flag this as a problem, because of its focus on tertiary education. The founders interviewed, however, agree with the LSE Growth Committee (2017) that vocational education should be improved and incentives for employing and training workers on the job should be strengthened.

Next to these aspects, our founder survey also highlights the importance of transparent and easily accessible information about venture creation, as well as stable and reliable regulation. Given that these aspects are not covered by the REDI data, the survey offers important complementary insights into how policy makers can still facilitate venture creation—even in a comparatively business-friendly environment as the UK. Founders repeatedly highlighted the importance of clear and reliable information about venture creation requirements, as well as stable regulation. Whenever founders are faced with uncertainty because of unclear requirements and frequently changing regulation, this substantially—and unnecessarily—hinders venture creation.

Taken together, our historical, quantitative and qualitative information for the UK, though necessarily limited in scope and depth, reveals enough information to now draw up a diagnosis for the UK and turn to a proposed treatment.

8.4 Step 4: Mapping onto the FIRES-Reform Proposals

Formulating a reform strategy to strengthen the entrepreneurial ecosystem is similar to treating a patient. In the previous sections, we have considered the medical history of the patient, used an advanced diagnostic tool to scan for their health problems, and asked the patient how they feel and what they believe would be good treatments. Based on all this information, we can reach a diagnosis, map that diagnosis onto the menu of available treatments, and propose a treatment that fits the patient.

For the UK, we conclude that its rich and long history has shaped its institutions in a unique way. And yet, British ventures compete in an increasingly global marketplace with innovative and efficient competitors for the favor of consumers around the globe. The UK is therefore well advised to improve its entrepreneurial ecosystem in order to face that competition.

Since the Thatcher years in the 1980s, the UK has relied on the private sector and market competition to assert its competitive position in the world, with mixed success. Its London-based financial sector has developed into one of the most advanced and developed markets in the world, while waning industries long lingered in the North. Policies that governments of different political orientation have implemented are often and still based on the tried and tested UK recipes of further liberalization and stronger market competition, resulting in the most liberal market economy in Europe characterized by a liberalized regulatory environment, flexible labor markets, well-funded elite universities, and strong protection of intellectual property rights. In such a system, the winner takes all, creating strong incentives to succeed. But low taxes and minimal social protection also imply high risks of failure, low investment in human capital, and eroding public infrastructures.

We argue below that the UK needs to start paying more attention to the public and collective infrastructures that the individual entrepreneur also needs to succeed. Making the UK entrepreneurial ecosystem more inclusive—regionally as well as across income groups and wealth classes—may well turn out to be vital to the long-run sociopolitical sustainability and global competitiveness of the UK model (Piketty 2014; Van Bavel 2016).

The UK boasts a strong entrepreneurial ecosystem in general, but the average masks some great disparities. London (as well as the corridor from London to Bristol) is the undisputed hotbed of entrepreneurship alongside lagging rural and old industrial regions. The geographic resolution of our data reveals that UK's entrepreneurial talent and resources tend to cluster in London, where returns to such skills and resources are highest. Quantitative data analysis then suggests large heterogeneity in entrepreneurial ecosystem performance. While this does not come out as a problem for the country as a whole, it creates a political divide, as the Brexit vote has clearly uncovered, for example.

The results from our survey do not reveal this heterogeneity. While they confirm that the challenges and bottlenecks in their ecosystem are not formidable, they still point to a lack of funding for small ventures, as well as a lack of skilled personnel. This, in turn, supports the insights obtained from the previous historical and quantitative analyses.

Our data analysis additionally reveals that entrepreneurship in the UK is less successful in adopting and commercializing high-tech knowledge developed in academic institutions and world-class R&D laboratories. New ventures in the UK score (comparatively) low in radically new products and technology absorption and its regions lack risk capital in the form of informal investment. These pillars in the ecosystem, together with non-transparent information about and frequently changing regulation of entrepreneurship, seem to be the weakest links in an otherwise business-friendly entrepreneurial ecosystem. The treatment needed should therefore help to overcome these weaknesses.

As the UK is to leave the European Union, it may be required to diversify its economy and regain its position in global markets also as a high-tech industrial exporter. This will require a well-trained labor force which is also available to nascent ventures that aim to grow into globally competitive firms. A healthy entrepreneurial ecosystem will be an asset and interventions to strengthen technology absorption and informal finance for more mundane and slow-growing industrial SMEs and start-ups will be beneficial.

Taking these prescriptions to our menu of policy interventions and reform proposals in Part I of this report, we can select the fifteen most suitable interventions. They are listed in Table 8.5. In Column 1, we find the number under which they are presented in Elert et al. (2019). Column 2 lists the policy area and 3 the full proposal, where Column 4 gives a brief motivation that links the proposal to the specific situation in the UK and the analysis presented above.

The first two proposals (2 and 4) refer to intellectual property rights and call for the UK to experiment and negotiate for less stringent and encompassing IPR. This may sound counterintuitive and goes against the mainstream thinking that strong IPR promotes innovation and growth by providing incentives to generate knowledge. In stakeholder dialogues and discussions, as well as academic research, however, that conventional wisdom is often turned on its head. Complex legal protection of IPR serves the interest of large incumbent corporates, who use IPR to maximize their profits. This rarely involves maximizing the generation and diffusion of new knowledge and technology through commercialization. The British experience in the industrial revolution, when IPR enforcement was expensive and scant, is a case in point. The reforms we propose would aim to restore IPR to its original purpose: Give credit to the inventor, while promoting further incremental innovation and commercialization by entrepreneurs. By opening up IPR, the UK would create opportunities for less sophisticated entrepreneurs to compete at the global frontier.

Table 8.5 FIRES-reform proposals for the UK[a]

No.	Policy area	Proposal	UK
2	Intellectual property	Limit the breadth, width, and span of patent protection to cover working prototypes and market-ready innovations only for a short period of time and permit economic actors to infringe upon patents that have not been commercialized.	IP is intended to promote the registration, diffusion, and commercial application of new knowledge and technology. But the system is gradually turning into a system where savvy lawyers help large corporates to prevent, not promote these things. To restore the system to its original purpose, the rights of inventors and infringers need to be better balanced. You can be the inventor/discoverer of an idea, but society only benefits if that knowledge is commercialized.
4	Intellectual property	Introduce and support existing experiments with open-source patent registration.	Open-source patents combine giving credit to the inventor, keeping a registry of useful knowledge and opening up that knowledge base for further expansion, also through commercial venturing. The UK after Brexit will remain a member of the European Patent Office but can offer to take the lead in experiments that will promote free flows of knowledge in society.
13	Private wealth	Allow for more wealth to accumulate and remain in private hands and make it possible, easy, and attractive to invest such wealth in entrepreneurial ventures.	This may sound counterintuitive as a policy to promote a more inclusive entrepreneurial society, but small, everyday entrepreneurs cannot access the increasingly formalized angel and VC markets. Their tickets are too small and returns too low to attract such funding. Thus, triple-F finance is, for now, their only recourse. This proposal aims to increase the availability of such funding. As we want to promote especially small tickets and amounts, tax exemptions can be capped at relatively low amounts. Small wealth that is actively invested in small, triple-F, equity investments should be treated differently from large fortunes, passively invested in global financial markets.

(continued)

Table 8.5 (continued)

No.	Policy area	Proposal	UK
18	Banks	Ensure that (appropriately anonymized) credit decision information becomes publicly available in the system of bank loan guarantees for start-ups.	Banks in the UK do not disclose information about credit they grant or credit they refuse (Barclays, 2017). Such information, if adequately anonymized, however, can be very helpful for other credit seekers and investors, also outside the banking sector. Access to such information should be supervised by the government and privacy must be protected.
19	Banks	Increase the mandatory equity ratio in banking gradually to 10–15 percent to allow them to take on more risk responsibly in their lending portfolios.	European and international minimum standards are applied in the UK but allow for rather low reserves and high leverage. The UK banks are among the largest and highest leveraged banks in the world, still posing a considerable risk for the UK economy while failing to serve the needs of especially SMEs. Financing entrepreneurship first requires more loss absorbing capacity in banking.
20	Banks	Introduce central bank digital currency to replace deposits at commercial banks as the dominant medium of exchange.	Following the logic of proposal 19, the Bank of England can reduce the need for strict bank supervision on the asset side of commercial banks' balance sheets after ensuring the stability of the decidedly public infrastructure for transactions and savings. By introducing a central bank digital currency, there is no need for guarantees of commercial banks liquidity and public deposit insurance that distorts banks financing costs. When payments and savings are secure, banks can once more invest on behalf of their clients for own profit, risk, and responsibility.

(continued)

Table 8.5 (continued)

No.	Policy area	Proposal	UK
26	Social security	Guarantee equal access to welfare state arrangements for all, regardless of tenure in a specific job or labor market status.	The LSE Growth Commission (2017) argued for a more level playing field between employees and self-employed on the premise that self-employed is currently favored in the UK labor market. We believe that in addition, both employees and self-employed face risks they cannot self-insure and that should not be a basis for competition. Small and risk ventures can only compete for employees on a level playing field when access to welfare state arrangements is equal for the important risks across labor market statuses.
31	Active labor market policy	Establish or strengthen training programs to prepare workers for new occupations.	Job creation and destruction are relatively high in the UK. Small firms are disproportionately responsible for this (Hijzen et al. 2010). This implies that a more entrepreneurial society, with more employment in small- and medium-sized firms in experimentation, will imply that employees need to be equipped with the skills to transfer between jobs and employers.
37	ICT	Invest in excellent, open-access digital infrastructure for European citizens and businesses.	Infrastructures benefit entrepreneurs and their clients at home and abroad and represent classic public goods characteristics and free rider problems. Efficient provision of such public goods is traditionally a government responsibility that the UK government should take up.

(continued)

Table 8.5 (continued)

No.	Policy area	Proposal	UK
38	ICT	Develop open but responsible standards and open regulation for the many digital platforms that emerge to facilitate peer-to-peer and business-to-business trade, services, and finance.	The digital revolution is beginning to change the way we do business across the board. It touches the very institutions that allocate capital, labor, and knowledge in society (Degryse 2016; Ferrari 2016; MacKenzie 2015; Lin et al. 2009). The UK is leading in platform-based financial innovation and is in a position to set the standards. A strong infrastructure with clear and well-designed open standards should be created to promote innovation and the creation of new services and create opportunities for all to contribute and participate. Crowdfunding, crowdsourcing, self-employment, and open innovation are all greatly leveraged with digital technology.
40	Insolvency	Set up publicly funded "entrepreneurial knowledge observatories" where knowledge accumulated in the entrepreneurial process is collected, curated, and freely diffused.	In the UK, there is a relatively high rate of firm formation and failure. This is beneficial and signals a healthy entrepreneurial ecosystem generating a lot of variety and selecting quick in a tough market environment. However, this also implies a lot of knowledge is lost. Incentives to retain and disclose experiences of in particular failures are low. Such knowledge constitutes a public good.
41	Education system	Reforms in primary and secondary education should provide pupils with a solid and coherent knowledge base and promote initiative, creativity, and a willingness to experiment.	The weakness in the UK we most try to address is low levels of absorptive capacity and firm-specific human capital. UK citizens are willing to start a firm, but not so much willing to work for one and invest a lot in its success. Fostering a more entrepreneurial mindset will in the long run make jobs in start-ups and new ventures more appealing, even for the non-entrepreneurs.

(continued)

Table 8.5 (continued)

No.	Policy area	Proposal	UK
44	Universities/entrepreneurial clusters	The link between universities and external stakeholders should be strengthened by encouraging universities to stimulate entrepreneurial initiatives and university spinoffs.	UK initiatives to form clusters around its academic centers of excellence can be strengthened and made more inclusive to focus on team formation and new firm foundation as opposed to licensing and exploiting IP in more traditional ways. It involves more active engagement of the universities.
48	Innovation policy	Develop highly competitive programs encouraging small businesses to engage research and development with the potential for commercialization.	This should predominantly be done in case of the UK by enhancing the resources of firms to invest in their personnel and providing incentives, other than regulation and legal protection, to retain workers and provide stable employment opportunities for loyal employees.
50	Innovation policy	Institute technology inducement prizes to further the development of commercially applicable knowledge in especially important areas, such as climate change.	Following LSE Growth Commission (2017)'s call for a mission-driven industrial policy, we would propose to shape such a policy still in an open way. That is, the government can direct innovation and entrepreneurial venturing toward societally relevant challenges, such as energy transition and circular business models, but the government should do so in a way that selects the best solutions, and not choose the incumbent firms that are best positioned to lobby for subsidies and support. We think innovation prizes could be a way to implement such an open mission-driven industrial innovation policy.

[a]Numbered as in Elert et al. (2019)
Source Authors' own compilation

Proposal 13 aims to increase the levels of informal investment in the UK. Allowing wealth to accumulate should not be understood as an across the board reduction in wealth or property taxes. Indeed, if our diagnosis calls for a more inclusive entrepreneurial ecosystem, such a proposal would be strange indeed. We should therefore add that this proposal is to be interpreted as interventions in the taxation of wealth that will promote the accumulation of small private fortunes to be invested in small, everyday entrepreneurial ventures, through good old personal networks, and modern crowd-based equity and lending platforms. Proposal 18 adds the credit information that banks typically consider proprietary. By disclosing that information at least for the publicly guaranteed loans, also the refused ones, private investors that can take on more risk can pick up on these opportunities to invest.

Proposals 19 and 20 also aim to have free up the banks' balance sheets for more risky financing of entrepreneurial and SME venturing. The role of banks in early-stage entrepreneurial finance is typically absent, but bank credit in the form of personal loans is an important source of finance for start-ups. Both new ventures in their growth stage as well as established SMEs would benefit from a banking sector that can take on more risk and banks on relationships rather than solid collateral and track records. To allow banks to take that traditional intermediation role (again), they need to finance their balance sheet with more equity (have more "skin in the game") and the savings and transaction money of ordinary people should not be at risk sitting as a liability in the form of deposits on their balance sheets. This implies that bank credit will become more expensive, but importantly, more risk tolerant.

Proposals 37, 38, and 40 are very much aligned with the above in strengthening the infrastructure on which platform-based financial (and other) services operate and creating central and publicly funded "observatories" that collect, curate, and disclose relevant and reliable information on entrepreneurial venturing and ventures, for entrepreneurs but also for (less sophisticated) investors.

Proposals 26, 31, 41, and 44 are directly aimed to promote the flow of talent into entrepreneurial venturing, specifically in the form of a well-trained and creative workforce. Proposal 26 creates a level playing field for small, risky ventures as employers while proposal 31 intends to make Britain's workers more resilient in the face of faster changing jobs and labor markets. Employability in a modern economy depends to a large extent on the ability to learn not just knowledge that was acquired in school. Therefore, proposal 41 aims to instill creativity and experimentation in primary and secondary education (with the required tolerance for failure), whereas proposal 44 continues this line in higher education in support of entrepreneurial behavior and venturing.

Proposals 48 and 50 then aim to also keep that spirit alive on the work floor, where the former should be interpreted in the UK context as a way to incentivize small businesses to also retain and train their employees, strengthening the accumulation and maintenance of human capital throughout the average British career, while the latter translates into the government giving direction to innovation, without exerting direct control.

The intentions of these proposals, individually and in combination, are to make British entrepreneurs and SMEs more inclined to hire workers and also train them on the job and maintain their skills. One may conclude that the proposals are insufficient to create the powerful incentives to invest in on the job training that exist in CMEs, but at least these proposals take us in the right direction and are consistent with the historically evolved institutional framework of the UK. Reforms in education aim to make workers more entrepreneurial while increasing their skills and flexibility, whereas reforms in the financial system and tax code aim to allow for more private wealth to accumulate and flow to the SMEs and start-ups that VC and angel investors have shunned. The interventions proposed do not limit the mobility of resources in the UK but will help to strengthen regional entrepreneurial ecosystems. Private wealth and informal investment, as well as training on the job in small- and medium-sized manufacturing firms, tend to strengthen local and regional ecosystems, without risking leakage of resources to the center. London, meanwhile, can attract resources from all around the world and still thrive as the entrepreneurial hotspot of the UK.

It is possible that, even though all regions stand to benefit from such interventions, the fact that density and clustering tend to promote the quality and impact of entrepreneurial venturing, will imply that the same policy improvements will benefit London most. Still, that should not stop policy makers from pursuing these interventions. It is the UK citizens, not its administrative units per se, that the national government should care about. In addition, the UK has effective automatic transfer systems in social security and the National Health Service that will help maintain a high quality of life throughout the country, even if the available entrepreneurial resources end up being deployed only in parts of the territory.

As a final point, it should also be stressed that policy makers should ensure that regulation is long-term oriented and does not change frequently, as this will deter entrepreneurial activities and makes it hard to plan for the future. Information about the requirements to create ventures could also be made more easily accessible for potential entrepreneurs and, if possible, of better quality.

Of course, these proposals will need a much more detailed discussion and form the starting point, not the final word on the policy debate. In this, we join the debate the LSE Growth Committee's 2017 report has sparked in UK policy circles. By focusing on strengthening economic resilience, we believe our interventions' success depends a lot less on uncertain political and technological processes the UK cannot hope to control. Based on our analysis of the situation, we propose the UK considers this set of interventions to improve and maintain the health of its entrepreneurial ecosystem. That will be a key asset for the UK, whatever the circumstances.

8.5 Step 5: The FIRES-Reform Proposals in Light of the Countries' Historical, Geographical, and Institutional Context

To put our proposed reform program in its proper context, it is important to discuss the diagnosis and proposed treatments with experts in the field. In this case that is British policy makers that are active in the field. Given the wide diversity of policy areas involved, it is furthermore important to not only discuss this with policy makers that are active in "entrepreneurship policy" in a narrow sense. Our approach emphasizes the importance of reforming institutions that determine the allocation of financial, labor, and knowledge resources to entrepreneurial activity in the broadest and most inclusive sense of the word. Entrepreneurship policy in the narrow sense has been around for some three decades or more and to date has achieved only limited success.

Because of its breadth, our reform agenda inevitably cuts across many policy areas, traditionally less associated with entrepreneurship policy, including wealth taxation, financial and labor market regulation, social security, and science policy. As the institutions in these areas have evolved historically and policy makers in these areas pursue different, equally relevant public policy priorities, the challenge is to discuss the proposed agenda in sufficient depth but with a sufficiently diverse group of policy makers and practitioners. Policies and institutions in these different areas overlap and interact in ways that affect the quality and performance of the entrepreneurial ecosystem (Stam 2015, 2018). The challenge is to not only propose policies and reforms that will strengthen the ecosystem, but to do it in such a way that other important policy priorities are also achieved.

In order to receive the first round of feedback on the proposals for the UK presented in Table 8.5, a policy roundtable was held at the London School of Economics on April 26, 2018. Participants included senior policy makers, consultants, and political advisors as well as entrepreneurs and suppliers of financial capital. This step can be seen as an attempt to allow our patient, or perhaps more accurately, her team of medical specialists, intimately familiar with our patient, to give feedback about our diagnosis and proposed treatments. What proposals does this team endorse, question or maybe even want to drop?

The participants agreed that a more proactive government policy making along the lines of the FIRES-report might be worthwhile considering carefully. However, policies to reduce failure and accelerate scale-up were proposed as important policies to generate more entrepreneurship, which some of the participants argued should be the main focus of the FIRES proposals. The participants also suggested that the notion of entrepreneurship itself and the meaning of the term was ambiguous, covering a variety of activities from forming major new companies to providing work for the socially excluded. It was important to link the policy proposals to the specific form of entrepreneurship under consideration.

The participants then discussed the proposals on experimenting with or abandoning IP protection laws. IP and patents are one of the few tangible components of an entrepreneurial project upon which investors can make evaluations. It was suggested that one could either increase renewal fees of patents or open IP systems to radical change toward "open source." This system would then mirror that of, for example, the culinary industry.

Some major UK issues such as immigration, human capital, and digitalization were pointed out as having not been sufficiently addressed in the study. The participants pointed to the importance of developing a dynamic entrepreneurial environment with a much more inclusive venture capital investment approach.

The participants furthermore expressed deep concern about the geographical concentration of entrepreneurial activity in UK, as discussed in the FIRES-report. There is a visible centralization of the entrepreneurial resources in London which only attracts a narrow demography and a lack of incentives for people to stay or go back home to the countryside.

As a final point, the need for developing a benchmark that enables this study to better evaluate the findings by comparing it to what is happening in the rest of the world was stressed.

8.6 Conclusions

This chapter on the UK illustrates the FIRES-approach to formulating a tailored institutional reform strategy to promote a more entrepreneurial society in Europe. It illustrates how one could systematically analyze the situation before selecting and proposing reforms within this area. After carefully analyzing the UK's historically rooted institutional foundations, this chapter triangulates historical, qualitative, and quantitative information to identify the UK's strengths and weaknesses. Based on this diagnosis, the most relevant proposals are selected from the menu of policy interventions and reform proposals in the companion volume of this book (Elert et al. 2019).

The UK's long and rich history has shaped its institutions in a unique way. The British Isles rose to unrivaled global supremacy in the nineteenth century, but in the twentieth century its rivals rapidly caught up. Like any other nation, the UK has to compete with innovative and efficient competitors for the favor of consumers across the globe. The UK has developed its distinct Anglo-Saxon model of capitalism with a relatively business-friendly regulatory environment, highly flexible labor markets, well-funded universities, and strong protection of intellectual property rights. At the same time, low labor protection reduces incentives for people to invest and accumulate (firm-specific) human capital. As a consequence, the UK has relatively efficient and business-friendly markets, but is also characterized by short-termism and economic rewards that are not always socially inclusive.

The UK as a whole performs relatively well by EU standards in terms of the entrepreneurial ecosystem. UK entrepreneurs are not short of spirit, and our survey suggests they are not held back by stifling bureaucracy (as they are in some EU countries). Moreover, its formal financial markets are world class.

The chapter discusses proposals concerning intellectual property rights, how to increase the levels of informal investment as well as how to strengthen the infrastructure on which platform-based financial services operate. It also discusses reforms to promote the flow of talent into entrepreneurial venturing and ways to strengthen the accumulation and maintenance of human capital.

The proposals individually and in combination aim to strengthen the knowledge base, talent pool, and capital base from which UK entrepreneurs can draw and aim to open opportunities for not only starting but also growing innovative firms in all regions in the UK. All regions stand to benefit from these interventions. But by strengthening informal investment and the skills and resilience of low wage workers, while fostering a more entrepreneurial spirit throughout, it is likely that all regions—even peripheral—will benefit. Of course, these proposals will need a much more detailed discussion and only form the starting point, not the final word in the policy debate. Moreover, even if eventually adopted, our proposals all require careful implementation and evaluation to complete the policy cycle.

References

3i Group (n.d.) About us. History. Retrieved from: https://www.3i.com/about-us/history/ on 14-04-2018

Acs ZJ, Audretsch DB, Lehmann EE (2013) The knowledge spillover theory of entrepreneurship. Small Bus Econ 41(4):757–774

Acs ZJ, Autio E, Szerb L (2014) National systems of entrepreneurship: measurement issues and policy implications. Res Policy 43(3):476–494. https://doi.org/10.1016/j.respol.2013.08.016

Acs ZJ, Braunerhjelm P, Audretsch DB, Carlsson B (2009) The knowledge spillover theory of entrepreneurship. Small Bus Econ 32(1):15–30

Anderson R (2016) University fees in historical perspective. History and Policy. Policy Papers. Retrieved from: http://www.historyandpolicy.org/policy-papers/papers/university-fees-in-historical-perspective on 14-04-2018

Ashmore G (1988) Government and business: reducing red tape. Public Money Manag 8(1):78–81

Ashton DN, Green F (1996) Education, training and the global economy. Edward Elgar Publishing, Cheltenham, UK

Bank of England (n.d.) About our history. Retrieved from: https://www.bankofengland.co.uk/about/history on 14-04-2018

Barclays (2017) What factors do lenders consider when making credit decisions? Retrieved from: https://www.barclays.co.uk/help/credit-rating/lender-decision/ on 16-04-2018

Barnes S (1996) England's civic universities and the triumph of the Oxbridge Ideal. Hist Educ Q 36(3):271–305

Bates T, Bradford WD (1992) Factors affecting new firm success and their use in venture capital financing. J Entrepreneurial Fin 2(1):23

Bathmaker A, Ingram N, Abrahams J, Hoare A, Waller R, Bradley H (2016) Higher education, social class and social mobility: the degree generation. Palgrave MacMillan, London

BBC (2008) Timeline: The Bank of Scotland. Retrieved from: http://news.bbc.co.uk/2/hi/uk_news/scotland/7620761.stm on 14-04-2018

BBC (2009) The history of payments. Retrieved from: http://news.bbc.co.uk/2/hi/business/7839823.stm on 14-04-2018

Birtles S (1999) Common land, poor relief and enclosure: the use of manorial resources in fulfilling parish obligations 1601–1834. Past Present 165(1):74–106

Brennan K (2010) Train to gain is money well spent. The Guardian. Retrieved from:https://www.theguardian.com/education/2010/apr/06/train-to-gain on 9-04-2018

British Council (n.d.) Higher education system. Retrieved from: https://www.britishcouncil.in/sites/default/files/higher_education_system_of_uk.pdf on 14-04-2018

Brosan G (1972) The development of polytechnics in the United Kingdom. Paedagogica Europaea 7:41–53

Brown W, Deakin S, Nash D, Oxenbridge S (2000) The employment contract: from collective procedures to individual rights. Br J Ind Relat 38(4):611–629

Cranfield D, Taylor J (2008) Knowledge management and higher education: case study. Electron J Knowl Manag 6(2):85–100
Choi WK (2010) Capitalism, unfree labor and colonial doxa: the master and servant act from Britain to Hong Kong, 1823–1932. J Hist Sociol 23(2):284–315
Clarke T (2001) The knowledge economy. Education+Training 43(4/5):189–196
Clegg HA, Fox A, Thompson AF (1985) A history of British trade unions since 1889: 1911–1933. Oxford University Press, Oxford
Collins M (2012) Money and banking: a history. Routledge, London
Cowling M, Mitchell P (1997) The self-employment: a study of government policy and the role of the macroeconomy. Manchester Sch 65(4):427–442
Craig R (2007) The history of employment law in England and Northern Ireland. Business Law, 8th edn. Cengage Learning. Retrieved from: http://cws.cengage.co.uk/abbott8/students/ni_supp/employ_law/hist_of_employ_law.pdf on 14-04-2018
Curthoys M (2004) Governments, labour, and the law in mid-Victorian Britain: the trade union legislation of the 1870s. Oxford Historical Monographs. Clarendon Press, Oxford
Davies H (2002) A review of enterprise and the economy in education. HM Treasury, London. Retrieved from: http://www.readyunlimited.com/wp-content/uploads/2011/09/Davies-Review-main-doc.pdf on 7-04-2018
Degryse C (2016) Digitalisation of the economy and its impact on labour markets. ETUI Research Paper—Working Paper 2016.02. Available at SSRN: https://ssrn.com/abstract=2730550 or http://dx.doi.org/10.2139/ssrn
Dilli S, Elert N, Herrmann AM (2018) Varieties of entrepreneurship. Exploring the institutional foundations of different entrepreneurship types through 'Varieties-of-Capitalism' arguments. Special issue on "Financial and institutional reforms for an entrepreneurial society." Small Bus Econ 51(2):293–320
Dutton HI (1984) The patent system and inventive activity during the industrial revolution, 1750–1852. Manchester University Press, Dover, NH
EC (1995) Green paper on innovation. European Commission. Retrieved from: http://europa.eu/documents/comm/green_papers/pdf/com95_688_en.pdf on 14-04-2018
Elert N, Henrekson M, Sanders M (2019) The entrepreneurial society: a reform strategy for the European Union. Springer, Berlin
Estrin S, Gozman D, Khavul S (2018) The evolution and adoption of equity crowdfunding: entrepreneur and investor entry into a new market. Small Bus Econ 51(2):425–439
Feld F (2011) The welfare state—Never ending reform. BBC History. Retrieved from: http://www.bbc.co.uk/history/british/modern/field_01.shtml on 14-04-2018
Ferguson N (2009) The ascent of money: a financial history of the world. Penguin, New York
Ferrari R (2016) FinTech impact on retail banking–From a universal banking model to banking verticalization. In: Chishti S, Barberis J (eds) The FinTech book: the financial technology handbook for investors, entrepreneurs and visionaries. Wiley, Chichester, pp 248–252
Goos M, Manning A, Salomons A (2009) Job polarization in Europe. Am Econ Rev 99(2):58–63
Goos M, Manning A, Salomons A (2014) Explaining job polarization: routine-biased technological change and offshoring. Am Econ Rev 104(8):2509–2526
Green F, Felstead A, Gallie D, Henseke G (2016) Skills and work organisation in Britain: a quarter century of change. J Labour Market Res 49(2):121–132
Hall PA, Soskice D (2001) Varieties of capitalism: the institutional foundations of comparative advantage. Oxford University Press, Oxford
Han L, Benson A, Chen JJ, Zhang S (2012) The use and impacts of bank support on UK small and medium-sized enterprises. Int Small Bus J 32(1):61–80
Hannon PD (2005) Philosophies of enterprise and entrepreneurship education and challenges for higher education in the UK. Int J Entrepreneurship Innov 6(2):105–114
Hay C (2010) Chronicles of a death foretold: the winter of discontent and construction of the crisis of British Keynesianism. Parliamentary Aff 63(3):446–470

Held L (2019) Part-time entrepreneurship: the role of institutions, venture and individual characteristics in entry and transition choices. In: Held L (ed) Unravelling the patterns in venture creation processes. Ph.D. thesis. Utrecht University, Utrecht, pp 25–55

Held L, Herrmann AM, Polzin F (2018a) Follow the money: the funding acquisition process of nascent ventures. Horizon 2020 Project on "Financial and Institutional Reforms for an Entrepreneurial Society" (FIRES), Workpackage 5, Deliverable 5.1; currently under review. Also available in Held L (2019) Unravelling the patterns in venture creation processes. Ph.D. thesis. Utrecht University, Utrecht, pp 91–122

Held L, Herrmann AM, Storz C (2018b) Whom do nascent ventures search for? Variance of linkage formation activities during new product development processes. Horizon 2020 Project on "Financial and Institutional Reforms for an Entrepreneurial Society" (FIRES), Workpackage 5, Deliverable 5.1; currently under review. Also available in Held L (2019) Unravelling the patterns in venture creation processes. Ph.D. thesis. Utrecht University, Utrecht, pp 123–150

Henkel M, Kogan M (1993) Research training and graduate education. The British macro structure. In: Clark BR (ed) The research foundations of graduate education: Germany, Britain, France, United States, Japan. University of California Press, Berkeley, CA, pp 71–114

Hepple B (2002) Social and labour rights in a global context: international and comparative perspectives. Cambridge University Press, Cambridge

Hepple B, Morris GS (2002) The employment act 2002 and the crisis of individual employment rights. Ind Law J 31(3):245–269

Herrmann AM (2019) A plea for varieties of entrepreneurship. Special Issue on "Entrepreneurship in context." Small Bus Econ 52(2):331–343

Herrmann AM (2020) On the institutional foundations of the varieties of entrepreneurship in Europe. In: Sanders M, Marx A, Stenkula M (eds) The entrepreneurial society. Reform strategies for Italy, Germany and the UK. Springer, Berlin

Heyck TW (2012) The idea of a university in Britain, 1870–1970. Hist Eur Ideas 8(2):205–219

Hijzen A, Upward R, Wright PW (2010) Job creation, job destruction and the role of small firms: firm-level evidence for the UK. Oxford Bull Econ Stat 72(5):621–647

HM Treasury (2003) Lambert review of business-university collaboration. HM Treasury, London

HM Treasury (2006) Leitch review of skills. Prosperity for all in the global economy—World class skills. HM Treasury, London

HM Treasury (2009) HM treasury annual innovation report. HM Treasury, London

HM Treasury (2010) HM treasury annual innovation report and accounts. HM Treasury, London

HMSO (1971) Report on committee of enquiry on small firms (Bolton Report), Cmnd 4811. HMSO, London

HMSO (1979) Interim report on financing of small firms (Wilson Report), Cmnd 7503. HMSO, London

Huggins R, Williams N (2009) Enterprise and public policy: a review of labour government intervention in the United Kingdom. Environ Plan C Polit Space 27(1):19–41

Intellectual Property Office (2014a) History of patents: the 18th century. Retrieved from: http://www.ipo.gov.uk/types/patent/p-about/p-whatis/p-history/p-history-18century.htm

Intellectual Property Office (2014b) History of patents: the 20th century. Retrieved from: http://webarchive.nationalarchives.gov.uk/20140603131909/ on 14-04-2018

Jones H (2018) Funding for lending scheme: how does it work? Express. Retrieved from: https://www.express.co.uk/finance/personalfinance/911166/funding-for-lending-scheme-bank-of-england on 9-04-2018

Kahn-Freund O (1944) The illegality of a trade union. Modern Law Rev 7(40):192–205

Leendertse J (2017) Entrepreneurship in the UK's renewable energy industry. Background paper for FIRES WP5, mimeo

Lewchuk WA (1984) The role of the British government in the spread of scientific management and fordism in the interwar years. J Econ Hist 44(20):355–361

Lin MJJ, Hung SW, Chen CJ (2009) Fostering the determinants of knowledge sharing in professional virtual communities. Comput Hum Behav 25(4):929–939

Lloyds Banking Group (n.d.) Our heritage. Timeline. 1695–1800. Retrieved from: http://www.lloydsbankinggroup.com/Our-Group/our-heritage/timeline/1695-1800/ on 14-04-2018
LSE Growth Commission (2017) LSE growth commission report 2017. Retrieved from: http://www.lse.ac.uk/researchAndExpertise/units/growthCommission/documents/pdf/2017LSEGCReport.pdf on 14-04-2018
Machin S, Vignoles A (2018) What's the good of education? The economics of education in the UK. Princeton University Press, Princeton
Machlup F, Penrose E (1950) The patent controversy in the nineteenth century. J Econ Hist 10(1):1–29
Mackenzie A (2015) The fintech revolution. London Bus Sch Rev 26(3):50–53
MacLeod C (1988) Inventing the industrial revolution: the English patent system, 1660–1800. Cambridge University Press, Cambridge
MacLeod C, Nuvolari A (2006) Inventive activities, patents and early industrialization. A synthesis of research issues. DRUID Working Paper No. 06-28
Mason C (2009) Public policy support for the informal venture capital market in Europe: a critical review. Int Small Bus J 27(5):536–556
Mason C, Harrison R (1989) Informal venture capital. In: Storey DJ (ed) Small business: critical perspectives on business and management. Taylor and Francis, New York
Mason C, Jones L, Wells S in collaboration with URS Corp (2010) The city's role in providing for the public equity financing SMEs. City of London, London
Merlin-Jones D (2010) The industrial and commercial finance corporation: lessons from the past for the future. Civitas. Retrieved from: http://www.civitas.org.uk/.pdf on 14-04-2018
Mokyr J (2005) Long-term economic growth and the history of technology. In: Aghion P, Durlauf S (eds) Handbook of economic growth, vol 1. Elsevier, Amsterdam, pp 1113–1180
Mollick E, Robb A (2016) Democratizing innovation and capital access: the role of crowdfunding. Calif Manag Rev 58(2):72–87
Morris D, Collier T, Wood G (2005) Effects of minimum wage legislation: some evidence from small enterprises. Int Small Bus J 23(2):191–209
Moser C (1988) The Robbins report 25 years after—and the future of the Universities. Oxford Rev Educ 14(1):5–20. Retrieved from: http://www.jstor.org/stable/1050360 on 14-04-2018
Mueller P, van Stel A, Storey DJ (2008) The effects of new firm formation on regional development over time: the case of Great Britain. Small Bus Econ 30(1):59–71
NAO (2014) Business perceptions survey. Retrieved from https://www.nao.org.uk/report/business-perceptions-survey-2014/ on 16-04-2018
NESTA (2008) History matters: unlocking innovation in British cities and regions. Policy briefing HM/26. Retrieved from: https://www.nesta.org.uk/sites/default/files/history_matters.pdf on 14-04-2018
Newton L, Cottrell PL (1998) Joint-stock banking in the English provinces 1826–1857: to branch or not to branch? Bus Econ Hist 27(1):115–128
NHS (n.d.) The history of the NHS in England. Retrieved from: https://www.nhs.uk/NHSEngland/thenhs/nhshistory/Pages/NHShistory1948.aspx on 14-04-2018
Nicholas T (2014) Technology, innovation and economic growth in Britain since 1870. In: Floud R, Humphries J, Johnson P (eds) The Cambridge economic history of modern Britain. Cambridge University Press, Cambridge, pp 181–204
OECD (2015) OECD reviews of vocational education and training key messages and country summaries. OECD, Paris. Retrieved from: http://www.oecd.org/education/skills-beyond-school/OECD_VET_Key_Messages_and_Country_Summaries_2015.pdf on 14-10-2019
OECD (2019) Average wages. OECD, Paris. Retrieved from: https://data.oecd.org/earnwage/average-wages.htm#indicator-chart on 14-10-2019
Parkinson M, Champion T, Evans R, Simmie J, et al. (2006) State of the English cities. A research study. Office of the Deputy Prime Minister, London. Retrieved from: http://image.guardian.co.uk/sys-files/Politics/documents/2006/03/07/StateoftheEnglishCitiespart1.pdf on 14-10-2019

Pike R (2017) How will the market adapt to the end of funding for lending? Mortgage solutions. Retrieved from: http://www.mortgagesolutions.co.uk/better-business/2017/08/08/will-market-adapt-end-funding-lending/ on 9-04-2018
Piketty T (2014) Capitalism in the 21st Century. Harvard University Press, Cambridge, MA
Potter J, Moore B (2000) UK enterprise zones and the attraction of inward investment. Urban Stud 37(8):1279–1312
Pratt J (1997) The polytechnic experiment: 1965–1992. SRHE and Open University Press, Buckingham. Retrieved from: https://eric.ed.gov/?id=ED415724 on 14-04-2018
Richardson HW (2011) Regional development agencies in England. In: Richardson HW, Bae CHC, Choe SC (eds) Reshaping regional policy. Edward Elgar Publishing, Cheltenham
Robinson E (1972) James Watt and the law of patents. Technol Cult 13(2):115–139
Rothwell R (1985) Venture finance, small firms and public policy. Res Policy 14(5):253–265
Rusly FH, Talib YYA, Salleh D (2017) The impact of minimum pay implementation on small businesses operating cost and sustainability: a case of service business. In: SHS web of conferences, vol 34. EDP Sciences, Les Ulis
Sanders M, Stenkula M, Grilli L, Herrmann A, Latifi G, Pager B, Szerb L, Terragno BE (2020a) A reform strategy for Italy. In: Sanders M, Marx A, Stenkula M (eds) The entrepreneurial society. Reform strategies for Italy, Germany and the UK. Springer, Berlin
Sanders M, Stenkula M, Fritsch M, Herrmann A, Latifi G, Pager B, Szerb L, Terragno BE, Wyrwich M (2020b) A reform strategy for Germany. In: Sanders M, Marx A, Stenkula M (eds) The entrepreneurial society. Reform strategies for Italy, Germany and the UK. Springer, Berlin
Schumpeter J (1911) The theory of economic development. Harvard University Press, Cambridge, MA
Schwanen D, Wyonch R (2018) Canada's innovation report card. C.D. Howe Institute e-Brief 273. Retrieved from: https://www.cdhowe.org/public-policy-research/canadas-2018-innovation-policy-report-card on 16-04-2018
Scott P (2014a) The reform of English higher education: universities in global, national and regional contexts. Cambridge J Reg, Econ Soc 7(2):217–231
Scott P (2014b) Robbins, the binary policy and mass higher education. High Educ Q 68(2):147–163
Shawl WF (1954) The repeal of the Combination acts 1824–1825. Graduate Student theses, Dissertations, & Professional Papers. University of Montana
Spicker P (2014) Social policy: theory and practice. Policy Press, Bristol
Stam E (2015) Entrepreneurial ecosystems and regional policy: a sympathetic critique. Eur Plan Stud 23(9):1759–1769
Stam E (2018) Measuring entrepreneurial ecosystems. In: O'Connor A, Stam E, Sussan F, Audretsch DB (eds) Entrepreneurial ecosystems. Springer, Cham, pp 173–197
Storey DJ, Tether B (1998) Public policy measures to support new technology-based firms in the European Union. Res Policy 26(9):1037–1057
Szerb L, Lafuente E, Horváth K, Páger B (2019) The relevance of quantity and quality entrepreneurship for regional performance: the moderating role of the entrepreneurial ecosystem. Reg Stud 53(9):1308–1320. https://doi.org/10.1080/00343404.2018.1510481
Szerb L, Vörös Z, Komlósi É, Acs ZJ, Páger B, Rappai G (2017) The regional entrepreneurship and development index: structure, data, methodology and policy applications. Fires Report D4.4. Retrived from http://www.projectfires.eu/wp-content/uploads/2018/07/d4.4-the-regional-entrepreneurship-and-development-index_-structure-data-methodology-and-policy-applications.pdf
Tate J (2001) National varieties of standardization. In: Hall PA, Soskice D (eds) Varieties of capitalism. Oxford University Press, Oxford, pp 442–473
Taylor J (2003) Institutional higher education: policy and outcomes since the end of the binary divide. High Educ Q 57(3):266–293
Teubner G (2001) Legal irritants: how unifying law ends up in new divergences. In: Hall PA, Soskice DW (eds) Varieties of capitalism—the institutional foundations of comparative advantage. Oxford University Press, Oxford, pp 417–441

Thirkell PC, Dau R (1998) Export performance: success determinants for New Zealand manufacturing exporters. Eur J Mark 32(9/10):813–829
Towers B (1989) Running the gauntlet: British trade unions under Thatcher, 1979–1988. Ind Labor Relat Rev 42(2):163–188
UK Government (n.d.) University Enterprise Zones. Retrieved from: https://www.gov.uk/government/publications/university-enterprise-zones/university-enterprise-zones on 7-04-2018
UK Government (2000) Financial services and markets act 2000. Retrieved from: https://www.legislation.gov.uk/ukpga/2000/8/pdfs/ukpga_20000008_en.pdf on 8-04-2018
UK Government (2015) 2010 to 2015 government policy: business enterprise. Retrieved from: https://www.gov.uk/government/publications/2010-to-2015-government-policy-business-enterprise/2010-to-2015-government-policy-business-enterprise#appendix-2-encouraging-private-sector-investment on 4-04-2018
University of Cambridge (n.d.) About the university. Early records. Retrieved from: https://www.cam.ac.uk/about-the-university/history/early-records on 14-04-2018
University of Edinburgh (n.d.) About. Our history. Retrieved from:https://www.ed.ac.uk/about/our-history on 14-04-2018
University of London (n.d.) History of University of London. Retrieved from: https://london.ac.uk/about-us/history-university-london on 14-04-2018
University of Oxford (n.d.) Introduction and history. Retrieved from: https://www.ox.ac.uk/about/organisation/history?wssl=1 on 14-04-2018
Van Bavel B (2016) The invisible hand? How market economies have emerged and declined since AD 500. Oxford University Press, Oxford
Varga A, Szerb L, SebestyénT, Szabó N (2020) Economic impact assessment of entrepreneurship policies with the GMR-Europe model. In: Sanders M, Marx A, Stenkula M (eds) The entrepreneurial society. Reform Strategies for Italy, Germany and the UK. Springer, Berlin
Walters A (2005) Personal insolvency law after the enterprise act – An appraisal. J Corp Law Stud 5(1):65–104
White LH (1992) Competition and currency: essays on free banking and money. NYU Press, New York
Whiteside N (2014) The Beveridge report and its implementation: a revolutionary project? Retrieved from: https://www.researchgate.net/publication/286702415_The_Beveridge_Report_and_Its_Implementation_a_Revolutionary_Project on 14-04-2018
Wilson T (2012) A review of business–university collaboration. HM Government, London. Retrieved from: http://dera.ioe.ac.uk/13842/1/wilson.pdf on 14-04-2018
Wilson W (1997) Student grants, loans and tuition fees. House of Commons Library Research Paper No 97/119
Wiltbank (2009) Siding with the angels: business angel investing—promising outcomes and effective strategies. Research report published by NESTA & BBAA
Wooden M, Sloan J (1998) Industrial relations reform and labour market outcomes: a comparison of Australia, New Zealand and the United Kingdom. Retrieved from: https://www.rba.gov.au/publications/confs/1998/pdf/wooden-sloan.pdf on 14-04-2018
Woods DC (1982) The operation of the master and servants act in the black country, 1858–1875. Midland Hist 7(1):93–115
Woodward D (1980) The Background to the statute of artificers: the genesis of labour policy, 1558–63. Econ Hist Rev New Ser 33(1):32–44
World Bank (2018) Doing business report. Retrieved from: http://www.doingbusiness.org/~/media/WBG/DoingBusiness/Documents/Annual-Reports/English/DB2018-Full-Report.pdf on 7-04-2018
WIPO (n.d.a) An explanatory note concerning the origins of the United Kingdom intellectual property legal regime. Retrieved from: http://www.wipo.int/export/sites/www/wipolex/en/notes/gb.pdf
WIPO (n.d.b) United Kingdom country profile. Retrieved from: http://www.wipo.int/wipolex/en/details.jsp?id=1623 on 14-04-2018

Chapter 9
What We Have Learned and How We May Proceed

Mark Sanders, Axel Marx and Mikael Stenkula

Abstract In this chapter, the editors conclude this volume and draw the most important lessons that can be drawn from the FIRES project. The editors highlight theoretical lessons, methodological innovations, and policy implications.

Keywords Entrepreneurship · Entrepreneurial society · Institutional reforms

This book marks the conclusion of the project *"Financial and Institutional Reforms for the Entrepreneurial Society" (FIRES)*—a European Union project launched in 2015 as part of the Horizon 2020 program to restore Europe's ability to innovate, grow, and create jobs over the coming decades. By 2015, the mood in Europe was gloomy. The global financial and ensuing Euro crisis had put severe strains on European solidarity and weakened especially the southern Member States. The ambitious Lisbon Agenda to make Europe the world's most innovative continent by 2010 failed to deliver on its promises. The Brexit vote, the Syrian refugee crisis, the backsliding rule of law and rise of populist movements in several European Member States and now the Corona pandemic have strengthened the need for the European Union to reinvent itself and return Europe on the path to inclusive, sustainable, and innovative growth. We therefore believe that since its start, the FIRES project has only gained in importance and urgency.

In the project, we identified the entrepreneurial society as the way forward. The entrepreneurial society is an open society in which ideas can compete on a level playing field and challenge the status quo. First described by Schumpeter (1911), an entrepreneurial society offers opportunity to all and organizes society to support productive entrepreneurship that will generate innovation, jobs, and growth while

M. Sanders (✉)
Utrecht School of Economics, Utrecht University, Utrecht, The Netherlands
e-mail: m.w.j.l.sanders@uu.nl

A. Marx
Leuven Centre for Global Governance Studies, University of Leuven, Leuven, Belgium
e-mail: axel.marx@kuleuven.be

M. Stenkula
Research Institute of Industrial Economics, Stockholm, Sweden
e-mail: mikael.stenkula@ifn.se

M. Sanders et al. (eds.), *The Entrepreneurial Society*, International Studies in Entrepreneurship 44, https://doi.org/10.1007/978-3-662-61007-7_9

solving the many social and ecological challenges that Europe faces. The European Union (EU) can only (re)assert its place on the global technology frontier by channeling more of its resources and talent to the small scale, innovative, and, therefore, also risky ventures that develop and test solutions for tomorrow, in business and beyond. In an entrepreneurial society, the institutions are such that productive entrepreneurial experimentation is both made possible and encouraged. In our project, we propose seven steps to design, implement, and evaluate reforms that help develop the entrepreneurial society across Europe.

In the companion volume to this book (Elert et al. 2019), our project identified 50 proposals for reform in six key areas of policymaking that would support the mobilization and allocation of human, financial, and knowledge resources for entrepreneurial activity. In this volume we explicitly recognize the diversity of institutional arrangements in the EU as well as the multi-level nature of EU policymaking. An entrepreneurial growth and innovation strategy for the EU cannot be a "one-size-fits-all" basket of proposals.

To identify the appropriate set of interventions in a given context, careful analysis is required. Hence, this volume highlighted the diverse and historically deeply rooted institutional foundations of EU Member States and introduced the tools we developed for analyzing the entrepreneurial ecosystem before turning to reforms. It has also introduced a policy analysis of how and at which levels of governance an effective reform strategy must be formulated in the context of European policymaking. Developing these tools required a broad, multidisciplinary approach. The project, including this book, has included thoughts and ideas of scholars from a range of different fields such as history, economics, geography, management, political science and law.

As the proof of the pudding is in the eating, we then illustrate the practical usefulness of our approach by analyzing Italy, Germany, and the UK in depth and formulate a reform strategy for these countries using our seven-step approach. These three countries were chosen to broadly represent Europe's institutional families.[1]

We draw some important lessons from this exercise. The first is theoretical: building on the work of Schumpeter (1911), Baumol (1990), and Audretsch and Thurik (2000, 2001), our project has confirmed that institutions enable or inhibit the allocation of resources to the challengers of the status quo that drive productive entrepreneurial venturing. Therefore, to build an entrepreneurial economy and society, institutional reforms are required. Our application of historical analysis, however, has shown that, due to strong path- and interdependencies, not all institutions are so easily reformed. Echoing the work of Williamson (2000) and new institutional economics, we recognize that some institutions are more deeply embedded than others. Moreover, it is the way institutions actually operate, not how they appear in law or data, that matters. Consequently, it is the functions that institutions perform, rather than the specific shape they take in any given context, that should be the focus of efforts to reform.

[1]In the Varieties of Capitalism (VoC) terminology they represent European examples of a mixed (or Mediterranean) market system, a coordinated market and a liberal market, respectively.

To make this more concrete, we can look at the example of universities. Based on cross-sectional and panel data evidence, many have concluded that the presence of a university promotes knowledge-intensive entrepreneurial venturing in its direct surroundings. The university campus serves as a hotbed for entrepreneurship. But university knowledge can spill over to economic activity through productive entrepreneurship in many shapes and forms. The most obvious is perhaps the campus-based university spinoff through a USA-style tech transfer office on a land-grant college that was indeed founded with a mission to disseminate knowledge to business. But that is as much a manifestation of USA history as it is a measure of knowledge spillovers. In a different, say German or Italian context, where universities have traditionally fought to minimize or exclude outside influences (e.g., the Church and the State) in research and curriculum, the same spillover may take the form of educated graduates joining an off-campus research institute and developing new ideas in close collaboration with incumbent firms. Given the deep-rooted institutional context of the German university, perhaps the reform should aim to facilitate the flow of knowledge from universities to firms via the channels that already exist, rather than setting up a tech transfer office and copying the USA Bayh–Dole Act in a context where the institutional framework simply does not support it.

These theoretical lessons have implications for the methods that should be applied in analyzing the need, scope, and opportunities for institutional reform in any specific country, region, or locality. As much as can be learned from comparing uniformly defined indicators and their impacts across regions and countries, doing so implicitly assumes that the same observed variables reflect the same underlying mechanisms across regions with potentially very different institutional contexts. Methodologically, we therefore stress the need to triangulate methods. It is a good start, but not enough to compare regions on a set of well-defined variables to identify their weaknesses, strengths, and bottlenecks. Such analyses need to be complemented with careful historical analysis to understand the specifics of the local, regional, and national institutional contexts as well as survey-based and qualitative information on how local entrepreneurial ecosystems function and how they could be improved.

These methodological innovations also have important policy implications. There are many ways in which an ecosystem can channel resources to (or away from) productive entrepreneurs. And there are many, potentially highly relevant, complementarities among these institutions. Proposing a one-size-fit-all reform strategy to promote the European entrepreneurial society is then beside the point. Bavaria cannot be(come) Silicon Valley or London, nor should it want to. Instead, the focus should be on promoting access to resources for challengers of the status quo in all of these specific institutional contexts.

The lack of a clear and unambiguous policy prescription also implies that policymakers have to make some tough choices, as there are inevitable tensions between the various approaches. First there is the tension between *universalist* and *particularist* analysis. The Varieties of Capitalism (VoC) and historical analysis approach in Chaps. 2 and 4 clearly stress that every constellation of institutions is unique, whereas the Regional Entrepreneurship and Development Index (REDI) and Geographic, Macro, and Regional (GMR) modeling approaches of Chap. 3 rely on uniformly defined, internationally comparable indicators and estimates of average effects to quantify bottlenecks and predict the impact of alleviating them. On the one hand, *particularists* will claim that every economy has to be analyzed separately, and no general model can be used to analyze the impact of a specific policy, strategy, or reform. Moreover, one cannot compare economies and extract "best practices" from one country and expect them to work similarly in another country. On the other hand, *universalists*—including most economists—will claim that the basic mechanisms under study are sufficiently similar across contexts, and the relevant diversity between them can be adequately addressed by including a broad variety of indicators in the overall index, carefully distinguishing between complements and substitutes in the ecosystem and controlling for institutional characteristics.

In this book, we do not want to argue the case one way or the other: We firmly believe that the approaches should complement each other. The entrepreneurial ecosystem approach (Stam 2015; O'Connor et al. 2018) brings the two approaches together and proposes universal theoretical concepts to systematize particularistic empirical data.

A second, perhaps somewhat related tension in our book exists between reforms that are *desirable* and those that are *feasible*. Once universalists and particularists have agreed on a set of desirable interventions in a specific context, there is always the reality check of their political and legal feasibility. Policymaking in the EU involves navigating the complex tangle of treaties, legislation, and agencies that have and give mandates and competences. The scope for encompassing reforms is often severely limited by the complexities of policymaking in the EU. Legal competencies are distributed between the EU and its Member States in a set of treaties that, although not set in stone, are politically difficult to change. Moreover, the allocation of these competencies was not arranged with making effective entrepreneurship policy in mind. The appropriate governance level for each of the 50 reform proposals in Elert et al. (2019) was identified and provided in that volume. Chapter 5 in this volume provides an analysis of Europe's current entrepreneurship policies to illustrate the complex interwoven structure of actors and competencies involved. Chapter 5 clearly conveys the message that implementing reforms at the appropriate level may be quite challenging in the existing legal frameworks. We need to be aware of this tension and consequently be *modest* in our expectations but, despite of this, *ambitious* in our efforts.

A final, politically highly relevant tension that the work in Chap. 3 and the country studies force us to address, is the one between the inclusion of *people* and of *regions*. In line with the aim of the Horizon 2020 program, the EU aims for *inclusive* and sustainable growth. We understood this to mean, inclusion of citizens. However, the proposals and reform strategies proposed in this volume are likely to benefit already prosperous cities and regions the most. Creating more opportunities for more people implies that people and resources become more footloose and will tend to concentrate in places where they can benefit from economies of agglomeration, knowledge spillovers, and network externalities. Unfortunately, hopeful models predicting an almost automatic trickle-down effect to the backward regions do not find much support in the data. This sits uncomfortably with policymakers that are elected and hope to be reelected by a geographically delimited constituency. The flexibility of people and resources throughout the EU is not likely to spread economic activity and prosperity equally across space. In fact, it may drive further divergence between core and peripheral, urban and rural, regions and countries. Chapters 3, 6, 7, and 8 in this volume address this issue. It is important to be aware that, even if all citizens benefit, not all regions in the EU will. In our project, it is the well-being of its people, not the fate of the politicians representing distinct administrative geographical units that is the primary concern in our reform proposals. That said, effective automatic transfer schemes that will help to maintain economic prosperity throughout the EU might be needed to ensure stable support in the long run.

In conclusion, the FIRES project ended formally on May 31, 2018, but the real work has only just begun. Policymakers at all levels in the EU now need to carefully navigate the tensions we discussed above and start experimenting with reforms that channel resources to challengers in their constituencies. More than a call for a set of specific reforms, our project is a call for experimentation. Carefully designed and evidence-based interventions now need to be tested on the ground. We stand ready to support policymakers who are willing to take up our call to action.

References

Audretsch DB, Thurik AR (2000) Capitalism and democracy in the 21st century: from the managed to the entrepreneurial economy. J Evol Econ 10(1–2):17–34

Audretsch DB, Thurik AR (2001) What's new about the new economy? Sources of growth in the managed and entrepreneurial economies. Ind Corp Change 10(1):267–315

Baumol W (1990) Entrepreneurship: productive, unproductive and destructive. J Polit Econ 98(5):893–921

Elert N, Henrekson M, Sanders M (2019) The entrepreneurial society: a reform strategy for the European Union. Springer, Berlin

O'Connor A, Stam E, Sussan F, Audretsch DB (2018) Entrepreneurial ecosystems. Springer, Berlin

Schumpeter J (1911) The theory of economic development. Cambridge University Press, Cambridge, MA

Stam E (2015) Entrepreneurial ecosystems and regional policy: a sympathetic critique. Eur Plan Stud 23(9):1759–1769

Williamson OE (2000) The new institutional economics: taking stock, looking ahead. J Econ Lit 38(3):595–613

MIX
Papier aus verantwortungsvollen Quellen
Paper from responsible sources
FSC® C105338

If you have any concerns about our products,
you can contact us on
ProductSafety@springernature.com

In case Publisher is established outside the EU,
the EU authorized representative is:
Springer Nature Customer Service Center GmbH
Europaplatz 3, 69115 Heidelberg, Germany

Printed by Libri Plureos GmbH
in Hamburg, Germany